MASCULINITY AT WORK

Masculinity at Work

*Employment Discrimination
through a Different Lens*

Ann C. McGinley

NEW YORK UNIVERSITY PRESS
New York

NEW YORK UNIVERSITY PRESS
New York
www.nyupress.org

References to Internet websites (URLs) were accurate at the time of writing. Neither the author nor New York University Press is responsible for URLs that may have expired or changed since the manuscript was prepared.

Library of Congress Cataloging-in-Publication Data
Names: McGinley, Ann C., author.
Title: Masculinity at work : employment discrimination through a different lens / Ann C. McGinley.
Description: New York : New York University Press, [2016] | "2016 |
Includes bibliographical references and index.
Identifiers: LCCN 2015049157 | ISBN 9780814796139 (cl : alk. paper) | ISBN 0814796133 (cl : alk. paper)
Subjects: LCSH: Discrimination in employment—Law and legislation—United States. | Masculinity—Social aspects—United States. | Sexual harassment—Law and legislation—United States. | Sex role in the work environment—United States.
Classification: LCC KF3464 .M348 2016 | DDC 344.7301/4133—dc23
LC record available at http://lccn.loc.gov/2015049157

New York University Press books are printed on acid-free paper, and their binding materials are chosen for strength and durability. We strive to use environmentally responsible suppliers and materials to the greatest extent possible in publishing our books.

Manufactured in the United States of America

10 9 8 7 6 5 4 3 2 1

Also available as an ebook

To Jeff, Ryan, Shanen, and Reed

CONTENTS

PREFACE

I first discovered masculinities scholarship while researching sexual harassment cases in which groups of blue-collar coworkers subjected women to severe or pervasive harassment. In cases like *Robinson v. Jacksonville Shipyards, Inc.* (1991) and *Jenson v. Eveleth Taconite Co.* (1997), male coworkers engaged in a pattern of harassing behaviors ranging from sexually explicit graffiti and posters displayed throughout the workplace to pinching and grabbing, offensive language directed at individual women, and comments that women did not belong in the workplace. One female worker found a used condom in her sandwich (*Sex, Power, and the Workplace* 2002); another, a corrections officer, alleged that she was handcuffed to the toilet and her head held under water. She claimed that her male colleagues punched her in the kidneys and placed an electrified cattle prod between her legs (*Reed v. Shepard* 1991).

I was surprised that men treated women so poorly and wondered why they did so. It was especially odd to witness the group hostility that men demonstrated toward women in these environments, which seemed a far cry from the sexual harassment that the courts imagined as occurring from an excess of romantic love. The behavior I noticed was hostile, not romantic. Men I knew did not place used condoms in a woman's sandwich to court her.

Soon I realized that while the worst blue-collar atmospheres were particularly egregious, men in predominantly male white-collar jobs also engaged in practices that created hostile work environments for their female colleagues. In white-collar environments, the behavior was often different in intensity and design, but men still let their female colleagues know that they were not welcome. Women were excluded regularly, had to work harder than men to advance, and often failed to receive credit for their ideas.

At the time, in the mid- to late 1990s, I was a law professor at Florida State University College of Law, where I met Patricia Yancey Martin and Irene Padavic, sociologists at Florida State who research, write, and teach about gender and masculinities. Pat and Irene introduced me to their work and the study of masculinities. Pat Martin had performed a number of ethnographic studies of corporate workplaces that revealed that women suffered from gendered practices enacted by male colleagues who appeared to be unaware that they were harming women. But they *were* harming them. Because these practices were not sexual or brutal in nature, they were less visible than those performed in blue-collar workplaces. In fact, Pat Martin explained, men describe the masculine practices in which they engage as work itself, thereby obscuring the gendered nature of their behavior. For example, when men spend long hours in the office talking about baseball, they consider themselves to be working even though women around them often see the men's behavior as wasting time. Much of this behavior forms bonds among the men, and excludes women. Even if they would like to become members of the informal group, many women have homecare responsibilities that prevent them from doing so.

I began to read the other social science researchers who wrote about masculinity, and to understand that there were social scientists who considered themselves feminists but who also believed that feminism described men in essentialist terms, and that feminism did not recognize the social pressures that men endured. In essence, men, too, suffered from the binary gender regime that drew fairly strict lines between acceptable behavior for men and acceptable behavior for women. This work by authors such as Raewyn Connell, Michael Kimmel, Richard Collier, and David Collinson explored the pressures that gender expectations place on men in society and the competition that the need to prove one's masculinity created among men.

While I was interested in men's role in society in general, men's behavior in the workplace and the importance of work to men's identity particularly intrigued me. While at Florida State, I worked on "unconscious discrimination," the concept that our cognition creates screens through which we unknowingly process information based on societal stereotypes. This information about cognitive processing raised serious questions about the intent requirement of the employment discrimination law. Given the information about stereotyping and cognition, Title VII of the 1964 Civil Rights Act, as interpreted by many of the courts, depended on an outdated view of the way discrimination occurs. Today, the concept of "unconscious discrimination" is expressed as implicit bias, and many social scientists, lawyers, law professors, and judges have concluded that most of us harbor implicit biases that affect our behavior.

The masculinities research that Pat Martin and Irene Padavic introduced to me fit with the concept of "unconscious discrimination," especially given that many masculine behaviors were invisible to the naked eye because they are considered to be a normal result of biological differences between the sexes. At about the same time, I met Nancy Dowd, a law professor at the University of Florida who was writing about fatherhood and masculinity. Nancy was one of the first law professors to use masculinities research to forward legal theory.

In my mind, one question kept coming up: what did the law do to recognize workplace behaviors as gendered, and how could the law remedy gender-based injuries? This inquiry led to cases where groups of men or boys harassed individual male employees or students in workplaces and educational institutions. The fact patterns of these cases were surprisingly similar to one another and not that different from sexual harassment cases brought by female employees in predominantly male workplaces. Male victims were often either new to the organization or outsiders because they were perceived to be less masculine or not to fit in with the group. Like Joseph Oncale, whose case was decided by the U.S. Supreme Court (*Oncale v. Sundowner Offshore Services, Inc.* 1998), male victims suffered humiliating physical and verbal abuse, sometimes culminating in rape. In the education cases, students were often punished by peers and authorities for reporting the behavior and for not fitting into the group (*Seamons v. Snow* 1996).

These fact patterns reminded me of a case that took place in Glen Ridge, New Jersey, in the early 1980s, memorialized in *Our Guys* by Bernard Lefkowitz (Lefkowitz 1998), where male high school athletes enticed an intellectually disabled teenage girl into a basement with the promise of a party and raped her with a baseball bat. One troubling aspect of all of these cases is that there was very little condemnation of irresponsible behavior. Many in Glen Ridge condemned the victim, and did not judge the boys. Perhaps even worse, many from Glen Ridge were more concerned about their decreasing property values as a result of the adverse publicity than the criminal behavior of the boys. In Utah, where

Seamons v. Snow took place, the plaintiff, a young high school football player who reported his abuse by his teammates, received threatening phone calls (Roche 1993). Somehow, group membership not only encouraged egregious behavior but also provided an excuse for it.

In 1999, I moved to UNLV Boyd School of Law in Las Vegas. Las Vegas presented an amazing laboratory for my research on gender and employment. At the same time, other scholars were writing about bullying in workplaces and educational settings, and I began to research bullying in workplaces and schools, which many scholars contended was unrelated to gender. When I looked closely at the bullying fact patterns, however, they were almost identical to the behaviors that occurred in sexual harassment cases (McGinley 2008). I began to write a number of articles about masculinities research and how it could be used to interpret Title VII cases. Years later, I made a proposal to NYU Press to write this book about how masculinities theory could help lawyers and judges interpret Title VII law. It was an exciting new field in the law, and only a few of us were writing about it.

Frank Rudy Cooper was writing at the time on masculinity, race, and the criminal justice system. I met Frank at a conference at the Southeastern Association of Law Schools (SEALS), where we spoke on a panel on masculinities and law with John Kang, Nancy Dowd, Joan Howarth, and Val Vojdik. Frank and I decided to move the discipline along by editing a collection on masculinities and the law, *Masculinities and the Law: A Multidimensional Approach* (Cooper and McGinley 2012). Our idea was to merge feminist legal theory and masculinities studies using an intersectional/multidimensional approach that would take into account not only gender but also race and other identity characteristics combined in the context of the experience. We solicited chapters from other law professors who were writing about masculinity. At approximately the same time, Nancy Dowd published one of the first books on law and masculinities, *The Man Question: Male Subordination and Privilege* (Dowd 2010).

The decision to publish an edited collection on multidimensional masculinities delayed my Title VII book, but the detour was well worth it. The work with Frank Rudy Cooper helped me understand how masculinities theory fit in with critical race theory and multidimensionality theory. While Frank and I were working on the edited collection, we sponsored a symposium at UNLV Boyd School of Law on "Masculinity and Law," where Devon Carbado and Russell Robinson delivered the keynote address jointly and where Athena Mutua, author of *Progressive Black Masculinities* (Mutua 2006), took a leading role. Around the same time, Nancy Levit, Nancy Dowd, and I presented at the University of Baltimore School of Law's Feminist Legal Theory Conference, where we spoke to feminist colleagues about how we believed that masculinities theory fit in with feminist theory. That presentation ultimately became a chapter included in Frank Cooper's and my edited collection on multidimensional masculinities.

As Frank and I were working on our edited collection, Martha Albertson Fineman and Michael Thomson dedicated a workshop at Emory's Feminism and Legal Theory Project to "Masculinities and Law." A group of nationally and internationally known scholars participated. At that conference I met Michael Kimmel and Richard Collins, top-rate sociologists from the United States and the United Kingdom, who, among others, ultimately participated in the edited collection and/or a symposium that the *Nevada Law Journal* published in 2013. Fineman's workshop culminated in another edited collection on law and masculinity, *Exploring Masculinities: Feminist Legal Theory Reflections* (Fineman and Thomson 2013), to which I contributed a chapter on disparate impact law and masculinity.

After Frank Rudy Cooper's and my edited collection came out, it became clear that there was still significant masculinity work to be done. The *Nevada Law Journal* of the UNLV Boyd School of Law dedicated an issue to *Men, Masculinities, and Law: A Symposium on Multidimensional Masculinities Theory* (McGinley 2013b), which I introduced and helped to edit. That symposium included seventeen masculinities scholars from across the country and Europe.

In the meantime, I continued to think and write about how masculinities theory could help us understand difficult interpretive problems in employment discrimination cases brought under Title VII of the 1964 Civil Rights Act. I also taught a seminar and first-year elective courses entitled "Masculinity, Law, and Popular Culture." In this course, participants studied masculinities theory and research, popular culture's creation and reinforcement of notions of masculinity, and legal doctrine's incorporation of concepts of masculinity.

During this time period, it was evident that serious gender- and sex-based group harassment of individuals continued to occur in predominantly male environments. Many of these cases have received significant media attention. From the Glen Ridge rape case to Jonathan Martin's claim that he was harassed as a player for the Miami Dolphins (Smith 2013); from Sayreville, New Jersey's alleged locker room rape of football neophytes (Petersen 2014) to an alleged attempted rape of a special needs student in a football locker room in the state of Washington (Hastings 2015); and from the Steubenville, Ohio, rape case (Perez 2014) to the brutal rape and murder of an Indian woman by a gang of men on a bus in New Delhi (Rawat and Daigle 2013), the common denominator is a group of men or boys acting in concert who subject a vulnerable victim (man or boy, woman or girl) to abusive and, often, criminal behavior. Only by studying masculinities can we begin to understand these behaviors and attempt to remedy them.

This Book

This book is a culmination of almost twenty years of study and work. It deals with how lawyers practicing in the field can use masculinities research to educate judges and juries about issues surrounding masculinity and gender in Title VII employment discrimination cases. In essence, it encourages lawyers, judges, and juries to see the behaviors described through a lens created by an understanding of masculinities theory.

ACKNOWLEDGMENTS

This book results from a long process in which I wrote articles, published other books, spoke at symposia, taught classes, worked on book chapters, and raised my children.[1] My husband, Jeff Stempel, has been supportive during this time, cheering me on, discussing how concepts of masculinity affect all of us, reading drafts of chapters, and suggesting book titles. My sons, Ryan and Reed McGinley-Stempel, contributed to my understanding of masculinity through observation and conversation, while my daughter, Shanen Stempel, gave me her unvarnished opinions about men and masculinity as well. I thank all of them and my mother, Mary McGinley, for her enduring support while I traveled around the country to give my views on masculinity and law.

My original editor at NYU Press, Debbie Gershenowitz, was great in helping me frame the book so that the press would agree to my proposal. She also edited *Masculinities and the Law: A Multidimensional Approach*, which Frank Rudy Cooper and I published in 2012. The process of editing that collection immensely improved my understanding of masculinities research and how it should apply to employment discrimination law. Thanks also to my current editor at NYU Press, Clara Platter, who artfully guided this book to its completion, and to all of the folks at NYU Press who worked on the book, especially Constance Grady, Alexia Traganas, and Emily Wright.

Frank Rudy Cooper, my coeditor of *Masculinities and the Law* and my coauthor of a number of law review articles, helped me understand the multidimensional aspects of masculinities theory. He also read and edited a number of my articles on masculinity and earlier drafts of this book. Nancy Dowd, author of *The Man Question*, commented on a number of articles and an earlier draft of this book; she was always there to talk about masculinities theory and how it played out in practice. Both Nancy Dowd and Nancy Levit discussed a number of draft chapters of the book with me and gave me excellent suggestions for edits once it was nearly completed. Elaine Shoben discussed a number of draft chapters of the book and articles on masculinities with me.

John White, former dean at the UNLV Boyd School of Law and former executive vice president and provost at UNLV, supported this project by financing summer research stipends, a research leave, and a workshop on masculinity at the law school. Former Dean Camille Nelson of Suffolk Law School also contributed to the workshop. Acting executive vice president and provost at UNLV, Nancy Rapoport, has always demonstrated her support on this project. Dan Hamilton, the current dean at UNLV Boyd School of Law, supported me financially, intellectually, and emotionally and encouraged me to finish this book. Like my other colleagues at UNLV Boyd School of Law, Dan was incredibly supportive.

The Wiener-Rogers Law Library at UNLV provided invaluable research support. Jeanne Price, a professor of law and the library director, oversaw the preparation of a significant bibliography of works on masculinity. She also purchased a substantial library on masculinity that rivals all others of its kind. David McClure, head of Research and Curriculum Services and library professor at UNLV Boyd School of Law, provided excellent research. Numerous UNLV law students worked with David throughout the years to support my research.

While I worked on the book, the *Nevada Law Journal* published *Men, Masculinities, and Law: A Symposium on Multidimensional Masculinities Theory* in its winter 2013 edition. *Nevada Law Journal* editors, in particular Jason DeForest, Aaron Haar, and Kendra Kisling, worked diligently on the symposium. The symposium brought together new works of seventeen scholars in law, social science, and women's studies from the United States and Europe who are experts in masculinity.

Student research assistant Skylar Young, who researched masculinities and other gender theory, edited the manuscript, and helped pull everything together, worked diligently on this book. She deserves my deepest gratitude. Cheryl Grames, Debra Amens, and Tess Johnson all provided invaluable research and editing earlier in the book's process. Finally, I wish to thank the law students at UNLV Boyd School of Law who taught me so much in my seminars and first-year elective courses on Masculinity, Law, and Popular Culture.

Introduction

Bullying Masculinities

In late October 2013, the news broke that National Football League (NFL) Miami Dolphins' right tackle, Jonathan Martin, walked out on the team and checked himself into a mental health institution in Miami. The original story stated that Martin had gone "AWOL" and insinuated that Martin could not take the pressure in professional football (Smith 2013). Within days, the story changed. News sources reported that Martin's teammates had repeatedly bullied him under the leadership of Richie Incognito, an experienced thirty-year-old Caucasian guard. Martin, a twenty-four-year-old African American player who was in the beginning of his second professional season, suffered serious emotional depression as a result. The initial response by the media was skeptical. How, commentators asked, can a 315-pound, 6'5" tackle for the Miami Dolphins be bullied (Dahl 2013)? Many opined that the harassment involved was merely locker room banter—roughhousing and hazing—which all football players endure. In fact, a majority of Jonathan's teammates—both black and white—seemed to express this sentiment. Other members of the NFL suggested that it is all in the game. One has to be tough. Richie and the others never meant to harm Jonathan. It was all in good fun (Murtha 2013; Phillips 2013). Boys will be boys.

Reports also emphasized that Martin's elite educational and personal background may have made him too "soft" to endure the rough-and-tumble atmosphere of a major league football locker room (Brinson 2013). Martin had graduated from a private high school and Stanford University; his parents were Harvard graduates who raised Martin in an upper-middle-class household, a fact to which some commentators attributed Martin's inability to stand up to roughhousing in the NFL.

A few days after the initial reports of bullying, the text of a voice-mail that Richie Incognito had left on Martin's phone on April 6, 2013, emerged. In the voicemail, Incognito stated, "Hey, wassup, you half-nigger piece of shit. I saw you on Twitter, you been training 10 weeks. I'll shit in your fuckin' mouth. I'm gonna slap your fuckin' mouth. I'm gonna slap your real mother across the face [laughter]. Fuck you, you're still a rookie. I'll kill you" (Wells et al. 2014, 99).

The voicemail caught the attention of management because it raised serious concerns about race and violence in the NFL; when the Dolphins discovered the voicemail, the team suspended Richie Incognito from play (Wells et al. 2014). The NFL hired Ted Wells, a well-known African American white-collar criminal defense lawyer who practices at the respected law firm of Paul, Weiss, Rifkind, Wharton & Garrison in New York City, to conduct an investigation into the facts surrounding the Martin/Incognito affair. After interviewing more than one hundred witnesses and with the help of a consulting psychologist, an expert in matters relating to workplace dynamics, Ted Wells and his colleagues published the *Report to the National Football League concerning Issues of Workplace Conduct at the Miami Dolphins* (2014; hereafter, Wells Report), which made factual findings but did not take a position on issues of legal liability. Wells and his colleagues had constant access to an expert psychologist, Dr. William H. Berman. The use of an expert in psychology was forward looking and important because many of the behaviors involved, especially those of the alleged victim, belied common expectations. The Wells Report documents serious verbal abuse, including bullying, mistreatment, and racial epithets directed toward Jonathan Martin, with Richie Incognito as the leader of a group of players who picked on Martin. It also documents similar serious verbal abuse of at least one other player and racist bullying of a trainer of Japanese origin. While the report concludes that upper management was unaware of the abuse and was serious about furthering respect among the players, it also suggests that at least two coaches knew of and/or participated in the abuse.

The Martin/Incognito story captured the media's attention because of the specter of a physically large professional football player who was unable to protect himself from childish antics of his teammates. Most were concerned about the racist comments directed at Martin. Issues of race and class were front and center. Here we had a white, lower-middle-class guard from New Jersey who was harassing a black player who had majored in classics at Stanford. The situation appeared to be a type of "reversal" in American society: here the young black male victim came from a more well-to-do and better-educated family than his white tormenter. Some compared Martin's background to that of Barack Obama, the well-educated but introverted black president of the United States.

In fact, the racism displayed was somewhat confusing to commentators. Other black members of the team goaded Martin for not being "black enough" (ibid., 31). Incognito and others—black and white—made derogatory and despicable comments daily about Martin's sister and his mother, announcing in crude terms that they were going to have sex with them. When asked about racism, many black teammates denied that it existed. Martin felt helpless to respond to the abuse because of his gentle manner, his belief that a response would only encourage more abuse, and the team's ethic of no "snitches" (ibid., 37).

The report documents a complicated relationship between Martin and Incognito, a relationship that may have led many to misunderstand what was happening. It finds that Martin and Incognito were close friends, but that Richie Incognito presented two different sides to Martin. At times, he was the protective mentor who helped Martin develop as a player, but at other times he engaged in serious abuse and bullying of Martin, knowing that he was damaging his colleague.

Martin's responses, too, were somewhat ambiguous. He often remained silent when offended. At other times, he laughed off the abuse and/or participated in the repartee in a half-hearted effort to fit in and diminish the abuse. The one thing Martin did *not* do is talk to management about the abuse, even though he engaged in a running commentary with his parents about his emotional difficulties caused by his teammates' bullying, and he had notified some members of management of his depression. One reason for nondisclosure was the "no snitches" ethic. The other was that Martin felt deeply ashamed that he wasn't strong enough to respond to the harassing behavior on his own (ibid.). In essence, Martin had absorbed the message: he was weak, not man enough to stand up for himself.

The report is particularly insightful because it documents the authors' initial doubts, many of which mirrored those of the general public and media commentators, and explains how and why the authors resolved those doubts with the help of the expert advice of a psychologist who specializes in workplace relationships. The report explains that it is not uncommon for victims of abuse to react as Martin did—to try to ignore the behavior in the hope that it will go away.

The Martin/Incognito story drew enormous interest from the public. For this reason, it is particularly noteworthy that the discussions surrounding the incident focus on race and class, but never acknowledge the issue of gender. For those of us who study masculinities theory, the locker room antics demonstrate a clear case of gender-based discriminatory harassment, in addition to race- and class-based harassment. Because the behavior occurred among men exclusively, however, the sex-discrimination/gender-based-harassment part of this story was and still is invisible to many. Most observers conceive of sex- or gender-based harassment victims as members of the "other" sex from the perpetrators. Even when members of the same sex engage in harassment against members of their own sex, many people tend to believe that the behavior occurs because of sex or gender only if there is a sexual motivation of a gay or lesbian perpetrator or if it is demonstrated that the perpetrator treats members of the two sexes differently from one another. Where women mistreat other women but not men, for example, this phenomenon is known as the "Queen Bee Syndrome" or "Mean Girls" and is attributed to jealousy or fear of losing one's exclusive place with the men.

When there are only men in a workplace or other environment, many conclude that the behavior is mere hazing or roughhousing that is insignificant and typical of male-on-male relationships. It happens everywhere—on male sports teams in school, in fraternities, on professional sports teams, at camp, in all-male workplaces—and, although some of the behavior is trivial, the law tends to excuse much more serious behavior because our society believes that it is normal or natural. Most people do not understand that the behavior occurs because of sex or gender and that it is sufficiently severe or pervasive to alter the conditions at the victim's school or workplace. In other words, the behavior satisfies the standards that the 1964 Civil Rights Act uses for determining whether illegal discrimination occurs.

The Martin/Incognito story demonstrates that as observers of others' behavior, people often use shortcuts that do not necessarily reflect reality, even though they believe that they do. Society presumes that victims are not victimized if they respond to harassing behavior in a manner that common sense indicates is unnatural. Unfortunately, common sense often betrays human beings when it comes to human behavior. Social science research demonstrates that victims often respond to harassment and bullying in ways that intuition would not predict. The Martin/Incognito story and the Wells Report validate lawyers' use of expert social scientists such as Dr. Berman to help them and the courts understand human behavior. Many legal scholars have advocated the use of social science research to help judges and juries explain behavior of parties before them, but courts have been reluctant to do so. This is not surprising given the lack of training of most lawyers and judges in the social sciences and the law's emphasis on reason over emotion.

But judges regularly reach conclusions on the basis of their own untrained common sense of how people should or do act in certain situations. These conclusions often stand in stark contrast to the research results. In complex situations involving motivation, intent, and perception, social science research is often crucial in helping judges and the fact finders figure out what happened and why.

Masculinities studies are particularly helpful in explaining behaviors that occur in all-male or predominantly male environments. Masculinities theorists posit that masculinity is not a biological given but a social construction of how men should appear and behave. It causes many, if not most, men to engage in performances of masculinity to prove their worth to other men. The locker room scene at the Miami Dolphins is a vivid example of how concepts of masculinity affect behaviors. Society encourages men to demonstrate their masculinity to other men. Men engage in intense competitions to prove their worth. Their relationships are homosocial; other men serve as their audience for their behaviors and must be convinced of their masculinity (Collinson 1988). To prove their masculinity and achieve power and status, men demean other men, especially those they perceive to be effeminate or soft, engage in competitive, crude group behavior, and, where women are present in small numbers, harass women to prove their masculinity to other men. Richie Incognito's behavior is a classic example of the performance of masculinities. When he was alone with Jonathan Martin, he ordinarily treated him as a friend—there was no opportunity to prove his manliness to others under these conditions. But when there was an audience,

Incognito used Martin as a foil to prove his own toughness to the other men on the team.

Courts have struggled with the enforcement of Title VII law, which prohibits discrimination because of sex, including discriminatory harassment that alters the terms or conditions of employment for the victim. In particular, in harassment cases, especially those happening among men, like the public that ignored the gendered aspects of Martin's treatment, courts do not always see the gendered aspect of the behavior. Consequently, they conclude that the behavior did not occur "because of sex." This conclusion represents a grave misunderstanding of the reasons for the behavior and an underestimation of Title VII violations as they occur in the workplace.

Of course, it is not only men who suffer in predominantly male environments. Women and girls also succumb to harassing gender-based treatment. But courts have at times concluded that even their treatment does not occur "because of sex" where the antifemale behaviors, jokes, and pornographic pictures existed in the workplace before women were hired. Some courts reason that the harassing behavior was present when the workplace was exclusively male. It follows, they conclude, that the behavior cannot occur because of the newly hired women's sex. An understanding of masculinities theory can help courts realize that although the male behavior is dominant and even commonplace, when it becomes sufficiently severe or pervasive to alter the terms or conditions of employment at work, it may be illegal under Title VII. It *does* occur because of sex or gender, *either because the person targeted does not live up to gender stereotypes or because the perpetrators are attempting to police the boundaries of male behavior and masculinity in the workplace.*

Without the understanding that men are not all equally positioned, women as a group will never achieve equality. Perhaps even more crucial for this book, masculinities studies help explain that workplace structures are themselves masculine and that masculine structures and behaviors are conflated with work. Women who attempt to assimilate into the masculine workplace must work harder because their lived experiences are often different from those of the men. Moreover, masculinities theory can explain that women, too, perform masculinities that may be harmful to other women or men. Because the behaviors are conflated with work and management techniques, often the gendered nature of the behavior is invisible.

Feminist legal theorists who engage with masculinities theory not only analyze the ways masculinities harm men but also ask how society might break down gender segregation and social gender barriers to the benefit of both men and women. We use masculinities theory to understand the social pressure on men, and to consider how social construction of men's roles can cause women's inequality. We argue that it is necessary to understand masculinities theory and the pressure that the gender order places on men in order to understand why women have had such difficulty achieving equality (Dowd, Levit, and McGinley 2012). Often, an understanding of masculinities helps to explain men's behaviors that harm women. These understandings permit us to suggest workable law reform that benefits men, women, and families.

While the Martin/Incognito story mirrors others in blue-collar workplaces such as the atmosphere at the oil rig where Joseph Oncale allegedly was seriously harassed by male coworkers in the shower (*Oncale v. Sundowner Offshore Services, Inc.* 1998), masculinity performances are not limited to blue-collar environments. In fact, even in the most elite law firms, there are masculinity performances that affect the working conditions of those harmed. In white-collar workplaces such as law firms, men tend to prove their masculinity in different, less physical ways than do men in blue-collar workplaces. White-collar workers often confuse performance of masculinity with work. Men engage in careerist behavior—working nonstop, acting aggressively, and engaging in self-promoting behavior—as a means of proving their masculinity.

For example, this book discusses the case of Ariel Ayanna, a male associate in a Boston law firm who sued the firm, alleging that he was fired because of his role as caretaker of his wife and children. Ayanna alleged that the firm expected men to work extremely long hours and to be available and visible even when there was no pressing work to be finished, and even when there was a crucial need for Ayanna to be with his family (*Ayanna v. Dechert LLP* 2012). These allegations are consistent with sociologist Richard Collier's study finding that law firms have cultures that demand bodily presence, visibility, and performances of hypermasculinity (Collier 2013).

As is obvious from the description of white-collar masculinities, masculinity performances do not always include harassing behaviors; they may also involve informal behaviors or expectations that affect the victim's career in the particular firm. These behaviors may be subtler than the reprehensible treatment that Jonathan Martin endured, but they, too, may create gender- or sex-based discrimination that is illegal under Title VII. To the extent that the expectations affect employees' careers and their employers cannot prove a legitimate defense, there may well be a violation of Title VII.

Finally, multidimensional masculinities theory, which is examined more thoroughly throughout the book, helps legal theorists and practitioners understand that we should not consider only gender and class when analyzing work situations and masculinity. Other identity factors and the context of the situation will come into play. As legal theorists and practitioners reconsider the Martin/Incognito affair, we cannot ignore the importance of race, combined with gender and class, in the context of professional football. For example, while the Wells Report recognized the harm Martin suffered because of the behavior of his football colleagues in ridiculing and telling false sexual stories about Martin's mother and sister, it does not mention that it is particularly problematic that teammates directed this behavior at two black women. Historically, black women suffer from false stereotypes of hypercarnality and sexually aggressive behavior. When Martin's teammates taunted him with imagined sexual escapades with his mother and sister, there was an underlying racist tinge to the behavior. One way of seeing this more clearly is to shift the lens by imagining how society would judge this behavior if the racial makeup of the players were different. If black professional football players made similar statements about a white teammate's white mother and sister, serious racial divisions might have arisen on the team. But in Martin's case, no one questioned the behavior at the time. To understand the situation, therefore, we need to shift the lens from race and class in the first instance to gender and then back to race to have a more complete understanding of the dynamics at the Miami Dolphins.

Another example of the intersection of race, gender, and class is Martin's black teammates' insistence that he was "not black enough." Some observers would conclude that these remarks are not based on race because of the identity of those making the remarks. Others would argue that because blacks can discriminate against other blacks, these remarks do indicate discriminatory motive. Even if observers would interpret these remarks as racially motivated, however, many of them would not connect these remarks to gender and class. Masculinities theory helps explain that the comment that Martin was "not black enough" is gendered because it relies on the stereotype of black *men* as threatening and dangerous—the bad black man. In the case of professional football, the stereotype has a positive connotation because the job of football requires players to be tough, threatening, and dangerous to the opponents. The stereotype relates to men, not to women, and to the way a black man performs his masculinity. Masculinities theory demonstrates the importance of certain masculine characteristics to black men. Moreover, the stereotype relates to poor or working-class blacks who come from minority neighborhoods who perform their masculinity in a more threatening manner. Thus, the remark is also about Martin's upper-middle-class presentation of a more cultured and less tough masculinity. By shifting the lens various times, observers can understand the multidimensionality of this comment. If the comment were made by white teammates, there would be little doubt that it was racially motivated. If the comment were made about a black woman, those making the comments would probably not mean that she was not tough enough or that she was not enough of a "bad-ass." It would have a different meaning. Courts should engage in similar lens shifting to understand the cases before them and to explain the proof to juries.

Martin's situation, therefore, demonstrates that lawyers and judges should use masculinities studies to understand the gendered and racial motivations for harassing behaviors in the workplace. Assuming the applicability of Title VII of the 1964 Civil Rights Act to a hypothetical lawsuit that Martin would bring against the Dolphins and/or the NFL, Martin's lawyers and the judge assigned the case should focus on masculinities theory and research to understand how to apply Title VII's prohibitions of a hostile work environment occurring because of sex and race. This is particularly important because under federal law there is no protection against general bullying and harassment in the workplace, and there is only sporadic coverage under state law. In essence, horrific behaviors, even criminal behaviors, do not provide recourse against an employer unless the employee proves under Title VII that the harassment was discriminatory on the basis of sex, race, or other protected characteristic.

In Jonathan Martin's hypothetical case against his employer, his lawyer would allege sex- and race-based harassment that creates a hostile work environment. In harassment cases, courts focus on whether the harassing behavior is sufficiently severe or pervasive to alter the plaintiff's employment and whether it occurred "because of sex." It is noteworthy that the Wells Report never even mentioned sex or gender. The gender-based harassment was invisible to the authors of the report. Masculinities theory can help courts see the gendered content of the behavior that is invisible to most observers. In this case, the court would also probably have trouble determining whether the behavior occurred "because of race." Indeed, even though Martin's teammates made offensive racist remarks, including remarks about shooting black people, the consultant's report declined to decide whether the behavior that took place was motivated by racial animus (Wells et al. 2014, 32). Masculinities theory would help Martin prove that the harassment was based on both race and sex, in addition to class.

More generally, this book proposes the use of masculinities studies to sharpen courts' understanding of discrimination under Title VII. My approach is both theoretical and pragmatic. It explains how masculinities theory can help lawyers, judges, and legal academics understand why the courts' views of motivations for specific workplace behaviors are often limited by their own personal experiences. It encourages courts to understand the unconscious bases for discriminatory behavior and treatment and to consider masculinities theory to determine whether illegal discriminatory behavior has occurred. It discusses how courts should use masculinities theory to help juries interpret behaviors to determine whether sex discrimination occurs. As Martin's case demonstrates, masculinities theory is particularly helpful in the sex- or gender-based harassment cases where the plaintiff must prove that the behavior occurred "because of sex" and that it was sufficiently severe or pervasive to alter the victim's terms or conditions of employment. But it is equally important in sex discrimination claims proved under disparate treatment or disparate impact analysis where stereotypes and implicit biases affect not only individual decision making but also the processes and structures in the workplace that further or limit an individual's success at work.

Part I of the book introduces the reader to research on masculinities and multidimensional masculinities theory, and discusses generally how this body of research and theory can help in the analysis of cases arising under Title VII of the 1964 Civil Rights Act, which forbids employment discrimination because of race, color, gender, national origin, and religion. Chapter 1 examines the origins of masculinities theory and its relationship to workplace behaviors, as well as its potential use in explaining why certain behaviors should constitute sex- or gender-based discrimination.

Part II describes Title VII law in sex- and gender-based hostile work environment cases and examines how courts can use masculinities theory to explain why and how a particular environment may violate Title VII. Chapter 2 discusses the history and interpretation of sex- and gender-based harassment law. Chapter 3 analyzes how masculinity studies can aid in establishing that the harassing behavior occurred because of the victim's sex. Chapter 4 uses a methodology of multidimensional masculinities theory—shifting the lens—to consider the proper standard for determining whether harassing behavior is sufficiently severe or pervasive to constitute an illegal workplace environment.

Part III analyzes Title VII law in disparate treatment and disparate impact cases and suggests how masculinities theory can help in resolving interpretive problems in those types of cases. Chapter 5 examines the history of Title VII jurisprudence and the doctrinal and proof differences between disparate treatment and disparate impact causes of action under Title VII. Chapter 6 discusses the requirement that plaintiffs prove intent to discriminate in disparate treatment claims and analyzes the different possible definitions of intent under the statute. With the background of the intent requirement in mind, chapter 7 analyzes various circumstances in which masculinities theory can enlighten a disparate treatment case. Chapter 8 evaluates disparate impact causes of action under Title VII and demonstrates that masculinities theory can aid lawyers and judges to understand disparate impact causes of action.

Part IV analyzes practical ways for legal actors to use masculinities research in litigation, and discusses how employers should prevent discrimination based on masculine structures and practices. Chapter 9 proposes concrete ways in which the courts should become educated about masculinities theory and other relevant social science research. It also discusses how lawyers and judges, through use of expert testimony and jury instructions, can convey to juries an understanding of the complicated gender- and sex-based behaviors in workplaces that should create liability under Title VII. The conclusion summarizes the theory, application, and admissibility of masculinities research and suggests that employers should educate themselves about masculine practices and structures, and alter their workplaces to eliminate them.

PART I

Masculinities Theory and Title VII

1

Masculinities' Relationship to Title VII

Understanding Masculinities: Social More Than Biological

Society views masculinity as a natural result of male biology. Masculinities research comprises an interdisciplinary field of research and theory that challenges this view. It posits that rather than being a natural biological characteristic, masculinity is constructed from social pressures and individual experiences. Men *are* not masculine; they *perform* their masculinity.[1] For example, from childhood on, social forces pressure boys and men to act like a "man," hide their emotions, refrain from crying, and demonstrate their emotional and physical strength to others. As boys and men internalize these admonitions, the resulting behaviors are not biologically driven but socially constructed.

Most masculinities theorists accept that gender is socially constructed, but they also understand the importance of reproductive capacity in shaping masculinity. They recognize that society assigns women the caregiving role because of their reproductive roles of carrying babies in their wombs and sees men as the protectors of and providers for their families because of their generally greater strength and body mass (Connell 2005). Expecting women to engage exclusively in caregiving and men to be the financial providers of their families is a societal construction that devolves from women's and men's bodily reproductive functions.

Masculinity has multiple forms; hence scholars use the term "masculinities" rather than "masculinity" to refer to many different behavioral variations. Men of different races, classes, sexual orientations, and national origins perform their masculinity in different ways and in relation to one another in varying contexts. For example, at the risk of stereotyping, white, upper-middle-class, heterosexual men may perform their masculinity by practicing a profession and earning a large salary, dressing in expensive clothing, driving high-powered cars, dating models or other high-powered women, and playing competitive tennis. In contrast, white, lower-middle-class men may perform their masculinity by working in blue-collar positions that require physical strength, driving powerful trucks or SUVs, playing and watching football, and visiting strip clubs. Young black and Latino men in poor or working-class neighborhoods may perform their masculinities by wearing "sagging" pants and their caps sideways, carrying weapons, joining gangs, and listening to hip hop. Some gay men may perform their masculinity by engaging in bodybuilding and aggressive sex with multiple partners. Many of the behaviors performed by men of color and blue-collar white men are stances in reaction to the "ideal" version of masculinity—the professional hegemonic white male. Of course, these serve merely as examples. I do not suggest that all men of a particular race, class, or sexual orientation act in identical ways. In fact, masculinities theory holds the opposite position—that there are multiple variations of masculinity that men perform. The important point is that a social need to perform masculinity often drives men's behavior.

As men age, their performances change. Moreover, depending on the context, the same men might behave differently. For example, a gay male lawyer who performs his masculinity to adhere to professional heterosexual norms in the law firm might perform his masculinity differently among friends in a gay bar. These examples, while incomplete, demonstrate that masculinities are cultural and contextual, performative, and constantly changing, rather than static, natural, and biological.

Applications of Masculinities Studies to Title VII

Masculinities theory draws much of its analysis from feminist and other theories but also offers explanations that other theories do not. It helps de-essentialize men, who, like women, are not all the same (Dowd 2010). Masculinities research explains the importance of recognizing the power differential among men and how it affects male experience and behavior. It demonstrates that although men as a group may have more power than women as a group (the "patriarchal dividend"), individual men may occupy less powerful positions than individual women. Moreover, a focus on men helps explain the complexity of the inequalities that exist because of male gender combined with race, class, national origin, sexual orientation, and other identities. Finally, masculinities research shows that even when men are privileged, privilege has costs (ibid.). One example of these costs is that men have less opportunity and community support for a true parenting relationship with their children. Another is the related pressure placed on men to serve as the breadwinner in a family (Carbone and Cahn 2014; Williams 2010).

Masculinities researchers consider how societal norms shape the behavior of individual men and women, how masculinities are embedded in the structure of institutions, and how individuals and groups perform masculinities within those institutions. The term "masculinities" therefore has multiple meanings. As I use it, the term defines both substance and methodology. Because this book deals with issues of masculinities and the workplace, I limit the *substantive* term to three different meanings that are relevant to work.

- First, the term describes a *complex social structure* that is embedded into organizations and determines and reflects power relationships at work.
- Second, it refers to the *construction of masculine identities* at work through performance.
- Finally, the term describes a *set of practices* and the active engagement in these practices by men and women. These practices, consciously or unconsciously, reinforce the gender hierarchy in workplaces by conflating "doing masculinity" with work itself (Martin 2003).

The next subsection discusses masculinities theory as methodology. A discussion of masculinities theory as substance follows the methodology discussion.

Masculinities Theory as Methodology

As a *methodology*, masculinities theory shifts the viewer's perspective by examining human behavior and organizations *through a different lens*. Using this process exposes how gender operates, and the presence of discrimination that we might not otherwise notice. It calls attention to both the obvious that we often ignore and the hidden that we often miss. For example, chapter 4 discusses the concept of the "reasonable woman" in sexual harassment law in the unusual case where a man alleges that he is a victim of sexual harassment by a woman. In the traditional case where a woman alleged that a man harassed her, the reasonable woman standard emerged in the 1990s in response to critiques of the traditional reasonable man (or person) standard for identifying whether harassing discriminatory behavior was sufficiently serious to constitute a violation of Title VII. My analysis in chapter 4 shifts the lens from the expected female victim to a male victim to help us understand how we should evaluate the standard. This lens shift enables legal scholars to consider the benefits and disadvantages of the reasonable woman standard and suggests an alternative that should benefit both male and female victims of sexual harassment. The chapter demonstrates that surprising stereotypes arise when courts use the reasonable man standard in a case where the victim is a man. If courts use a reasonable man standard to determine whether the behavior was sufficiently severe to pollute the male victim's work environment, it becomes obvious that society expects men to suffer much more serious harassment than it would expect of women. In fact, many people believe that men would feel lucky to be sexually harassed by women in the workplace, a stereotype that courts would not want to engrave into law. This lens shift also makes it possible to consider the stereotypes and problems that are built into the reasonable woman standard when applied to a female victim. One example is that the standard assumes that all reasonable women, despite the context and other aspects of their identities, will react in only one identical manner rather than in a range of different manners, all of which are reasonable.

Masculinities scholarship can also help shift the lens from race to gender and vice versa. For example, chapter 8 discusses a case challenging the City of New Haven for throwing out the results of a promotional firefighter examination whose use would have created a nearly all-white class of captains and sergeants. The city believed that using the results of the promotional examination would result in an illegal disparate impact on black and Latino firefighters. Although the theory of the case and the analysis of the Court focused on race, masculinities scholarship suggests that using a gender lens that exposes the history of employment practices in fire departments that favor white men who traditionally passed the jobs down from (white) father to (white) son, and other white masculine practices, would illuminate the effects of these practices on men of color and all women.

Likewise, analyzing Jonathan Martin's victimization at the Miami Dolphins through a lens of gender as well as race will make visible gendered behavior that was hidden from the media and its audience. Only upon shifting the lens to gender is it clear that much of Martin's harassment occurred because he did not adhere to gendered stereotypes of what an NFL player should be. The harassment probably resulted from his tormentors' need to reinforce their own masculinity and the masculinity of professional football itself by drawing gendered boundaries around the players. In other words, an NFL player should act in a particular way that reinforces his own masculinity and that of the entire group. A player who does not engage in the accepted behavior undermines not only his own reputation but also that of all of the other players, the team, and the league.

This shift to considering gender does not ignore race; in fact, in the Jonathan Martin situation, it enhances our consideration of race because it allows us to pinpoint the different stereotypes and expectations that society harbors regarding black men as opposed to black women. Black men are supposedly angry and tough, a stereotype that often works to their disadvantage. But in the NFL, anger and toughness are valued personality traits. Hence, Martin's coworkers may not have related to the soft-spoken black classics major from Stanford. Unless the law considers race and gender, it presents an incomplete picture of the possible motivations for the harassers' behaviors.

Masculinities Theory as Substance

1. Masculinities as Complex Social Structure

Gender is embedded in the structure of organizations (Connell 2005). Assumptions about gender inform the way work is organized (Martin 2003). While individuals bring their gender identities into the workplace and perform them at work, gender is also a structure that supports the organizational design (and vice versa) (Connell 2005; Whitehead 1998). For example, historically a workplace or business has worked most efficiently when men are the primary or sole breadwinners. The ideal is the man as breadwinner who is totally dedicated to his job because of his responsibilities to provide for his family. In return, his wife or partner performs many of the personal tasks for the man so that he can concentrate solely on his work. Thus, the organization benefits from the sole breadwinner's total dedication to work (as well as his partner's contribution) and his willingness to work long hours to finish the task at hand. In effect, the man as sole or primary breadwinner is more responsive to hierarchical demands than his counterpart who is not the primary breadwinner because he is expected to support the family's physical needs and to protect its members from economic and physical harm.

This organization is not only gendered but also classed and raced: it presumes an intact, two-parent, heterosexual family or a single person with no family. Only intact middle- or upper-middle-class families can afford the luxury of a stay-at-home parent. And, even black and Latino families who earn middle- or upper-middle-class incomes have less money in savings; it is more difficult in an intact two-parent black or Latino family for one parent to stay home to care for the home and the children.

In sum, institutions are structured around male bodies and reproductive systems; they view heterosexual white men as the norm, and measure all others against that norm. The invisible gendered premise accepted by most organizations is that employees should work to their utmost capacity and, in many cases, be available to work at all hours in order to get the work done. Underlying this concept is the implicit assumption that the worker has a male body that does not bear children and a partner or wife who deals with his outside needs (Williams 2001, 1–3).

Blue-collar workers may not regularly work the long hours that white-collar workers do, but they typically have considerably less autonomy when compared to their white-collar counterparts. Blue-collar workers have inflexible schedules, mandatory overtime, and little vacation or personal leave time. Even when they are due leave, blue-collar workers encounter difficulty getting approval for proposed leaves. Because of these inflexible schedules, many working-class women work part-time hours, and make 21 *percent less per hour* than their full-time counterparts (Williams 2010). Because of the unavailability of quality, affordable childcare, many working-class families rely on relatives and spouses for childcare. These relatives often engage in "tag-teaming" to cover the childcare because they, too, have job commitments (ibid., 45).

Organizational behavior enacts gender in varying and complex ways (Martin 2003). Organizations assign genders to certain jobs; the expectations of persons doing those jobs reflect a traditional division of labor in the family (ibid.). Jobs whose holders perform the primary and most respected work of the institution are gendered male. In contrast, women generally work in the jobs that serve the auxiliary role of helping the men in their work. This division of labor reflects and reinforces the traditional roles of men and women in the family (Williams 2001). Thus, jobs of bankers, lawyers, engineers, and doctors are gendered male while jobs of administrative assistants, paralegals, and nurses are gendered female.

In the white-collar workforce, jobs that are gendered male enjoy status, respect, privacy, and power. They benefit by having a "helper" who takes care of the insubstantial work, the dirty work, and the emotional labor so that the boss can do the more important substantive work of representing the client, designing a bridge, or diagnosing a patient's illness. Jobs that are gendered female lack status (in relation to the male jobs), respect, privacy, and power. As the wife and mother in the family puts the interests of her husband and children above her own and acts to support others in the family rather than to further her own interest, those holding female jobs put their boss's interests first and work to further their boss's careers and work over their own.

The status of the female job holder is linked to that of her boss. The administrative assistant, for example, makes travel reservations, arranges for food to be brought into meetings, and assures that the boss's documents are filed and in order. The nurse does the important dirty work, caring for patients after surgery, cleaning them up, and watching for changes in their conditions. Both the administrative assistant and the nurse also engage in emotional labor. Emotional labor assures that relationships in the office and in the hospital run smoothly. Male jobs ordinarily confer the privacy of an office and some relief from the stress of the job; female jobs generally do not. Persons holding female jobs are interruptible, and located in the open with little privacy. More status and respect are conferred upon those performing male jobs. The holder of a male job has a title such as Mr. (or Ms. or Mrs.) or Dr. or Professor. The boss, coworkers, and the public often address those holding female jobs by their first names.

In the blue-collar context, male jobs are generally paid better and require strength and endurance. Machine workers, firefighters, construction workers, and automobile workers engage in high-paying jobs with significant status. Female jobs such as housekeeping may be equally taxing on the worker's body, but because the work is considered "women's work" and the physical labor and strength required to do these jobs are underestimated, these jobs suffer from lower pay and status than blue-collar male jobs.

Workplace culture also reinforces gendered norms. Even when women occupy male jobs, they often experience lower status and poorer working conditions than those of their male counterparts. In jobs that are predominantly held by men, male colleagues look to their female counterparts to perform "female" tasks such as answering the phones, performing emotional labor, and doing committee work (McGinley 2009a; Martin 2003). Conversely, colleagues do not expect men occupying traditional female jobs to perform the same kind of emotional labor or dirty work that women holding those jobs perform. In fact, others expect men in women's jobs to ride the glass elevator out of the female job itself (Pierce 1995). Insiders and outsiders often confuse women in traditionally male, higher-status jobs with those belonging to a lower-status group while they believe that men occupying the lower-status, female-gendered jobs belong with the men holding higher-status jobs. For example, in law firms, partners and clients assume that female lawyers are paralegals or secretaries, but mistake male paralegals for lawyers (ibid.). Women holding high-status jobs with the ability to hire and fire and to set others' pay tend to suffer more stress and depression than men holding the same jobs because coworkers tend not to consider women as legitimate authority figures. This failure of legitimacy contributes to higher stress levels in women (Pudrovska and Karaker 2014).

2. The Construction of Masculine Identities through Performance

Masculinities are plural. There are multiple forms of masculinity that are affected by time, place, social class, race, gender, sexual orientation, disability, and national origin. Thus, masculinities theorists prefer the term "masculinities" to "masculinity." Moreover, masculinities are not static, but are active and changeable.

The normative masculinity in many American workplaces is aggressive, competitive, and anxious (Kimmel 2004). Although numerous masculinities exist in tension with one another, "hegemonic masculinity" defines the most powerful version of masculinity in a particular place at a particular time (Connell 2005, 77). In the United States, the hegemonic masculinity is white, educated, upper-middle-class, and heterosexual. Our culture rewards white middle-class men who compete to prove their masculinity, who exclude women from power because they lack masculinity, and who exclude men from power who do not live up to the normative definition of masculinity (ibid.). The competition is a "homosocial event" that requires men to test themselves to prove to other men that they are masculine (ibid., 186). The pressure to prove one's masculinity is constant, and the competition is keen.

Masculinity is antifemininity and "is defined more by what one is not rather than who one is" (ibid., 185; Karst 1991). It involves a flight from the feminine, and a fear of homosexuality. Men prove their masculinity to other men to gain acceptance (Kimmel 2004). Many men who perform masculinities see homosexuality as feminine behavior; homophobia "is a central organizing principle of our cultural definition of manhood. Homophobia is more than the irrational fear of gay men, more than the fear that we might be perceived as gay" (ibid., 188). It is a fear that other men will recognize that one is not as masculine as one pretends to be (ibid.). This fear creates shame and leads to an unwillingness to stand up for others who are being harassed (ibid.). Moreover, it compels men to enact exaggerated masculine behaviors and to project attitudes that women and gays are "the other" with whom straight men compare themselves to establish their own "manhood" (ibid., 191).

Masculinity is fragile. Men compete to prove their masculinity, but the vast majority of men cannot achieve the ideal hegemonic form of masculinity. When men fall short, they suffer, and to reinforce their own masculinity, they often cause others who are subordinated to them to suffer as well (ibid.). Some men prove their masculinity to other men at work by demonstrating their superiority to female colleagues and by engaging in harassment of women. Others harass gender-nonconforming men who do not live up to the hegemonic ideals. Still others engage in more subtle forms of masculine practices that I discuss below. In any event, masculinities theory is important because it helps to explain the motivations of men who compete to prove their masculinity in the workplace and the harm the competition does to women and men.

Concepts of the preferred masculinity are transferred through social means. Our society barrages boys and young men with images and comments about what it means to live up to this form of masculinity. Comments such as "Don't be a girl" and "Man up," and accusations that a particular man or boy has no "cojones" or is a "wimp" are criticisms of men or boys who are not performing their masculinity in the aggressive or competitive manner sanctioned by society. Even in the political realm, these comments happen regularly. Sharron Angle, for example, who ran for the United States Senate against Senate Majority Leader Harry Reid in Nevada in 2010, told Reid to "man up" as she criticized him in their televised debates for his position regarding Social Security (Silva 2010). These types of comments disparage the boy or man by directly comparing him to a woman or girl and creating doubt as to his masculinity. They not only police the barriers of masculinity but also reinforce a gender hierarchy: masculine men are always superior to women.

Men who do not have the power to engage in hegemonic masculinities perform subordinated masculinities. Often, subordinated masculinities are subversive. They resist the hegemonic form of masculinity and present a more forceful or violent form of masculinity.

An example of subversive masculinities includes the hypermasculinities performed in the shop cultures described by sociologist David Collinson. In his study of masculinity in shop-floor relations, Collinson found that in many blue-collar work environments, competing masculinities are stark (Collinson 1988). Laborers, who are powerless to adopt the white-collar hegemonic masculinity, perform subversive masculinities to resist their more powerful managers (ibid.). Because blue-collar workers' masculinity is subordinated to the hegemonic masculinity of the white-collar worker, blue-collar workers often react to and resist hegemonic masculinity. The resistance can include hypermasculine behavior and comparisons of their white-collar superiors to women ("pansies") (ibid.). Male blue-collar workers often direct these performances of hypermasculinity at women who work in "men's jobs" (ibid.). They also harass men who are outsiders because these outsiders do not conform to the definition of hypermasculinity that is required of the men on the job (ibid.).

Social scientists like David Collinson have studied the performance of masculinities in workplace environments that are exclusively or predominantly male. Even in the absence of female workers, men enact masculinities in relationship to one another. For example, they engage in competitive ritual behaviors such as sexual humor, aggressive derogatory comments, and physical touching and grabbing of other men's genitals. The men compete aggressively by engaging in these behaviors to prove their masculinity to one another.

Men use humor to build a sense of solidarity, to break the monotony of their jobs, and to resist the tight control exercised over them by the managers. Collinson studied the relationship between humor and masculinity and found that the men working on the shop floor developed a "shared sense of masculinity" by adopting exaggerated nicknames for each other and by using hypermasculine banter on the shop floor, "permeated by uninhibited swearing, mutual ridicule, [and] displays of sexuality and 'pranks'" (Collinson 1988, 185–86). By contrasting their own hypermasculinity to what they characterized as effeminate behavior of management, the men actively resisted their subordination by management (ibid.). They couched their resistance in explicit gender terms, seeing management as effeminate "twats" and "nancy boys" (ibid.). This humor gave them a sense of power and authority at work, permitting them to "negate and distance" their managers, even though the shop jobs required monotonous, repetitive tasks (ibid.).

Men also used humor to pressure group members to conform to working-class masculinity. The shop followed the concept of "survival of the fittest" (Collinson 1988, 187). For example, workers expected other male workers to take a joke and to laugh at themselves and spar with others, act aggressively and critically, treat others disrespectfully, and embarrass others (ibid.). Newcomers were especially vulnerable to mistreatment. They "had to negotiate a series of degrading and humiliating initiation ceremonies" designed to teach them how to take a joke and be a man (ibid., 188). Surviving these rituals signaled to the group that the initiate would willingly follow the precepts of the group. The ridicule included displays of "tough masculinity" and testing others' limits. Jokes centered on a "preoccupation with male sexuality and the differentiation of working class men from women" (ibid., 190). Through these performances, the workers constructed their identities as independent, powerful, and sexual, and dismissed women as passive and dependent (ibid.).

Men perceived as outsiders were kept at a distance or endured the joking in order to gain the group's acceptance. For example, the researcher, an outsider to the blue-collar workplace because of his education, suffered derogatory comments comparing him to a woman—a "lazy cunt" (ibid.). After he proved his endurance and that he would not challenge the power dynamics at the workplace, the men gave him a card accepting him into the "dumb fuckers club" (ibid., 190).

Much of the behavior described by Jonathan Martin at the Miami Dolphins strongly resembles the conduct observed by Collinson in the shop in England. Martin alleges that his teammates regularly ridiculed him and subjected him to humiliation. The Wells Report found that they also engaged in racist slurs, crude discussions of women, and sexual fantasies about Martin's mother and sister. Martin's response was to ignore the ridicule, attempt to joke, or stay silent.

In Collinson's study, the men emphasized two competing masculine identities on the shop floor: sexual conqueror and breadwinner. Younger men displayed their sexuality through active construction of women as sexual objects. Derogatory comments about women as sexual objects and boasts of sexual conquests combined with nude photographs of women displayed openly on walls of the shop floor created an atmosphere of explicit compulsory male heterosexuality. Older men regarded their role as breadwinners as crucial to their self-respect (ibid.). All engaged in peacocking behavior—strutting their masculine prowess—by using foul language and rough discussion of women.

Collinson observes, however, that many of the men admitted to him privately that they did not act this way at home (ibid.). Indeed, their work behavior was merely a performance that established their identities as masculine men, a performance that was necessary to survive the work environment. The men's gender identities were socially enacted at work through their performances and their interactions with one another (ibid.). Legal scholars Devon Carbado and Mitu Gulati explain that the performance of identities helps an outsider become more acceptable in the workplace, but may become a denial of oneself (Carbado and Gulati 2000). While masculine behaviors in the shop context serve as resistance to supervisors, these behaviors also appear to be identity performances designed to gain acceptance among fellow blue-collar workers.

Collinson found that men used humor to mask serious criticism and fragile relationships. Humor accusing a fellow worker of laziness often touched a nerve and led to battles and unwillingness to talk to coworkers (ibid.). Ironically, a number of the workers admitted that joking sometimes went too far and that they engaged in the practice to comply with the culture's demands (ibid.). Often a worker would "snap" as a result of the joking aimed at him; in one case, the victim of the jokes suffered a "total emotional breakdown" (ibid., 194). This finding suggests that Jonathan Martin's emotional distress and passive response to Incognito's and others' harassment may be more common than popular belief presumes.

Women and effeminate men may be harassed to undermine their competence, to force them out of the job, and to preserve the job as a masculine enclave (Schultz 1998). As in fraternities studied by anthropologist Peggy Sanday in which pledges were humiliated (Sanday 2007), men in workplaces also harass newcomers and those who have been in the workplace for a longer period to assure that they conform to the group's masculine norms. In the workplace, these behaviors assure the job's masculine identity, and the masculinity of the men holding the jobs.

Collinson's shop workers expressed and constructed their masculinity in resistance to the hegemonic forms of masculinity. They also subordinated others as they performed their masculinity, and violently disparaged other men who did not live up to the ideals of masculinity.

Probably because of a fear of betraying their masculine identities at work, male workers in blue-collar jobs even risked their jobs to avoid telling their bosses that they could not work overtime because of childcare responsibilities (Williams 2010).

Joan Williams's Center for WorkLife Law studied ninety-nine arbitrations of employee disciplines, many of which occurred because the employee refused to work overtime without sufficient notice. Despite union representation, employees were fired or penalized for putting their families first in situations where work and childcare conflicted, even though the workers had tried to arrange alternate care.

Williams's research reveals a fascinating truth about childcare and men: despite working-class men's more complete engagement with childcare than their white-collar counterparts, they do not readily admit to this division of labor (ibid., 56–57). Although there was no case involving a female worker who flatly refused to discuss the work-family conflicts with her supervisors, a number of men willingly risked discipline or firing rather than explain to the employer that they had to leave work to care for their children (ibid.).

Male workers asked their employers to excuse their absences, but when pressed, refused to explain that they had family care responsibilities. In one case, mandatory overtime was posted too late for a male worker to make up the overtime before his regular work hours, and the worker refused to stay after regular work hours because he had to care for his grandchild. When the supervisor asked why the worker could not stay to work overtime, the worker told him that it was none of the supervisor's business. The worker refused to work overtime and was fired for insubordination (ibid.). In other cases, male workers were fired or disciplined for refusing to work when they had major child- or family care commitments. When asked for their reason for not working, the men told the supervisors that they had "family commitments" or that it was "personal," or the worker refused to explain, even though in at least one case the employer had permitted a failure to work if the justification was reasonable (ibid., 58).

Williams attributes the men's failure to explain their predicaments to their employers to the men's sense of masculinity and the "hidden injury of class" that working-class men feel when they are unable to support their wives and families on their salaries alone (ibid., 59). Many working-class men see their inability to support their families on their salaries as a failure, in essence, a downhill slide from their parents' lives. Much of the sense of failure affects the men's sense of masculinity because the breadwinner role is key to their concept of masculinity (ibid.).

Masculinities theory suggests that it is a performance of masculinity for a working-class man to refuse to discuss his childcare responsibilities with his male coworkers and supervisors. The injuries caused by an admission that a man has family care responsibilities may be invisible, but such an admission would undermine his masculinity in his own eyes and in the eyes of his fellow workers.

These examples demonstrate that masculinities are dynamic and are created through action and performance. Masculinity is not a stable, fixed notion, but social concepts of masculinity are malleable. Individuals construct their masculinity in response to the behavior and expectations of others.

3. Masculine Practices at Work

There is substantial overlap between the previous subsection on constructing identities through performance and this subsection on masculine practices, but I separate the two discussions to emphasize that individuals construct their identities actively by performing their masculinity in various ways and that particular practices themselves become referred to as "masculinities." This subsection deals with the practices themselves that are termed "masculinities." These practices include authoritarian and careerist behaviors in white-collar workplaces as well as physical and verbal abuse of women and unmanly men in blue-collar workplaces.

Masculine practices become so conflated with work and success at work that they are often invisible to those who practice them and others. Moreover, because of their association with the norm at work, both women and men engage in these behaviors. These practices vary depending on the type of workplace, but their dominant characteristic is that they have a disparate negative effect on women and gender-nonconforming men in the workplace.

WHITE-COLLAR MASCULINITIES

Collinson and Hearn identified five types of masculinities practiced in white-collar workplaces. They include

- authoritarianism,
- paternalism,
- entrepreneurialism,
- informalism, and
- careerism (Collinson and Hearn 1994).

Managers who practice *authoritarianism* broach no dissent or difference, are unwilling to engage in dialogue, and prefer coercive power and control over subordinates. Managers who model themselves on the father in a family enact *paternalism*. They emphasize personal trust and loyalty. The effect is to ensure the subordinate's cooperation and to enhance the manager's power. *Entrepreneurialism* is a highly competitive style that elevates efficiency and managerial control over other values. It requires subordinates to work long hours, to be mobile geographically, and to meet tight deadlines. *Informalism* is a method of building relationships based on shared interests that simultaneously screens out female colleagues and some men. It includes talk about women, sex, and sports. *Careerism* is a masculinity ordinarily enacted by middle-class white managers whose masculine identity is linked to hard work and upward movement in their careers (ibid., 13–14).

A good example of the white-collar workplace is on display in a case brought by a male associate, Ariel Ayanna, in a Family and Medical Leave Act (FMLA 1993) and sex discrimination lawsuit under the Massachusetts employment discrimination law against a large Boston law firm from which he was fired (*Ayanna v. Dechert LLP* 2012).[2] Ayanna alleged that he was a father of two children whose wife suffered from several chronic and episodic mental illnesses. As a result, there were times when she was unable to care for herself and their children.

Ayanna's sex discrimination claim alleges that the firm had a "macho" culture and that it discriminated against him for his failure to meet the stereotype of macho lawyer. According to the complaint, Dechert's masculine culture "equate[s] masculinity with relegating caretaking to women and working long hours in the office" (Amended Complaint and Jury Demand, Introduction, *Ayanna v. Dechert LLP* 2012). The macho culture "praises and encourages male associates and partners to fulfill the stereotypical male role of ceding family responsibilities to women" (ibid., par. 11). The complaint further alleges that "caregiving is for wives of male attorneys and tolerated only for female attorneys. The firm culture does not require female attorneys to conform to the 'macho' stereotype" (ibid.). Because Ayanna was an equal coparent and he rejected the "macho" stereotype, Ayanna alleged that he advocated for more equitable treatment of attorneys who cared for their children (ibid., par. 15).

Assuming the veracity of Ayanna's allegations, the law firm culture was polluted with masculine practices identified by Collinson and Hearn, including authoritarianism, entrepreneurialism, and careerism.

These behaviors differ from those in blue-collar workplaces, but the motive for engaging in them is the same. Men engage in masculine practices to prove to others their own masculinity and the masculinity of the job in question. At the same time, the behaviors are inextricably intertwined with the definition of an ideal worker. Thus, work itself is defined as masculine, an attitude that operates against both female workers and male workers who do not conform to workplace masculinity (and work) norms.

BLATANT MASCULINITIES

In more blatant forms, masculinities may include physical and/or verbal abuse of women in predominantly male workplaces and of male victims who are homosexual or otherwise do not conform to masculine stereotypes. These forms of masculinities appear often in blue-collar workplaces where the men in the "men's job" are threatened by having a woman do the work. If women can do the work, then the job does not grant to the male workers the masculinity they desire. The same is true if a gender-nonconforming man does the job. His presence and ability to perform the job threatens the masculinity of the male workers.

MASCULINITIES PRACTICED AGAINST FEMALE WORKERS

The case of Vanessa Hernandez presents an example of masculine practices that are directed against female victims in workplaces.[3] Hernandez worked for Brand FX Body Company, which made fiberglass truck bodies. She alleged that employees and supervisors subjected her to severe and continuous verbal harassment and that when she complained to supervisors and Human Resources, the company did nothing to improve the situation, the harassment escalated, and she was ultimately fired. Among other harassment, Hernandez alleged that she suffered propositions for oral sex and a coworker who told her the length of his penis, showed her a photo of his penis on his phone, and told her that if she were "fucking" him, she would be in a better mood and "not such a bitch" (Complaint and Jury Demand, *Hernandez v. Brand FX Body Co., Inc.* 2013, par. 10). When the plaintiff complained to her supervisor about her coworker's behavior, the supervisor told her to go ahead and "fuck" the harasser (ibid., par. 11). On another occasion, the same supervisor told Hernandez that he hired her because she was a "bitch" and that he would like to see some "girl on girl action" (ibid., par. 14). He offered to sell tickets and to bring the Jell-O. As Hernandez was walking behind a coworker, another male coworker yelled, warning that Hernandez was going to "fuck" him "with her strap on" (ibid., par. 18).

Crude rap music with racist and misogynistic lyrics played in the background of the workplace; another female worker was physically and verbally assaulted. Despite the escalating harassment, and Hernandez's numerous complaints to the Human Resources Department, the company refused to do anything and the HR director told the plaintiff that sexual harassment training was too expensive. Ultimately, when the plaintiff told the HR director that she intended to file a lawsuit, the plaintiff was fired (Complaint and Jury Demand, *Hernandez v. Brand FX Body Co., Inc.* 2013). This exhibit of masculinities, behaviors practiced by men to force women out of the workforce, is not unusual in blue-collar workplaces when women occupy jobs that were traditionally exclusively male.

MASCULINITIES PRACTICED AGAINST MALE WORKERS

Examples of masculinities practiced against male workers include Jonathan Martin's treatment at the Miami Dolphins and the case of Joseph Oncale. Joseph Oncale's case is typical of male-on-male harassment cases where blatant masculinities occur. Oncale alleged that his male coworkers and supervisors on the employer's oil rig picked on him all of the time, called him a name suggesting homosexuality, restrained him while one placed his penis on Oncale's neck, and on Oncale's arm on another occasion, threatened him with forcible homosexual rape, and used force to push a bar of soap into Oncale's anus while another worker restrained Oncale as he was showering on Sundowner premises (*Oncale v. Sundowner Offshore Services, Inc.* 1998).

MASCULINITIES' HARM TO MEN AND WOMEN

Whether the victim is female or male, the behavior occurs to prove the abusers' masculinity and the victims are harmed because of their gender. Women suffer severe hostility and sexual harassment when they are the objects of the behavior. The harm to gender-nonconforming men is obvious: they are pushed, prodded, threatened, ridiculed, and even raped at work. The degradation of men occurs through taunts and practices that compare the male victims to women or that ascribe traits to the victims that are considered feminine. This behavior, which assigns to women or the feminine the most humiliating characteristics, offends women's dignity. When directed at men, the behavior is devastating because it raises issues about the men's very qualifications to be men.

Moreover, by openly abusing men who do not conform to gender stereotypes, men police the social and gender order at work, reinforcing the definition of certain jobs as masculine and closed to gender-nonconforming men and most women. Even the women who adopt the masculine characteristics that are necessary for the job, as defined by the hegemonic masculinity at work, are punished by their coworkers because they do not comport with the stereotypes traditionally attributed to women. Finally, and perhaps most importantly, the abusive behavior toward gender-nonconforming men reinforces the gendered institution of work, an institution that privileges masculine heterosexual men over women and homosexual or nonmasculine men. While these behaviors are very harmful to the victims, courts have been reluctant to recognize that they occur because of sex. Consequently, much of this behavior escapes sanction by Title VII.

MULTIDIMENSIONAL MASCULINITIES

Jonathan Martin's situation also suggests that he suffered not only because of his gender but also because of his race and class. In other words, multidimensional masculinities theory would analyze race and class as well as gender to explain Martin's perpetrators' behaviors and his reactions to them. Multidimensional masculinities theory investigates how concepts of masculinity interact with other identity categories in different legal contexts. Multidimensionality theory concludes that categories of identity are (1) always intertwined with one another and (2) experienced and interpreted differently in different contexts (Cooper 2010). When multidimensionality theory applies to masculinities theory, it demonstrates that masculine practices, performances, and structures differ depending on the context of the situation and the other categories of identity with which they overlap (McGinley and Cooper 2012).

This book develops multidimensional masculinities theory to suggest new definitions of "discrimination" and interpretations of employment discrimination law. These interpretations describe sex discrimination against women, but they also deal with men who may suffer discrimination because they do not meet the norms of hegemonic masculinity. While focusing on gender, this book also examines the interaction of race, class, and sexual orientation because these variables cannot be understood without an understanding of the masculinities produced by the intersection. As we shall see in subsequent chapters, without an understanding of multidimensional masculinities, courts often do not acknowledge that the discriminatory behaviors are rooted in gender and that the resulting injury should be compensable under Title VII.

A Practical Recapitulation: Analyzing Masculinity in the Workplace

To summarize masculinities theory and its applicability to Title VII cases: masculinities theory comprises a substantive analysis as well as a methodology. The substance includes the examination of three aspects: (1) masculine structures and practices in the workplace; (2) the performance of masculinity-enhancing behaviors in workplaces; and (3) masculine practices themselves that take place at work, but that are often invisible because they are defined as work.

Additionally, masculinities theory uses a methodology of shifting lenses to consider other potential identity characteristics of the victims and perpetrators and how they may react or be treated in different contexts. This book considers both the substance and the methodology and how this analysis would affect the interpretation of Title VII cases.

Next, part II examines the role of masculine practices and structures in sexual- harassment hostile work environment cases and suggests how courts can use multidimensional masculinities theory to understand the hostile harassing behaviors that men and women suffer in many workplaces.

PART II

Focusing on Gender- and Sex-Based Harassment

If the Wells Report findings are accurate, it appears that Jonathan Martin suffered a hostile working environment at the Miami Dolphins because of his race and sex. Assuming that Martin could meet the threshold requirement of proving that he had an employment relationship with the Dolphins or the NFL or both, Martin would file a charge with the Equal Employment Opportunity Commission (EEOC) and, ultimately, sue in federal court under Title VII. Martin could not sue his teammates individually under Title VII, but he could potentially sue them alleging violations of common law tort or state statutes prohibiting harassing behaviors.

Because the masculinities described in part I would frequently be litigated under sexual, gender, and/or racial harassment under Title VII, part II focuses on the potential Title VII liability based on sex or gender and racial harassment and how masculinities research could help make visible the gender-based injuries to Jonathan Martin. To cover this topic, part II has three chapters. Chapter 2 describes the historical and theoretical background of the creation of the hostile work environment cause of action under Title VII. Chapter 3 analyzes the term "because of sex" and shows that Martin could use masculinities studies to demonstrate that the alleged behavior occurred because of sex under Title VII. Chapter 4 discusses the proper standard for determining whether the behavior is sufficiently severe or pervasive to alter the terms or conditions of an employee's employment. As a whole, part II discusses the history and current legal standards of Title VII and demonstrates that masculinities research can illuminate difficult issues the courts have identified in proving a hostile working environment. Furthermore, it shifts the lens to permit a better understanding of how masculinities research can inform the courts' questions. Finally, part II demonstrates that as the law stands today, masculinities theory can help judges and juries decide hostile work environment cases. Chapters 3 and 4 also propose that courts adopt new legal interpretations and standards in light of masculinities research.

Alternative theories of litigation under Title VII would be disparate treatment and disparate impact claims that I will analyze in part III.

2

Background to Gender- and Sex-Based Harassment Law

Historical, Legal, and Theoretical Background of Gender- and Sex-Based Harassment

In 1986, the United States Supreme Court decided *Meritor Savings Bank v. Vinson*, which held that Title VII of the Civil Rights Act of 1964 forbids sexual harassment that creates a hostile working environment (*Meritor Saving Bank v. Vinson* 1986). *Meritor* reflected the changes in attitudes toward women that resulted from the feminist movement in the 1960s and '70s, and made it possible for women to hold jobs that men had previously held exclusively.

The express language of Title VII of the Civil Rights Act of 1964 prohibits discrimination in employment because of an individual's race, national origin, color, religion, and sex, but the Act does not mention harassment or hostile work environments. Beginning in 1971, however, lower federal courts began to hold that racial harassment constituted illegal race discrimination under Title VII (*Carino v. University of Oklahoma Board of Regents* 1984; *Vaughn v. Westinghouse Electric Corp.* 1980; *Rogers v. E.E.O.C.* 1971).

At the time, however, courts viewed sexual harassment as different from racial harassment. In their view, sexual harassment was not a violation of the Act because sexual propositions and encounters, even if not welcomed by female employees, were seen as natural and private. Finally, in 1977, the D.C. Circuit Court of Appeals held in *Barnes v. Costle* that Title VII created a cause of action for a woman who alleged that her boss fired her because of her refusal to have an affair with him. There was still a question, however, about employer liability if the employer did not know about the harassment (*Barnes v. Costle* 1977).

Two years later, Catharine A. MacKinnon published *Sexual Harassment of Working Women: A Case of Sex Discrimination*, in which she argued that employers should be vicariously liable for sexual harassment in the workplace under Title VII (MacKinnon 1979). In 1980, a year after the publication of MacKinnon's book, the Equal Employment Opportunity Commission (EEOC) promulgated a new guidance that adopted MacKinnon's theory and distinguished quid pro quo and hostile work environment sexual harassment claims. Quid pro quo claims were linked directly to an economic quid pro quo. Hostile work environment claims were based on harassment that altered the terms or conditions of employment without an economic detriment. Both types of harassment were actionable, according to the guidelines, if they had the "purpose or effect of unreasonably interfering with an individual's work performance or creating an intimidating, hostile, or offensive working environment" (29 C.F.R. § 1604.11(a)(3) (2007)).

Because EEOC interpretive guidances are not binding on the courts, the next move was up to the courts. Lower federal courts followed the guidance and held that there was a cause of action under Title VII for sexual harassment (*Katz v. Dole* 1983; *Henson v. City of Dundee* 1982). But it would take the Supreme Court to apply the law nationwide. The Court took this step in *Meritor Savings Bank v. Vinson* (1986).

The allegations in the complaint were stark. Mechelle Vinson, a nineteen-year-old black woman who worked at the bank, alleged that Sidney Taylor, a middle-aged black bank manager, forced her to engage in sexual relations with him, raped her, and exposed himself to her. She testified that he engaged in similar wrongful behavior with other women in the bank. In a bench trial, the federal district court held that if sex had occurred between Taylor and Vinson, it was voluntary and not a Title VII violation (*Vinson v. Taylor* 1980).

The D.C. Circuit Court of Appeals reversed and held that a cause of action can exist for a hostile work environment under Title VII even if there is no economic harm (*Vinson v. Taylor* 1985). On certiorari, the United States Supreme Court affirmed that in the absence of economic harm, an employer's creation of a hostile working environment can lead to employer liability. If the plaintiff demonstrates that the sexual harassment was sufficiently severe or pervasive to alter the employee's work environment, the behavior constitutes sex discrimination under Title VII. In 1993, the Court clarified this ruling in *Harris v. Forklift Systems, Inc.*, where it held that it was not necessary for the plaintiff to prove psychological harm in order to recover in a sexual harassment case (*Harris v. Forklift Systems, Inc.* 1993). She merely had to prove that the harassment was sufficiently severe or pervasive from the perspective of a reasonable person to alter the terms or conditions of the plaintiff's employment and that the plaintiff subjectively perceived it to be severe or pervasive.

The Supreme Court also held in *Meritor* that plaintiffs do not have to establish that the behavior was involuntary, but merely that it was unwelcome, in order to prove a hostile work environment. This holding demonstrates that the Court recognized the potentially coercive power a supervisor holds over employees.

Nonetheless, unlike the court of appeals, the Supreme Court held in *Meritor* that an employer is not automatically strictly liable for its supervisors' harassment of subordinates. The Court instructed lower courts to use agency principles to determine whether an employer would be liable for a supervisor's actions. This ruling led to confusion in the lower courts about the conditions under which employers should be liable for sexual harassment.

In 1998, the Supreme Court reconsidered the issue of employer liability in hostile work environment cases in *Burlington Industries v. Ellerth* and *Faragher v. City of Boca Raton* (*Burlington Industries, Inc. v. Ellerth* 1998; *Faragher v. City of Boca Raton* 1998). In *Ellerth* and *Faragher*, the Court held that an employer is strictly liable for a supervisor's sexual harassment of a subordinate if there is a tangible employment action such as a demotion, firing, or failure to promote. If there is harassing behavior that falls short of a tangible employment action, the employer can avoid liability by proving a two-pronged affirmative defense: (1) that it exercised reasonable care to prevent and correct promptly any sexually harassing behavior; and (2) that the plaintiff unreasonably failed to take advantage of any preventive or corrective opportunities afforded by the employer. The Court also noted that ordinarily an employer can escape liability if it creates an antiharassment policy and effective investigation and reporting procedures, if it educates its employees on how to use them, and if the victim fails to report the harassment in accordance with the procedures (ibid.).

The Supreme Court decided another case in 1998 that is extremely important to the application of masculinities theory in Title VII hostile environment law. *Oncale v. Sundowner Offshore Services, Inc.* held that harassment by a person of the same sex is illegal under Title VII so long as it occurs "because of sex." The Supreme Court clarified in *Oncale* that because the creation of a hostile working environment is sex discrimination that occurs because of the sex of the victim, it is not necessary that the harasser be motivated by sexual attraction or that the behavior be sexual in nature. Instead, a harasser may have gendered rather than sexual motivations. For example, illegal harassment of an employee can occur if the perpetrator's motive is to encourage women or men to leave the workforce either because the perpetrator does not believe that women or men belong in that type of work or because the individual does not live up to accepted stereotypes of how women or men should act (McGinley 2008).

Gender Harassment

The Court has also interpreted Title VII's prohibition of sex discrimination to forbid discrimination and harassment because of an individual's gender. As used here, "sex" refers to the biological sex of an individual whereas "gender" refers to the social norms that are ordinarily associated with a biological sex. In *Price Waterhouse v. Hopkins*, Ann Hopkins sued her employer and alleged that it failed to promote her to the partnership at Price Waterhouse because of her sex (*Price Waterhouse v. Hopkins* 1989). She argued that the evidence demonstrated that the defendant partners at Price Waterhouse voted against her promotion because of her failure to conform to traditional stereotypical expectations of how a woman should dress and behave. The Supreme Court agreed that to discriminate against a woman because of her failure to conform to feminine stereotypes equals sex discrimination, especially in cases like *Price Waterhouse* where women are placed in a "catch 22: out of a job if they behave aggressively and out of a job if they do not" (ibid., 251). Hopkins's job required certain aggressive or masculine behavior, but the partners who voted against Hopkins did not approve of her acting in a masculine fashion. While *Price Waterhouse v. Hopkins* was not a sexual harassment case, it is an important precedent for hostile work environment cases. It stands for the proposition that it is illegal sex discrimination under Title VII for a supervisor, coworker, or customer to harass or discriminate against a woman because of her failure to conform to gender stereotypes.

Protecting Gender-Nonconforming Men

Moreover, a number of courts have recognized that *Price Waterhouse* also protects men from discrimination and harassment occurring because of their failure to live up to masculine stereotypes. This is a particularly thorny area of Title VII law because courts have uniformly agreed that Title VII does not prohibit discrimination based on sexual orientation or perceived sexual orientation. Thus, courts have held that it is illegal under Title VII to discriminate because of a man's or woman's failure to comport with masculine or feminine stereotypes, but it is not illegal to discriminate against an individual because he is gay or she is a lesbian. Courts have a very difficult time deciding cases where the victims of the harassment are gay or lesbian or even if they are perceived to be gay or lesbian. Where the harassing behavior involves derogatory terms that are associated with homosexuality, such as "faggot" or "butch," some courts grant summary judgment for the defendant, and hold that as a matter of law the plaintiff was harassed because of his or her sexual orientation or perceived sexual orientation, not because of his or her failure to live up to gender stereotypes. Judge Richard Posner has gone so far as to assert that there is no gender discrimination cause of action in a situation where persons of the plaintiff's sex hold the job predominantly, and that gays and lesbians do not have a cause of action under the sex stereotyping doctrine (*Hamm v. Weyauwega Milk Products, Inc.* 2003). Other courts disagree. In *Rene v. MGM Grand Hotel, Inc.*, a plurality of the Ninth Circuit concluded that a victim's sexual orientation is not relevant to the question of whether he or she has suffered discrimination because of sex (2002).

These cases often arise in the context of harassment by members of the same sex. In *Oncale v. Sundowner Offshore Services, Inc.*, the U.S. Supreme Court held that Title VII prohibits harassment by members of the victim's sex (1998). But, the Court warned, without much elaboration, that the behavior must occur because of the victim's sex if it is to be illegal. This "because of sex" requirement has created significant difficulty for lower courts, which often conclude that behavior among men is "roughhousing" or "hazing" and, therefore, does not occur because of sex, or that it occurred because of the victim's sexual orientation or perceived sexual orientation.

As we shall see in subsequent chapters, masculinities theory is an important tool to help establish that attempting to distinguish between behavior that occurs "because of sexual orientation" and "because of sex" is fruitless. Masculinities theory recognizes that men conflate gay sexual orientation with a lack of masculinity, even though in reality many gay men perform their masculinity in traditional ways. It recognizes that men perform their masculinity, often excessively, because their most important goal is to prove that they are not women or gay. In essence, masculinity is an absence of gayness or femininity. Consequently, any behavior that is at all woman-like, or that appears to be weak and not masculine, may subject the victim to harassment.

Consider again Jonathan Martin's story. There was no allegation that Jonathan Martin is gay, but his teammate Incognito bullied and harassed him by calling him a "pussy" and "my bitch" because of what he perceived to be effeminate characteristics: an interest in reading, a love of the classics, an excellent education, and a gentle personality (Wells et al. 2014, 11, 118). Martin's experience at the Miami Dolphins supports studies that demonstrate that even when the harassing language apparently refers to sexual orientation, the perpetrators may actually be more concerned with policing the masculinity of the individual and of the group. Therefore, if we are to accept the courts' rulings that harassment based on gender is illegal but harassment based on sexual orientation is not, it is virtually impossible for a judge to ascertain on summary judgment the motives of the perpetrators by referring to the language used.[1]

Masculinities theory is particularly helpful when a group of men harasses an individual man. Experts in masculinities theory can help the judge and the jury understand that the behavior occurs because of gender, even if the language appears to pertain to sexual orientation. Moreover, expert testimony or reference to authoritative texts on masculinity should aid judges and juries to understand that behaviors appearing to be normal among men may occur because of sex or gender.

Furthermore, masculinities theory encourages a methodology that allows courts to "shift the lens" to gain a better understanding of legal theory and analysis. The next two chapters discuss how masculinities theory can help courts analyze two major elements of the hostile work environment claim. Chapter 3 uses masculinities theory to discuss the "because of sex" requirement of hostile work environment discrimination and to demonstrate how many men and women conflate masculinity with heterosexuality. It further explains why certain behaviors occur because of sex. Chapter 4 discusses the standard used to determine whether harassing behavior is sufficiently severe or pervasive to alter the terms or conditions of employment. In so doing, it shifts the lens to consider whether the "reasonable woman" or "reasonable person" is the proper objective standard by analyzing the nontraditional case of a male victim of a female coworker's sexually harassing behavior.

3

Evaluating Harassment Occurring "Because of Sex"

As noted in chapter 2, Title VII does not explicitly make harassment illegal, but the courts have interpreted Title VII's broad prohibition against sex discrimination in employment to ban sex- and gender-based harassment that creates a hostile working environment. The development of the law is the result of judicial interpretation over more than a thirty-year period, reflecting input from litigators, the EEOC, legal scholars, lower courts, and the U.S. Supreme Court.

To demonstrate an illegal sex- or gender-based hostile work environment under Title VII, the plaintiff must show that the harassing behavior was unwelcome, that it was sufficiently severe or pervasive to alter the terms or conditions of the victim's employment, and that it occurred because of the victim's sex. This chapter deals with the thorny issue of whether an individual's harassing behavior occurs "because of sex."[1] Courts have traditionally become confused when attempting to determine whether behavior occurs because of sex, often granting motions for summary judgment or to dismiss plaintiffs' claims in situations where their common sense leads them astray. Common sense can be problematic because socially constructed gender structures and behaviors can often appear normal and thus be invisible to judges and juries making these determinations. Masculinities theory can aid the courts and juries in determining whether behavior occurs "because of sex."

Questions Raised by the "Because of Sex" Standard

The meaning of "because of sex" in Title VII harassment cases has created significant trouble for courts and scholars who have grappled with the question. As a proof matter, courts have no difficulty determining that sexual advances by an individual man toward an individual woman and vice versa satisfy the "because of sex" requirement of the statute. Courts struggle, however, with many of the other cases that occur in different contexts such as same-sex harassment of a man by a group of men or where the harassment includes both sex- or gender-based behavior and behavior that is sex or gender neutral. The problems in hostile work environment law result from an inadequate theory to explain why sex- or gender-based harassing behaviors equal sex discrimination.

Theorizing in this area is particularly difficult because there are many moving parts that contribute to the broader question of whether the behavior occurs "because of sex." Many different contexts, motivations, and behaviors exist in cases that occur because of sex, but courts tend to revert to their own understanding of gender relations and focus on sexual relationships and/or differential treatment of men and women at work. This narrow focus creates conceptual difficulty in what courts see as unusual cases: same-sex harassment cases, workplaces where both men and women suffer harassment, and female-on-male harassment cases. Take the Jonathan Martin case. Commentators ignored the obviously gendered nature of Martin's treatment and characterized it as normal male behavior in the context of professional football. But when we consider masculinities theory, we can understand that the behavior directed at Martin occurred because of sex or gender.

There are legitimate concerns, of course, that come into play. Courts do not interpret Title VII as enforcing civility rules; rather, Title VII's purpose is to prohibit *discrimination* because of sex and other protected characteristics. Drawing lines between civility rules and illegal discrimination is often difficult. While courts must draw these lines, they should go beyond their own experiences to understand how sex and/or gender are intricately involved in many of the behaviors that courts examine to determine whether the behavior occurred because of sex.

Hostile work environment law relies heavily on analysis of the motivations for human behaviors in the context of the workplace. The law fails, however, when, without resorting to social science research, it relies on commonsense assumptions about why human beings engage in particular behaviors. Social science research in gender, masculinities, and workplace dynamics is an important tool for developing a comprehensive theory of what behaviors occur because of sex and why. With insight from masculinities theory, combined with other social science research, this chapter attempts to offer a comprehensive legal theory that explains why a variety of behaviors stemming from different motivations in different workplace contexts can occur because of sex.

This chapter identifies the problems courts have in interpreting whether harassing behaviors occur because of sex, explains the importance of power as not only a prerequisite to but also a goal of sexual harassment, and analyzes the different variables present in workplace situations involving sex- or gender-based harassment. It presents examples of different types of sex- or gender-based harassment, with different perpetrators and victims and varying behaviors, and explains why the harassment in these examples can be understood as occurring "because of sex." This theoretical analysis creates the legal justification for creating a presumption that behavior occurs because of sex where sexualized or gender-based behavior occurs. The theory offered here supports this presumption and should make judges' decisions more uniform and less confusing to litigants and employers who are responsible for preventing sex- and gender-based harassment. *The bottom line is that where the plaintiff offers evidence of sex- or gender-based behavior, a presumption should arise that the harassing behavior occurred because of sex.* The presumption would shift the burden to the defendant to prove that the behavior did not occur because of sex. The following discussion uses masculinities theory to justify the presumption.

Theorizing Sexual Harassment: Problems with Interpreting "Because of Sex"

The courts have difficulty with the "because of sex" requirement in atypical sex- and gender-based harassment cases. In what courts view as the typical case, where an individual man harasses an individual woman using sexual language or behavior, courts assume that harassment occurs because of the woman's sex. The theoretical justification relies on the assumption that sexual harassment results from overly exuberant sexual attraction. Moreover, a presumption that the male perpetrator is heterosexual leads to the conclusion that the male perpetrator would not be sexually attracted to a man and, therefore, he would not behave in the same way toward a man. Thus, the courts conclude, the behavior occurs because of the woman's sex. In essence, the courts decide, the woman's sex is a but-for cause of the harassment.

A similarly easy case for the courts occurs where an individual homosexual man harasses another individual male employee using sexual behavior and/or language. The courts readily agree that this situation resembles the fact pattern of a heterosexual man who harasses a woman in sexual terms. Because the harasser in this case is homosexual, the courts assume that the motivation for harassment is sexual attraction. The reasoning is that because the perpetrator is homosexual, the behavior is sexualized, and the target is of the same sex as the perpetrator, the behavior occurs because of the sex of the victim. A homosexual male perpetrator would not harass a woman, the theory explains. Here, the male victim's sex is a but-for cause of the harassment.

Although the cases occur less frequently, the courts have little trouble concluding that the behavior occurred because of sex in cases where a heterosexual woman harasses a man and where a lesbian harasses another women. In both cases, the courts find fairly automatically that the behavior occurred because of sex; that is, the victim's sex is a but-for cause of the harassment, presumably because the courts see sexual attraction as the nearly exclusive reason for sexual harassment.

But these easy cases do not represent the entire universe of sex- or gender-based harassment cases. The courts struggle with what they would consider the atypical cases: same-sex cases where the alleged perpetrator or perpetrators are not openly homosexual, "equal opportunity harasser" cases where the harasser or harassers subject men and women to the same harassing conditions or where they direct harassing behaviors at both men and women, and cases where a female coworker or a group of female coworkers harasses a male colleague. In these cases, even where the behavior is explicitly sex or gender based, the courts have difficulty concluding that the behavior occurs because of the sex or gender of the victim. This confusion is due to the courts' view that sex- or gender-based harassment results from sexual attraction, and their lack of understanding of the many other possible motivations and factual variations in which harassment can present itself.

Moreover, the confusion also results from a pure differential treatment approach in determining whether behavior occurs because of sex—that is, the theory that a heterosexual man treats a woman differently than he would treat a man because of his sexual attraction to the woman. This approach ignores the existence of important power differentials that allow the harassers to accomplish sex- and/or gender-based harassment in the workplace and the varying motivations for harassing others because of sex or gender. Finally, it results from a lack of understanding of the malleability of sexual attraction and orientation and of the ways in which unconscious attraction or fears of attraction can affect behavior.

While a power differential between perpetrators and victims is necessary to accomplish sexual harassment, plaintiffs should not have to prove that such a differential exists in order to prevail in a sexual harassment case. Rather, if we are to understand sexual harassment, we must be aware of the power dynamics that lead to its accomplishment. Awareness allows us to construct a theoretical explanation that identifies certain behaviors as occurring "because of sex."

In her groundbreaking book, *Sexual Harassment of Working Women: A Case of Sex Discrimination*, Catharine MacKinnon argued that sexual harassment of female subordinates by their male supervisors is sex discrimination. She based her argument on two different theories: the inequality theory, which she later described as "dominance" or "antisubordination" theory, and the differences theory, which others later called "anticlassification" theory. MacKinnon, who subscribes to inequality or dominance theory, explained that men's position socially and in the workplace is superior, whereas women occupy inferior positions. This differential between men and women in social, organizational, and economic power is not biologically essential or natural. It gives men the opportunity in the workplace to demand sexual favors of female subordinates as a condition of employment. Female victims are in the unenviable position of deciding to forgo their work or to accede to their employer's sexual demands. Even where the supervisor's demands are not a quid pro quo for beneficial treatment at work, the male supervisor's sexual jokes, advances, and liberties taken with his female subordinate become a discriminatory term or condition of the woman's work. MacKinnon translated her antisubordination theory for the courts into a differential treatment theory that is explicitly based on a presumption of heterosexuality. She explained that because male supervisors would not make sexual advances toward their *male* subordinates, the harassing behavior against female subordinates occurs because of sex (MacKinnon 1979).

The courts have accepted this explanation almost to the exclusion of all others, and have adopted a symmetrical view of how female and male harassers should be treated. Thus, if courts presume that harassment by a male supervisor of a female subordinate occurs because of sex, the same viewpoint applies to female supervisor harassment of male subordinates, of male coworkers' harassment of their female coworkers, and of female coworkers' harassment of their male coworkers. All occur because of sex. But this false symmetry obscures the reason why sex- or gender-based harassment constitutes illegal discrimination.

It is the power differential that makes harassment possible. When we consider harassment by a female coworker of her male coworker, courts automatically assume that the behavior occurs "because of sex," even though there are troubling concerns as to potential power differentials between a female coworker and her male colleague. If we were loyal to MacKinnon's theory, we would ask how a female coworker, who presumably has no organizational, social, or economic power over her male coworker, can harass him at work. While courts may subconsciously consider female sexual power so compelling as to permit the harassment, courts never ask the question of how a female with no greater organizational or economic power can accomplish a harassing situation with a male coworker. This is the case because the courts' views are rooted in differential treatment as a basis for discrimination law and the idea that what is good for the goose is good for the gander.

In contrast to the male-on-female, female-on-male "easy" cases where courts presume the behavior occurs because of sex, the courts often do not recognize that harassing behaviors by heterosexual male coworkers toward other heterosexual male coworkers occur because of sex. Masculinities theory can help us understand how power dynamics play out at work and lead to harassment, and how they are related to the "because of sex" requirement. It can do so because it not only explains gender dynamics and the fluidity of masculine performances at work but also takes into account the identities of the different participants and the context of the situation.

While MacKinnon's original theory covers some potential fact patterns of sex- or gender-based harassment, there are many more. Sex- and gender-based harassment often involves many variables that derive from power and contribute to it. The next subsection discusses the power prerequisite to sexual harassment and the possible variables in cases where behavior can occur because of sex or gender.

Prerequisites and Moving Parts

A theory of sexual harassment must explain many variables if it is to account for different types of harassment, all of which can be sex or gender based. The current jurisprudence, however, does not account for these moving parts, and a differential treatment approach that merely considers whether men and women are treated differently in the workplace underestimates the occurrence of sex- or gender-based harassment. A differential treatment approach ignores important issues that are crucial to understanding what sex- or gender-based harassment is and tends to reinforce a binary, biological view of human nature that ignores the social construction of gender. Moreover, as applied by the courts, it often fails to recognize that there are many possible different iterations and scenarios in which discrimination can occur because of gender. It relies heavily on the concept of sexual attraction as the only or the dominant reason for sex- and/or gender-based harassment, and it springs from the heteronormative impression that sexual harassment occurs because of a sexual interest in another person that has gone wrong in the workplace. Sometimes the fact pattern supports this assumption, but often it does not.

It is essential to understand the different variables in order to create a comprehensive theory of sex- and gender-based harassment. The variables include (1) the existence of power differentials that permit the accomplishment of the harassment; (2) whether the harassment is accomplished by an individual or a group of persons in private or in public in the workplace; (3) the motivation of the person/persons engaged in the harassing behaviors; (4) the harassing behaviors themselves; and (5) whether the employer's response contributes to the harassing environment.

Power Differentials: Prerequisite to Harassment

A power differential between perpetrators and victims is a prerequisite to the accomplishment of harassment. Without a power differential, the victim would be able to resist the harassing behavior by using his or her equal or superior power. Catharine MacKinnon first envisioned this differential as the power derived from organizational position (combined with social and economic power), which, she theorized, provides an opportunity for male supervisors to harass female subordinates who are relatively powerless in the job because of their lower organizational status, the lower sociocultural status of women, and their lower economic status (MacKinnon 1979).

An understanding of power in the workplace should consider not only power derived from organizational position but also sociocultural power mediated by a person's identity (race, class, sex, sexual orientation, etc.) and power gained from group dynamics in the workplace and other sources. In fact, power derived from organizational position may not suffice to compensate for a differential in sociocultural power.

Scholars who discuss "contra-power harassment" note that men who have less organizational power sometimes harass women in positions of superior organizational power in both employment and educational settings (Juliano 2007; Benson 1984). These male perpetrators accomplish the harassment as a result of their greater sociocultural power, combined with the diminished power that women who occupy positions that are predominantly held by men have in comparison with their male colleagues.

Men, even young men, have more power generally in the culture than many women occupying superior positions. This power is enhanced in the work and university settings when a female supervisor or professor works in a job that is historically occupied by men. In some workplaces where women occupy supervisory and/or professorial roles, male colleagues believe that the women hold their jobs illegitimately. When this is the environment, male university students and subordinates at work take advantage of their own superior sociocultural power to harass their professors or supervisors.

Research demonstrates that both women and men suffer harassment at the hands of subordinates, and it appears that for women, contra-power harassment is more prevalent the more education she has. A federal study demonstrates that 2 to 4 percent of women suffer contra-power harassment in federal jobs; a military study found that 8 percent of military women suffer from cross-gender contra-power harassment. These numbers seem fairly low, scholars theorize, because men are most frequently the perpetrators in contra-power harassment and only a small percentage of women supervise men (Juliano 2007).

The contra-power harassment example also demonstrates that power is not only a prerequisite but may also be a goal of the harassment. The harassment of the female supervisor or professor can occur because of power differentials. In turn, the harassment diminishes the female supervisor's power and enhances the power of the male harasser, and of men in general. Therefore, the previously established gender order is solidified.

Another example of differential power can occur in blue-collar workforces. Men working in blue-collar jobs may resist the power of their white-collar bosses and may even create a superior power of their own by engaging in harassing behaviors that emphasize their own physicality and the "nerd" factor of the white-collar bosses (Collinson 1988). By degrading their male supervisor as a "wimp" or less manly, these subordinates construct their own masculinity in contrast to those in the better-paid jobs. Whether these blue-collar men will get away with this behavior depends on whether their enactment of power actually overcomes the superior organizational and sociocultural power that the white-collar managers have over their blue-collar subordinates. But to the extent that blue-collar male workers have superior sociocultural power in a given context, they may be able to engage in some harassing of their male supervisors.

There are many other sources of sociocultural power differentials that courts and commentators tend to ignore when discussing sex or gender-based harassment. In addition to sex, other identity factors such as race, color, class, immigration status, sexual orientation, gender identity, age, disability, and religious affiliation contribute to dynamics in the workforce to exacerbate or create power differentials between supervisors and subordinates, and among coworkers.

Besides organizational and sociocultural power, moreover, the context matters. The workplace itself creates power dynamics that vary across different industries and workplaces within industries. The key fact to remember is that sex- and/or gender-based harassment will not thrive without power differentials between perpetrators and victims. Requiring victims of harassment to prove the power differential, however, should not be necessary because where no power differential exists, the targets of sex- or gender-based harassment can resist the harassment. In other words, if the target has more power than the harassers, harassment, if it takes place at all, will not last long.

Individual or Group Harassment

A key variable in analyzing sex- or gender-based harassment is whether the perpetrators are individuals acting alone or a group of employees acting in concert. Individuals and groups derive their power to harass from different sources. Harassment by individuals of other individuals often occurs in private and is often sexual in nature—the type of sexual harassment that Catharine MacKinnon identified in her work.

Harassment by groups often occurs in public spaces in the workplace and may use sexual or gendered means to accomplish the harassment, but is not overtly spurred by sexual attraction. While it may result in part from hidden sexual attraction (especially in the case of same-sex harassment), it ordinarily results from a more complicated set of emotions relating to the gender of the perpetrator(s), the gender of the victim(s), and the gender identified with the jobs held by the perpetrator(s) and the victim(s).

A few examples will clarify this point. When women move into jobs that are traditionally occupied by men, they often suffer harassment and bullying by groups of men. Men leave cruel notes in their lockers, refuse to back them up in difficult safety situations, make sexual jokes and references to "dumb women," and refuse to train the women. This behavior does not ordinarily occur because the men want to date the women. Masculinities theory explains that masculinity derives more from relationships among men than from those between men and women (Dowd 2010). Men often engage in harassment of women in order to perform their masculinity in front of other men, to prove themselves to other men, and to engage in competition with other men (ibid.). Moreover, men reinforce their own masculinity by proving that women and less masculine men cannot do the job.

For example, when Richie Incognito and his teammates harassed Jonathan Martin, there was no indication that they were interested in having sexual relationships with Martin. Granted, harassment of men by other men may be situated in deep-seated attraction and the fear resulting from it, but the situation of a group of men harassing another man is often not based primarily on sexual attraction. In Martin's case, it appears that his teammates harassed him to ensure the group's masculinity by "toughening him up" and to distance themselves from what they perceived to be Martin's failed masculinity.

Motivations

The motivations of harassers vary greatly, but even when the motivation is not sexual attraction, the behavior can still occur because of sex or gender. The motivation that is most commonly expected is sexual attraction. Harassment whose motivation is sexual attraction often is perpetrated by one individual on another individual, but is not limited to this pattern. It can be heterosexual, homosexual, or bisexual. A second motivation for harassing behaviors is hostility to men or women as a group in the workplace or in a particular job. This motivation may include an interest in preserving a particular job as belonging to a particular sex. For example, men tend to harass women who work in jobs that are considered to be "men's jobs." This behavior occurs in part because the men who occupy the job need to prove their own masculinity through their position. Women's ability to do the job undermines men's masculinity. Men may also wish to undermine the competence and confidence of women entering the job in order to ensure that the job remains an all-male enclave (Schultz 1998). A third motivation may include hostility toward a particular man or woman for failure to live up to expected norms or stereotypes of men and women, or for failure to subordinate their gendered identity to the group's gender identity.

These are some examples of the possible motivations that may exist, but reality is actually much more complicated because motivations for harassment may combine or change as the dynamic workplace environment changes. For example, a man who sexually harasses a female subordinate may be sexually attracted to her. As she rebuffs his advances, however, he may become hostile toward her. Now, his harassing behavior may occur for hostility or retaliatory reasons.

As in Jonathan Martin's case, a group of men may sexually harass an individual man whom they believe is too weak or "wimpy" in the workplace. Masculinities theory explains that although not all men in the group are similarly situated, most will engage in the harassment to negotiate their own position within the group. Some are motivated to punish the "wimp" for his failure to live up to masculine stereotypes; others engage in the behavior to demonstrate to the group leader and the other members of the group that they themselves are not "wimps," thereby increasing their own reputations for masculinity.

This motivation seems also to explain the situation of Joseph On-cale (*Oncale v. Sundowner Offshore Services, Inc.* 1998). Coworkers and a supervisor brutally harassed Oncale, who was physically small and vulnerable, in the shower as he worked on an all-male oil rig. He finally gave up the job after his superiors and coworkers punched and prodded him, threatened him with rape, and forced a bar of soap into his anus. In both Martin's and Oncale's cases, the selection of the victim and the harassment itself occurred because of sex or gender of the individual and because members of the group sought to establish their own masculine credentials.

Harassing Behaviors

Another set of variables is the means by which the harassers accomplish the hostile work environment. Many men who harass women use sexual means such as sexual advances, sexual jokes, and the display of pornography to harass women, but these means do not necessarily demonstrate sexual interest in the women. Others use gendered means, such as hostile comments about women, and disparaging treatment (*Harris v. Forklift Systems, Inc.* 1993). Still others may use a combination of sexual, gendered, and neutral means. For example, male workers may harass their coworkers using pinups and sexual gestures, but they may also use sex- and gender-neutral means such as denying them training or backup in important situations.

When faced with this evidence, some courts wrongfully disaggregate the sex- or gender-oriented behaviors from those that are hostile but neutral in substance (Schultz 1998; *Harris v. Forklift Systems, Inc.* 1993; *King v. Board of Regents of University of Wisconsin System* 1990). Courts must understand that even when accomplished by a combination of sex-based, gender-based, and neutral behaviors, all such behaviors contribute to the hostile working environment, and the harassers' motivation is the sex or gender of the victim. Thus, in determining whether the behavior is sufficiently severe or pervasive and occurs because of sex, the courts must consider all of the behaviors involved, rather than disaggregating them (*Alfano v. Costello* 2002).

Finally, some harassers are savvy enough to use only neutral means even when their motivation is to harass because of sex or gender. For example, a male supervisor who does not like his female subordinate because she is too masculine and too aggressive may harass her in non-sexual/non-gender-based ways. He may change her working hours or be ever vigilant in his supervision of the woman. Or, he may yell at her constantly. Or, he may give her bad assignments. Even though all of this harassment is not obviously sex or gender based, the supervisor's motivation for the harassing behavior is due to the subordinate's failure to live up to feminine stereotypes. Under *Price Waterhouse v. Hopkins*, the behavior occurs because of sex.

It is important for courts to understand that a power differential is both a prerequisite to and a goal of harassment. This understanding, combined with the other different possible variables at play in harassing situations, should allow courts to recognize new theories that expand beyond sexual attraction and differential treatment theory as the sole models for sexual harassment.

In *Oncale v. Sundowner Services, Inc.* the Supreme Court acknowledged that male-on-male harassment can be motivated by more than sexual or romantic interest. It listed three examples of situations that can account for same-sex harassment because of sex. These include harassment of someone of the same sex by a homosexual harasser; harassment by someone of the same sex because the harasser demonstrates hostility to persons of that same sex in the workplace ("the queen bee syndrome"); and harassment based on differential treatment of men and women as a group. These examples are merely illustrative and do not occupy the field of possible motives for behaviors that could occur because of sex. They form an insufficient basis for a comprehensive theory of sexual harassment, its causes, and the reasons it violates Title VII. In fact, in a celebrated example from *Oncale*, the Court emphasized the importance of social context: it distinguished a coach's swatting a football player on the rump (which is not sexual harassment) from the same coach's patting his secretary's buttocks (which is sexual harassment). But even this example of social context is severely limited in scope because it sees polar opposite examples as the defining contours.

Moreover, the Court in *Oncale* seemed to carve out same-sex harassing behaviors as often constituting merely "roughhousing" rather than harassment. As precedent, lower courts have used the examples in *Oncale* as the rule in same-sex harassment cases, concluding nearly invariably that the harassing conduct looks much less like the male-on-female supervisor-on-subordinate harassment and much more like the rough-housing or horseplay that the Court evidently does not consider to be actionable harassment.

Employer's Reactions

The law currently looks at the employer's reactions to the harassment only for purposes of determining whether the employer is liable for the hostile work environment. While the employer's knowledge of the harassment and reaction to reports of harassment are obviously important in determining employer liability, the employer's reaction may actually contribute to the harassing environment. Courts should consider the employer's reaction carefully to determine not only whether the employer should be liable but also whether the behavior enhanced the hostile work environment for the victim. A good example of this phenomenon is the reaction of the employer in Rudolpho Lamas's case in *E.E.O.C. v. Prospect Airport Services, Inc.* (2010). When Lamas reported to his supervisors that a female coworker was harassing him, the employer did not take Lamas's complaints seriously. In fact, one of his supervisors told Lamas that he should be pleased that Sylvia Munoz was pursuing him. This attitude led to an increase in the harassment that Lamas suffered, not only by Munoz but also by a group of coworkers who teased Lamas and questioned his sexual orientation. Even though the employer's behavior apparently increased the severity of the hostile working environment that Lamas endured, the court never discussed this behavior as a possible source of liability for the defendant.

Practical Applications

To analyze how power and the other variables identified above play out in different harassing situations, let's examine a number of different contexts in which harassment occurs: those perpetrated by individuals and groups; by superiors, equals, and subordinates; and by men and women. The following examples illustrate why in different contexts harassing behavior can be considered illegal sex discrimination under Title VII when courts employ antisubordination theory (power plus gender or sex). While the motivations and sources of power underlying the different scenarios differ according to the identities of the harassers and the victims and according to the context, a uniform approach to proof requirements and litigation is possible. These examples should help courts reach a legal justification for deciding when harassing behaviors occur because of sex in the workplace.

Familiar Patterns of Harassment

The most commonly understood forms of harassment are those in which the harasser is a supervisor and the victim is a subordinate or in which a male coworker harasses a female coworker.

SUPERVISOR HARASSER/SUBORDINATE VICTIM

In the individual-male-harasser-on-individual-female-victim cases, where the harasser has organizational power because he is a supervisor and the woman is a subordinate (the case envisioned by Professor MacKinnon), the male harasser harnesses both his social power and the organizational power of the employer to engage in sexual advances or gendered hostility toward the victim. Doing so is illegal sex discrimination under the antisubordination principle, as MacKinnon explained, because the man uses his organizational power to make sexual demands or impose gendered working conditions upon his subordinate that alter the terms or conditions of her employment because of her sex. This familiar pattern of sexual harassment appears in the early Supreme Court cases such as *Meritor Savings Bank* (1986) and *Harris v. Forklift Systems, Inc.* (1993).

As explained in more detail in chapter 2, in *Meritor Savings Bank*, the plaintiff, Mechelle Vinson, alleged that the vice president of the bank, Sidney Taylor, had subjected her to severe sexual harassment, including repeated unwelcome sexual intercourse, rape, and exposing himself to her. She also alleged that Taylor fondled her in front of other employees and engaged in similar unwanted behavior with other female employees (*Meritor Saving Bank v. Vinson* 1986).

In *Harris v. Forklift Systems, Inc.*, the manager of an equipment rental company alleged that Charles Hardy, the company president, subjected her and other women to derogatory comments about their gender and unwanted sexual innuendos, including comments about the women's clothing. The magistrate found that Hardy called Harris a "dumb ass woman" among other derogatory names, and that Hardy suggested that they settle their differences at a hotel (*Harris v. Forklift Systems, Inc.* 1993, 19). Hardy also told female employees to get coins out of his front pockets and to retrieve objects that he had thrown on the floor (ibid.).

These cases demonstrate that in male-on-female harassment, the harasser's motivations may vary: he may sexually desire the subordinate, or he may be interested in demonstrating his power over women or his hostility toward women to enhance his own masculinity and sense of superiority (or perhaps both). From Hardy's behavior toward the women, we can infer that he was establishing his own superior power through his harassing antics.

A subordinate's gender nonconformity or excessive gender performance such as hypermasculinity or hyperfemininity provides another motivation for a supervisor to use superior organizational power to harass a subordinate. Although it is not a harassment case, *Price Waterhouse v. Hopkins,* described in more detail in chapter 2, is a sex discrimination case in which the Supreme Court held that the refusal to promote a woman because of her failure to conform to gender stereotypes, at least in a job where masculine traits are necessary or preferred, was gender discrimination prohibited by Title VII.[2]

Where the other requirements in a harassment case are met—severe or pervasive unwelcome behavior—a motivation of gender nonconformity or excessive gender performance at work should demonstrate that the behavior occurred because of sex. Since *Price Waterhouse,* a number of lower courts have held that the same analysis applies to men: if a male employee is harassed or discriminated against because of gender nonconformity, that harassment occurs because of sex under Title VII (*E.E.O.C. v. Boh Brothers Construction Co.* 2013; *Prowel v. Wise Business Forms Inc.* 2009; *Rene v. MGM Grand Hotel Inc.* 2002; *Jones v. Pacific Rail Services* 2001; *Bibby v. Philadelphia Coca-Cola Bottling Co.* 2001; *Nichols v. Azteca Restaurant Enterprises* 2001; *Doe v. City of Belleville, Ill.* 1997). So, too, a number of courts have held that transsexual individuals who dress or behave contrary to the gender expected of their birth sex can also use Title VII to redress discrimination for their failure to exhibit appropriately masculine or feminine behavior (*Lopez v. River Oaks Imaging & Diagnostic Group, Inc.* 2008; *Smith v. City of Salem* 2004).

A supervisor may harass or fire a subordinate because of the victim's hyperfemininity or hypermasculinity (Meltzer 2013; *Nelson v. Knight* 2013). For example, a male supervisor might harass a female subordinate for dressing in an inordinately sexy fashion or for acting in a very submissive way. In her book *Camouflage Isn't Only for Combat*, Melissa Herbert interviewed hundreds of female soldiers. She found that about half of these women feel pressured to be more masculine to prove that they deserve to be in uniform alongside the men. Although conveying that masculine traits are important, many of the women said that if they are too masculine, their male counterparts would accuse them of being a "dyke." To avoid this sexual harassment, many of them found a balance of both masculine and feminine attributes (Herbert 1998). Whether the harasser engages in the harassment because of desire, hostility, or sex stereotyping about the proper forms of femininity or masculinity, as in the case of female soldiers, the behavior occurs because of sex.

Where a female supervisor harasses a male subordinate, she too, uses the organizational power conferred upon her by her position to accomplish the harassment because of the man's sex. Like her male counterparts, she may engage in the behavior because of sexual desire, hostility, or her victim's gender nonconformity or hypermasculine gender performance.

For individual male-on-male harassment of subordinates and female-on-female harassment of subordinates, the same motivations explain why the behavior occurs because of sex. A male supervisor may harass a male subordinate because he desires to engage in a sexual relationship, he has hostility toward other men, he harbors an unconscious hostility to his own sexual interest in other men, or he wishes to prove his own masculinity by ridiculing an effeminate man. Or, if the subordinate is perceived not to be sufficiently masculine, a male supervisor may harass him to enforce gender norms of the job in question.

If the subordinate exhibits a hypermasculine gender performance, the male supervisor may harass him to regulate or punish the failure to adhere to expected gender and class norms in the particular workplace, which vary depending on the workplace and the type of work performed. Masculine norms on Wall Street, for example, vary significantly from those on the construction site. A lawyer working on Wall Street may be harassed or otherwise discriminated against by male supervisors for his excessively masculine style—an inordinate number of tattoos, excessive display of muscles, use of profanity, or attitudes toward the more "refined" Wall Street lawyers—whereas the victim's behavior and appearance may be considered appropriate among male employees in the shipyard. Harassment for failure to conform to the gender norms that are socially appropriate for the type of workplace occurs because of sex.

A female supervisor may harass a female subordinate because of sexual interest, hostility or, sexual stereotyping. For example, if the female harasser dislikes excessively feminine or sexy women, she may harass a female subordinate who has a hyperfeminine or hypersexual presentation.

For all of these different types of cases, the motivations may change as the harassment continues. For example, a male supervisor might have a sexual interest in a female subordinate, but if she rebuffs his advances, his interest might turn into hostility and anger over his failure to dominate. All of the cases involve use of organizational power combined with some gender- or sex-based behavior. And, except for the pure sexual attraction cases, which I suspect number in the minority, the motivation of the supervisor might also include a desire to diminish the power of the harassee(s).

MALE COWORKER HARASSER/FEMALE COWORKER VICTIM

Individual male coworkers engage in sex- or gender-based harassment of female coworkers because of the same motivations described above. If the male harasser is a coworker, he may not have the organizational power that a superior ordinarily has, but he may still have other forms of power that allow him to harass the woman. Given that men have more sociocultural power than women in our society, he may have social power over the woman that he can exercise in the form of sexual demands, or by treating her in a hostile manner because of her gender.

This social power derives from the history of patriarchy, and in particular, the dominance of men in the sphere of the workplace. This social power differential, often combined with physical size and strength, supports the harasser's project. The power differential increases when the man is a member of a relatively more powerful social or identity group (based on race, sexual orientation, class, age, or disability) and the woman belongs to a racial-minority group or possesses other identity factors that contribute to her relative powerlessness. The research demonstrates that individual male harassers often intentionally select victims who are relatively powerless (Mulroy 1995). Thus, single mothers who are economically at risk are particularly vulnerable to sexual advances by male perpetrators at work (ibid.).

Contra-power Harassment

Male Subordinate Harasser/Female Supervisor Victim

As noted above, even where an individual man is a subordinate to the woman he harasses, he is often able to exercise social power that derives from his position in society and his interpersonal relationships at work to enact contra-power harassment on a female superior. A number of scholars have recognized "contra-power harassment" as illegal under Title VII (Juliano 2007; Benson 1984).

The types of harassing behaviors scholars have observed in contra-power harassment include unwanted sexual teasing, sexualized interactions including groping, explicit sexual propositions, obscene phone calls, letters, sexual assaults, and, in the academic setting, offensive comments about a woman's body or clothing in student evaluations (Juliano 2007). While these behaviors are sexualized, male subordinates' motivations to harass female supervisors do not ordinarily derive from sexual desire. Male subordinates who harass may feel resentment or hostility toward a female supervisor because of her failure to conform to gender norms of submission to male authority. In effect, the woman's organizational power, combined with her gender, motivate the harassment in which the perpetrator uses his social power as a man to put the supervisor in her place. The perpetrator may also derive interpersonal power at work from other men and their dominant position at work or in society, even though he may have inferior organizational status to the female supervisor. Legal scholar Ann Juliano notes that men who engage in contra-power harassment of their female supervisors "reinforce the inferior gender status of women by negating their higher organizational status" (Juliano 2007, 504). These men actually enhance their own power at work and diminish that of their female supervisors by harassing them.

Female Subordinate Harassers/Male Supervisor Victim

In situations where female subordinates harass their male supervisors in a sexual or gender-based fashion, the motivation may be sexual desire, hostility toward men in authority positions, or hostility toward the individual male supervisor for his gender-nonconforming behavior, whether it is effeminate or hypermasculine. As I explain more fully below, the power may derive from a number of possible sources. First, in the context of contra-power harassment, because the subordinate woman has inferior organizational power and, presumably, inferior sociocultural power, it is necessary to consider other sources of power. Potential sources of power include the woman's membership in a socially more powerful group based on race, ethnicity, sexual orientation, class, or color. Another might be the woman's adherence to and the man's failure to conform to gender expectations. Still another might be that the woman belongs to a group of women or a mixed-gender group that gives her interpersonal power in the workforce. As noted below about a female coworker's harassment of a male coworker, because a man would ordinarily be expected to endure harassment or to take care of it himself and not to complain of it, we can presume that a man who complains about this type of behavior probably has insufficient power to rebuff the woman's harassment and must therefore rely on the employer to stop the behavior. Because this is the case, there is a justification for creating a presumption that a female's sexual harassment of her male supervisor occurred because of sex. Here, once again, consistent with my arguments above, sexual or gendered harassment requires a power differential along with a motivation that is gender or sex related.

One situation raises concern because it reinforces stereotypes: when a woman uses sex to harass her supervisor and her power comes exclusively from her sexuality. This fact pattern reflects the classic "siren" stereotype and the supervisor who cannot resist the woman's sexual power, even though it is unwelcome. When the source of power of the female aggressor may be purely sensual, it makes sense to permit the presumption that the harassment occurs because of the superior's sex.

The courts would have no trouble with this situation because they would assume that the female subordinate would not engage in the same behavior if the supervisor were a woman. Of course, we cannot be sure of this conclusion, but we do know that the female subordinate is using her sex as a means of altering the terms or conditions of her boss's employment. This is a case where the presumption should affix; if there is no gender or sexual motivation, the employer can prove the affirmative defense that I propose below.

Same-Sex Contra-power Harassment

Where there is same-sex contra-power harassment, masculinities research demonstrates that men engage in harassing behavior to police the gender norms in the workforce and to assure that men comply with those norms (McGinley 2008). Men may also harass other men who are their superiors in order to demonstrate their own masculinity; a common theme in blue-collar workforces, for example, is the "limp-wristed" white-collar supervisor whom the blue-collar workers resent for his higher salary and supervisory power (Collinson 1988). The motivation may be the perceived or real gender failures of the supervisor in this situation and the resulting affirmation of men who harass that they are "real men." Because the harassment is ordinarily a group enterprise, the power derives from the group's interpersonal relationships. It serves as a means of proving to one's group how manly the perpetrators are.

Finally, men might harass male superiors because of their sexual interest in them. Once again, the power to harass in this situation does not come from organizational power, but it may derive from sociocultural power if the individual harasser belongs to a more powerful race, class, national origin, or other group. Even if he does not, he may acquire power to accomplish the harassment through his interpersonal relationships at work or outside of work.

Women may harass their female supervisors because of the supervisors' failure to conform to female gender norms—their adherence to a masculine style or to a hyperfeminine style. While female subordinates lack organizational power, they use power derived from workplace dynamics and interpersonal relationships to accomplish the harassment, especially if they form groups to harass the superior. Similar to the female subordinate who harasses a male supervisor, a female subordinate may also harass her female superior because of sexual desire, and her power in certain instances may derive from her sexuality.

Lateral Harassment

Group of Male Coworker Harassers/Female Coworker Victims

In male-on-female coworker harassment, the behavior can be sexual in nature or nonsexual and hostile. Both types of behavior often occur because of the woman's sex and are possible because of a social power differential between men and women outside and inside the workplace. When groups of men engage in harassing behavior of individual women or groups of women, the men's social power is magnified by interpersonal relationships and workplace dynamics, especially in workplaces that are historically predominantly occupied by male workers. Thus, their harassing behavior, whether sexual in nature or not, may occur as a result of a power differential between the men and women at work and because of sex. In predominantly male workplaces, male coworkers enhance their social power by engaging in gender harassment of the few women in the workplace, often with the motive of proving their masculinity to one another, undermining the confidence and competence of the women on the job, and/or maintaining the job as a man's job. Doing so enhances the masculinity of the men performing the work.[3]

An example of this type of harassment appears in *Robinson v. Jacksonville Shipyards* (1991). In *Jacksonville Shipyards*, the plaintiff, one of a few women working as a craft worker in the shipyard, alleged that the defendants created a hostile working environment because of sex. In a bench trial, the court found that pornography and pinups depicting women as sex objects were pervasive in the workplace and that several of Robinson's male coworkers made sexualized and gender-based derogatory comments to her and her female coworkers (ibid.). Robinson's expert witness, Dr. Susan Fiske, a prominent psychologist, testified that the prevalence of highly sexualized pinups and posters, especially in a workplace where there are few women, leads to stereotyping of women and negatively affects evaluation of women's work performance. The court concluded that the employer violated Title VII by permitting a hostile working environment that altered the terms or conditions of the plaintiff's working environment. Dr. Fiske's testimony established a theoretical basis from which the court concluded that the behavior occurred because of sex and was severe or pervasive (ibid.).

In a few cases after *Jacksonville Shipyards*, lower courts have concluded that in predominantly male workplaces, a pervasive environment of sexually explicit materials and behavior to which both men and women are exposed does not occur because of sex (*E.E.O.C. v. National Education Assoc.* 2005; *Petrosino v. Bell Atl.* 2003; *Ocheltree v. Scollon Productions, Inc.* 2002; *Steiner v. Showboat Operating Co.* 1994). They reason that if the behavior occurred before women were introduced into the workplace, the behavior does not occur because of sex. These courts take a cramped view of causation, especially in the situation where there are displays of pornographic or offensive materials. Most of these cases have been overturned on appeal because the courts conclude that there is some behavior that is targeted at the women and not at the men. Moreover, as in *Jacksonville Shipyards*, the sexualized materials, comments, and behaviors do not treat men and women equally. They depict women, but not men, in scant clothing and sexually submissive positions, and the men in the workplace often use the sexualized materials as references for their comments to and behaviors toward their female coworkers.

Masculinities research supports a finding that these environments occur because of sex. Men engage in homosocial competitive behavior to prove their masculinity to other men (Kimmel 2004). The process of constructing masculinity, social scientists conclude, is not only about demonstrating the commonalities among men; it also requires a highlighting of difference (Prokos and Padavic 2002). Women's presence in the organization, especially if they are performing what are considered to be men's jobs, creates an incentive for male workers to prove their manhood to other men by abusing the women. This behavior, which includes the exploitation of women and the derogation of the feminine, reinforces the masculinity of the job and the men performing it, and creates structural disincentives for women to work in these jobs (Schultz 1998).

Vicki Schultz notes that women are harassed most frequently when they occupy jobs that are predominantly male. In jobs historically occupied by men, women suffer harassment because men associate their jobs with masculinity and police the jobs by harassing women and gender-nonconforming men. A workplace in which both men and women are exposed to misogynistic behavior and/or language and jokes creates a hostile environment for women because of their sex: it enhances the men's masculinity and the superior position of men in the job while negatively affecting women's confidence and working opportunities.

Group of Male Coworker Harassers/Male Coworker Victims

Men also exhibit power over other men because of their sex.[4] Especially in situations where a group of men harasses an individual man, the behavior often involves competitive performances of masculinity (McGinley 2008). The group is motivated to assure that all men comply with the group's masculinity requirements and by doing so, to ensure that the job or workplace remains masculine. The harassing behavior occurs because of sex in two ways. First, the harassers enhance their own masculinity in the eyes of their peers, and in their own eyes, by engaging in hostile harassing behavior. Thus, the behavior occurs because of sex (or gender) in that it undermines the victim's masculinity in order to prove and enhance the masculinity of the harassers. Second, the harassers select as their victims other men who do not perform masculinity in an acceptable manner. The male victims are usually small, weak, or nonconforming in their gender presentations. The perpetrators harass them because of their gender nonconformity (because of their sex) (ibid.). This appears to describe what happened in Jonathan Martin's and Joseph Oncale's situations.

Harassing behaviors exhibit a surprising similarity across workplaces, and even in playgrounds, where boys learn to harass gendernonconforming boys (ibid.). Often, the harassers engage in teasing and name calling, but the behavior escalates to physical touching, and penetration of the anal cavity of the victim. The symbolism of penetration is that the person penetrated is feminine, not a "real man," and those doing the penetrating are "real men." Some men see homosexuality as the passive act of being penetrated by a man (Case 1995; Valdes 1995).

As to power in this situation, even where the perpetrators and the victims are equals in the organization, the perpetrators have more social power due to their numbers and their understanding that they are the masculine "real men" who set the standard for male workers in the particular workplace. Moreover, because of their numbers and interpersonal relationships at work, they are able to engage in harassing behavior. The victim has less power because he is alone and because he does not conform to the group's definition of who is a real man.

If it is a hazing situation, the group may not select the victim because of his failure to conform to gender norms, but the behavior still occurs because of sex. The group has an interest in assuring that the job and the workplace conform to masculine stereotypes. Thus, hazing is a method of gender policing in the workplace environment. The power derives from the group's behavior and the fact that the person hazed is a male newcomer in the organization. By definition, newcomers in all-male workplaces suffer for being not "man enough."

Although in *Oncale v. Sundowner Offshore Services, Inc.*, Justice Scalia stated that hazing is ordinarily not sufficiently severe or pervasive to create liability, many courts seem to see hazing as not occurring because of sex (*In re Smurfit-Stone Container Corp.* 2005; *Shafer v. Kal Kan Foods, Inc.* 2005; *E.E.O.C. v. Harbert-Yeargin, Inc.* 2001). Certainly, where hazing does not rise to the level of severity or pervasiveness, an employer would not be liable in a hostile work environment claim (*Oncale v. Sundowner Offshore Services, Inc.* 1998). But, where the hazing occurs in an all-male workplace and there is severe and/or pervasive verbal or physical harassment, such as in the *Oncale* case, where the plaintiff was subjected to escalating physical and verbal harassment in the showers, hazing can create a hostile work environment. Masculinities theory explains that the competitive nature of the environment occurs in order for the harassers to prove their masculinity to other harassers, to demean the victim's masculinity, and to police the boundaries of masculinity in the job in question. This behavior clearly occurs because of sex.

Group of Female Coworker Harassers/Female Coworker Victims

Women may harass their female coworkers because of the coworkers' failure to conform to female gender norms, e.g., their adherence to a masculine style or to a hyperfeminine style. In fact, the predominance of powerful men in the workplace may create a dynamic that creates competition among women. Robin Ely's research has found that where there are few women in positions of power in a predominantly male workplace, women in less powerful positions have more competitive relationships with one another and demonstrate a lack of social support for one another (Ely 1994).

While female coworkers lack organizational power, they use power derived from workplace dynamics and interpersonal relationships to accomplish the harassment, especially when they form groups to accomplish the harassment. The movie *Erin Brockovich* is useful in explaining how this behavior takes place. In *Erin Brockovich*, which is based on a true story, the protagonist goes to work for a small personal injury firm and convinces her boss to bring a case against Pacific Gas & Electric for polluting a small California town's water and causing cancer in its residents. Erin dresses in a manner that is hypersexual—a style that her female colleagues at work dislike. Her colleagues, in response, make degrading comments to her and shun her at work because of her failure to conform to proper female dress and presentation at work (*Erin Brockovich* 2000). This harassing behavior occurs because of sex because the victim does not perform her gender or sexuality in a manner that her coworkers find acceptable, and they engage in harassing behaviors as a result of her "failed femininity." Similar behavior is alleged to have occurred in *Durkin v. Verizon N.Y., Inc.*, where female coworkers were fixated on the plaintiff's breasts, disliked and harassed her because of her breast size, spread rumors that she was "loose" and did not wear underwear, and attributed her success to her breast size (*Durkin v. Verizon N.Y., Inc.* 2009, 128).

Female Coworker Harasser/Male Coworker Victim

While it seems almost impossible that an individual female harasser will have sufficient power to create a hostile working environment for her male coworker, some instances of female harassment of male colleagues occur. Lawsuits alleging this fact pattern are unusual probably because an individual female will not ordinarily have sufficient power to overcome the power of her male coworker. In *E.E.O.C. v. Prospect Airport Services, Inc.*, however, an individual female coworker harassed an individual male coworker (2010). Both Sylvia Munoz and her coworker, Rudolpho Lamas, worked at the Las Vegas airport pushing wheelchairs and guiding persons with disabilities to their planes. Lamas complained to management repeatedly that Munoz was sexually harassing him, but his managers did little to prevent Munoz's behavior. Moreover, other coworkers began to harass Lamas, questioning his masculinity and his sexual orientation because he did not respond to Munoz's romantic advances. Here, we have coequals who appear to have the same amount of organizational power. One would presume that because women as a group generally have less social power, Munoz, the female perpetrator, would have insufficient social power to accomplish the harassment.

The courts have not concerned themselves with this question. They merely assume the symmetry of the law. In other words, because male-on-female harassment is presumed to occur because of sex, female-on-male harassment is also assumed to occur because of sex. But because this symmetrical theory results from a presumption that both parties are heterosexual and that the motivation of the harasser is sexual attraction, it is based on inadequate theoretical foundations. Masculinities theory offers a richer, more contextualized view of this situation. Many employers and coworkers would not consider a man's complaint legitimate because of stereotypical views of how men should respond to sexual advances: they should either enjoy the advances or be able to handle them on their own. Thus, because of the significant deterrents to male complaints, it is likely that men who can engage in self-help will do so. Men who complain about harassment by a female coworker do so because they cannot handle the situation themselves: they do not have sufficient power to rebuff the advances on their own. This powerlessness probably derives from a particular man's failure to conform to masculine stereotypes, either as the sole factor or in combination with other identity factors such as race or class.

Given that men who do not conform to the gender stereotype cannot rebuff the advances without complaining to management, their position parallels that of female victims. Where female victims of male colleagues' sexual advances often lack the power to rebuff the sexual advances due to a history of patriarchy causing social or organizational factors that place women at a disadvantage, male victims of female harassers lack the power to rebuff unwanted advances by virtue of their failure to conform or their fear of being perceived as failing to conform to gender stereotypes. It would make sense, therefore, to presume that a man who brings suit on the basis of a female coworker's sexual advances is a victim of illegal discrimination because of sex. Here, I am using "because of sex" to incorporate a power differential between perpetrator and victim. This is not the symmetry that the courts use to support their reasoning because the reasons supporting the presumption that the behavior is illegal and occurs because of sex are different for men and women, but the use of a symmetrical approach to the "because of sex" requirement has underlying support based on feminist and masculinities theories.

Let's consider the situation of Sylvia Munoz and Rudolpho Lamas. Munoz is a tiny woman—less than five feet tall—who is light-skinned; Lamas is a large man who is six feet three inches tall and is dark-skinned. As a woman, Munoz belongs to the socially less powerful class whereas Lamas, a man, belongs to the socially more powerful class. Both are equals at work. It appears, given these facts, that Munoz would be incapable of harassing Lamas. But the case gives us some hints about the superior power that Munoz was able to marshal throughout because of the workplace context and the employer's unwillingness to become engaged in the situation. First of all, there is a color differential between Munoz and Lamas. Munoz, a light-skinned female, may have more social power than Lamas, a dark-skinned male, based on their racial/color differential. Second, Lamas is a recent widower and convert to fundamentalist Christianity.

The power differential here arises from Munoz's bold play for a vulnerable man, combined with the employer's refusal to take Lamas's complaints seriously, and the escalation of harassing behavior by Munoz and other workers. Even assuming that at first Munoz was attracted to Lamas as a man, once he showed his unwillingness to engage in a sexual relationship, Lamas's superiors and coworkers treated him as if he were not a "real man." His immediate supervisor, Rhonda Thompson, never spoke to Munoz about her behavior even though she agreed to do so when Lamas complained; the general manager, Dennis Mitchell, did nothing more than tell Munoz that he did not want to get involved in a personal situation. This admonition did not stop the harassment. The assistant general manager told Lamas that he should sing to himself, "I'm too sexy for my shirt" (*E.E.O.C. v. Prospect Airport Services, Inc.* 2010, 995). In other words, Lamas should have felt flattered by Munoz's advances. All signs were that Lamas did not act like a real man. A real man would have enjoyed the sexual advance and taken Munoz up on it.

But perhaps the worst behavior belonged to Lamas's coworkers and the employer's failure to stop it. At Munoz's encouragement, coworkers urged Lamas to go out with her, and when he rebuffed her advances, they turned on him, questioning whether he was gay and questioning his masculinity. All of this behavior occurred after Lamas had complained many times to his supervisors. Thus, the coworkers' behavior attempted to enforce a gender regime—that men should accede to a woman's sexual advances, and if they don't, they are not real men. Their mistreatment of Lamas occurred because of his sex. His colleagues pressured him to act like a man, and when he did not in their view, they ridiculed him for not being a real man.

Masculinities theory explains why the workplace environment is problematic. It acknowledges that men as a group have power. There is, indeed, a hegemony of men. But it also recognizes that because of the pressure to prove masculinity and the competition among men to perform and prove their masculinity, individual men often feel powerless. This feeling of powerlessness appears to describe Lamas's predicament. As a man, Lamas is a member of the gender with the greater social power, but Munoz marshaled the power of her coworkers and of the employer to create a situation for Lamas that called into question his very manhood. Given the pressure in society to conform to gender roles, this abuse occurred because of Lamas's sex—his failure to live up to stereotypical gender norms of masculinity. In essence, Lamas suffered a harassing environment, and lost his job because he did not live up to the stereotypical ideal of the way a man should have handled the situation.

The court understood the case as mere heterosexual attraction and romantic advances. Sylvia's sexual advances may have resulted from sexual attraction to the male victim, but the negative reactions of the supervisor and the coworkers also occur because of Lamas's sex. These reactions are attempts to require that a man live up to a stereotype—that he not be gay and not be effeminate. The employer, by failing to correct the behavior, ratifies the harassment and allows it to escalate, thus throwing the organizational power behind the harassers. This case is not only about sexual attraction; it is also about enforcing gender norms in the workplace. Requiring an employee to live up to gender norms or stereotypes at work is sex discrimination, according to Price Waterhouse v. Hopkins (1989).

Masculinities theory demonstrates that it is important not to make generalizations about how women and men should behave at work. Because of the power differentials in very segregated workplaces, it is ordinarily true that women have less organizational power than men. Moreover, because women on average still have less economic and social power than men, women are more often targets of sexual harassment. Women should not have to endure this behavior at work when it is related to their inferior positions in society and at work. But this theory should not immunize an employer who permits a woman to harass a male coworker. This is the case because even if the stereotypes may be true in a general sense, individuals may differ from the stereotype. The law should not reinforce gender norms and stereotypes when there is individual variation. By the same token, it is necessary to articulate a reasonable theory explaining why men (at least some men) can suffer illegal sex discrimination as a result of harassment by their female coworkers.

E.E.O.C. v. Prospect Airport Services demonstrates that courts need to take into account the complicated multidimensional identities of the plaintiff, his individual vulnerabilities, his status at work, the workplace context, and the location of organizational and social power. While men are generally more powerful socially, even if they are in equal positions at work, there are exceptions to this general rule. Furthermore, some of these exceptions themselves are related to gender and gender nonconformity. While the law merely states that the harassment should occur "because of sex," harassment "because of sex" is illegal because of a power differential between the harasser and the victim. The differences approach presumes that male-on-female and female-on-male harassment occur because of sex. This approach is based on a presumption of heterosexuality. Nonetheless, this presumption, if rebuttable, is supportable in both male-on-female and the female-on-male harassment cases, even though for different reasons.

Equal Opportunity Harassers

A few courts have concluded that when the same manager harasses both men and women at work, the harassment does not occur because of sex. This conclusion is squarely based on the differences approach, which concludes that the behavior does not occur because of sex if both men and women are subjected to it. It also focuses on the concept of differential treatment as the most important indicator of illegal discrimination. Courts call this individual harasser the "equal opportunity harasser" (*Holman v. Indiana* 2000, 402). There are multiple scenarios in which the same harasser may subject both men and women to harassment because of sex. The simplest motivation is that the harasser is bisexual and harasses both men and women because of sexual desire for both. But other scenarios may be even more likely because, as we have seen, harassment does not necessarily occur because of sexual attraction. In *Steiner v. Showboat Operating Co.*, for example, the Ninth Circuit rejected the defendant's argument that because the plaintiff's supervisor yelled at both men and women, his behavior was not directed at Steiner because of her sex (*Steiner v. Showboat Operating Co.* 1994). The court noted that the supervisor's abusive treatment of men and women differed—his yelling at women was of a sexual or gender-specific nature, whereas the abuse of the men did not include gender-specific terminology (ibid.).

Furthermore, the court observed that the supervisor could not cure his abuse toward the women by using "sexual epithets equal in intensity and in an equally degrading manner against male employees" because the standard in the Ninth Circuit for determining whether a hostile work environment exists is whether a reasonable woman would find the environment hostile (ibid., 1464). Finally, the court refused to rule out the possibility that both men and women may suffer from sexual harassment against the same supervisor (ibid).

One could argue that an environment that preexisted women's entry into the workplace cannot "alter the terms or conditions of employment" because that environment actually constituted a term or condition of employment at the time the women entered the previously all-male workplace. But the better approach is to interpret the environment as harassing because of sex even if the behavior is not specifically directed at women in the workplace and even if much of the behavior occurred before women were introduced into the workplace. Otherwise, it will be difficult to rid workplaces of misogynistic environments that may harm the working opportunities of most women and some men.

Moreover, as in *Steiner v. Showboat Operating Company,* even though a perpetrator might harass men and women, the harassment directed at men and women might differ significantly in style. But even if the harasser abuses the victims in the same way using the same intensity, a harasser's abuse of both men and women does not necessarily prove that the harassment does not occur because of sex or gender, especially if the harassing behaviors are gendered or sexual in nature. The supervisor who harasses both men and women may be motivated by sexual attraction to men and women, by hostile feelings toward both men and women (as groups or individuals) because of their failure to conform to gender norms, or because of their excessive conformity with gender norms. Or, he may be attempting to establish gender norms in the workplace by policing the role of men and women at work and maintaining a power differential between them. Finally, he may be trying to prove his masculinity and power by demeaning men and women in a sex- or gender-based manner.

A number of courts have explained why this behavior, occurring in the presence of both men and women, occurs because of sex. For example, in *Ocheltree v. Scollon Productions*, the plaintiff was the only woman working in a shop that produced costumes, along with ten or eleven men (*Ocheltree v. Scollon Productions, Inc.* 2002). During her first year, the shop became increasingly polluted with sexual banter and sexual conduct. Three incidents were directed specifically at the plaintiff: a vulgar song, a showing of a book of men with pierced male genitals, and pantomimes of sexual acts with mannequins. There was also evidence that male coworkers touched mannequins in sexual ways when the plaintiff walked by, and that the plaintiff was berated for calling her son, who was home recovering from a broken tailbone. A vice president commented that if the plaintiff did not like the rule against using the telephone for personal reasons, she should go home and be a housewife because she was not cut out for work at the defendant's place of business (ibid.).

Additionally, there was daily sexual banter that included use of profanity, male coworkers' use of explicit sexual insults to bother one another, and protracted discussion of their sexual exploits with their wives or girlfriends in extremely graphic terms. Much of this discussion took a decidedly misogynistic tone. For example, the workers made comments about sexual experiences such as "she swallowed, she gave good head. . . . I fucked her all night long." One employee spoke about his wife's "sucking his dick and swallowing and letting it run down the side of her face" (ibid., 369).

The Fourth Circuit panel concluded that the plaintiff had not proved her case. Three incidents that were obviously directed at the plaintiff were not sufficiently severe or pervasive to alter the terms or conditions of her employment. Other comments and gestures were not directed specifically at the plaintiff, and were therefore ignored. Finally, the behavior could not have occurred because of her sex because much of the behavior was not directed at the plaintiff specifically.

The dissent argued that there was evidence in the record from which one could reasonably conclude that men and women were treated differently and posited that based on the context of the sex-segregated workplace and the tone of the comments, a reasonable jury could conclude that the harassment of the plaintiff was "rooted in male resentment of Ocheltree's intrusion into their workplace and in resentment of her demands that they clean up their act" (ibid., 372). It noted that the behavior of the men portrayed women as sexually subordinate to men and could be considered sexual harassment because the comments reinforced a hierarchical gender regime in which men are portrayed as sexual subjects and women as sexual objects (ibid.). It appears that it is a permissible inference that the men subjected Ocheltree to severe, misogynistic behavior in order to undermine her competence, drive her from the workforce, and establish the shop and the job as masculine (Schultz 1998).

Sitting en banc, the Fourth Circuit overturned the panel decision and held that there was sufficient evidence from which a reasonable jury could have concluded that the discussions that took place in the plaintiff's presence were aimed at the plaintiff to make her uncomfortable (*Ocheltree v. Scollon Productions, Inc.* 2002). Curiously, the en banc court's opinion did not discuss whether it agreed that behavior that is more offensive to women because of its degrading content may occur because of sex even if it is not directed specifically at women in the workplace.[5] The en banc court did not reach the thorny question of whether a plaintiff may prove that offensive behavior occurs because of sex if the behavior is not directed specifically at women but has a disparate effect on women because it is more offensive to them.

A few other courts have reached this question and have concluded that the courts should consider subjectively different reactions women may have to similar treatment. For example, in *Petrosino v. Bell Atlantic*, the Second Circuit overturned the lower court's grant of summary judgment to the defendant on the hostile work environment claim. The court reasoned that even though both men and women were exposed to the hostile environment and even though the conduct ridiculed some men, it "also frequently touted the sexual exploits of others" (*Petrosino v. Bell Atlantic* 2004, 222). Moreover, the court stated, "the depiction of women in the offensive jokes and graphics was uniformly sexually demeaning and communicated the message that women were available for sexual exploitation by men" (ibid.). The court concluded, "Such workplace disparagement of women, repeated day after day over the course of several years without supervisory intervention, stands as a serious impediment to any woman's efforts to deal professionally with her male colleagues" (ibid.).

In a case that took place in a predominantly female workplace, *E.E.O.C. v. National Education Association*, the EEOC brought suit on behalf of three women who worked for the NEA, alleging that they were subjected to a hostile work environment (*E.E.O.C v. National Education Association* 2005). According to evidence in the record, the interim director created a general atmosphere of intimidation in the workplace, and women were afraid of him. The trial court granted the defendant's motion for summary judgment, concluding that there was insufficient evidence that the treatment was "because of sex." The Ninth Circuit overturned the lower court's grant of summary judgment, concluding that the lower court erred when it held that defendant's acts must be either of a sexual nature or motivated by discriminatory animus against women. The Ninth Circuit stated that in a workplace where there is a majority of women, the evidence raised the inference that the interim director was "more comfortable when bullying women than when bullying men" (ibid., 845).

In determining whether a hostile work environment is "because of sex," the Ninth Circuit looked to the differences between the objective treatment of men and women and the subjective effects of that treatment. The court noted that there was sufficient evidence in the record to conclude that the women were treated more harshly than men and that there was a marked difference in subjective effects on the women. This case goes beyond *Steiner* because it concluded that evidence of differences in subjective effects of the behavior on men and women is relevant to the question of whether the behavior occurred because of sex "even where the conduct is not facially sex- or gender-specific" (ibid., 845–46).

The key question in these cases is whether "because of sex" requires a conscious intent to create a hostile working environment for women because they are women. Cases holding that the hostile work environment is not actionable if both men and women are exposed to the same environment read the statute to require that the creator of a hostile work environment have the conscious intent to do so. In chapter 6, I analyze Title VII jurisprudence and conclude that the "because of sex" requirement refers to causation rather than a conscious intent in discrimination cases. Other authors have agreed (Hart 2005; Derum and Engle 2003). Whether other discrimination cases require a conscious intent or not, hostile work environment cases have never required a conscious intent on the part of the perpetrator. This is obvious from the EEOC guidance that was promulgated in 1980 and that courts have applied ever since. The guidance clearly requires that plaintiffs prove that either the intent or the effect of the behavior was discriminatory because of the person's sex or gender rather than a conscious intent to offend because of sex (E.E.O.C. Policy Guidance on Current Issues of Sexual Harassment 1990).

A reading of "because of sex" that takes into account a woman's reasonable reaction will better further the purposes of Title VII to create equal employment opportunity through the elimination of discriminatory terms and conditions of employment. Workplaces that are saturated with misogynistic comments and behavior, whether or not they are specifically directed at women, or whether or not there is a conscious intent to harm women, make it more difficult for many women to perform their work. Women in these workplaces are seen not as colleagues and competent workers but as inferior intruders because they are women. This environment is antithetical to one's ability to succeed at work (*Garcetti v. Ceballos* 2006). Moreover, these behaviors and comments ordinarily focus on the subordinate position of women and therefore, when they occur in the workplace, should fulfill the "because of sex" requirement.

Let's shift the lens to see the situation more clearly. It would be im-
plausible for a court to conclude that racially derogatory language and
behavior did not occur because of race merely because the same language and behavior occurred in the workplace before blacks were hired
to work there. The same reasoning should apply to sex.

Masculinities theory supports this interpretation. Men engage in homosocial competitive behavior to prove their masculinity to other men
(Kimmel 2004). One means of constructing their masculinity in front
of other men is to highlight their superiority over women. A workplace
in which both men and women are exposed to misogynistic behavior
and/or language and jokes will create a hostile environment for women
because of their sex; by making it more difficult for women to be taken
seriously as workers, a misogynistic environment has a disparate negative effect on women's terms or conditions of employment.

This behavior is not limited to blue-collar jobs. Sociologists Margaret and David Collinson studied sex- and gender-based harassment
of female managers in insurance sales (Collinson and Collinson 1996).
Women were isolated not only from the men but also from one another. The men used a "divide and conquer" strategy in which they
spoke disparagingly to each woman about the other women (ibid., 43).
In response, the women used different techniques. They variously dis-
tanced themselves from the other women at work, spoke out against the
harassment, ignored the harassment, or tried to be "one of the guys."
No matter the women's response, management enabled the harassers
by blaming the harassment on the women's reaction (ibid., 42–43). The
authors found that the small number of women in the male environment occupying traditional male jobs "seems to reinforce men's highly
masculine culture and solidarity. Reducing female employees to sexual
objects of ridicule, the dominant male culture reproduced and reinforced itself" (ibid., 45).

The introduction of the women into the male-dominated workplaces
in the Collinsons' accounts resulted in harassing behavior that courts
would agree is sufficiently severe or pervasive to constitute a hostile
working environment. Masculinities theory demonstrates that courts
should also agree that there is at least a question of fact concerning
whether the behavior occurred because of sex.

Creating a Reasonable Presumption

The above discussion demonstrates that using a differential treatment approach to determine that a behavior occurred because of sex tends to underestimate the incidence of illegal discrimination. To accomplish illegal harassment, the perpetrators must have some source of power over the victims. This power has many possible sources such as organizational position, sociocultural power, group dynamics, or a combination of factors. This discussion of the power differential is helpful in understanding how this behavior compares to behavior that Catharine MacKinnon described as supporting a cause of action based on antisubordination principles. We should presume that if an employee or group of employees suffers harassment and is unable to use self-help to stop the behavior, those employees lack sufficient power to stop the harassment. Thus, proof of the harassing behaviors themselves, when they have sexual or gender-based content, should be sufficient to establish the power differential.

Behavior occurs because of sex in many different situations. An important clue for determining whether the behavior occurs because of sex is the behavior itself. Harassment that is sex or gender based or a combination of the two should suffice to create a presumption that the behavior occurred because of sex. Once the presumption arises, the burden should shift to the defendant to prove that the behavior did not occur because of the victim's sex.

Where the behavior itself is neutral, there is little basis for the presumption. Neutral harassing behavior can occur because of sex, however, and if it does, and fulfills the unwelcome and severity or pervasive requirements, it too can create a cause of action for illegal sex discrimination. But where the behaviors are exclusively neutral with no gendered or sexual behaviors, the plaintiffs should have to prove something extra to establish the "because of sex" requirement. Possible means of proving something extra would be proof of differential treatment of men and women (*Kopp v. Samaritan Health Servs. Inc.* 1993) or the fact that the plaintiff does not fulfill common expectations of his or her gender. These are not the only means of creating a presumption in the situation where the behaviors are neutral, but proof of one of these should be sufficient to create the presumption.

In sum, courts should be entitled to presume that harassing behavior that is sex or gender based on its face is more than legal sexual behavior: absent defendant's rebuttal proof, it occurs because of sex in the Title VII sense as demonstrated by the sex- or gender-based content. Defendants' rebuttal of the presumption should require an affirmative defense. Defendants would then be entitled to prove by a preponderance of the evidence that the alleged perpetrator did not harass the plaintiff because of sex. To meet this requirement, the defendant would prove that the perpetrator was motivated by a reason other than sex. In making their affirmative defenses, defendants should offer evidence of the organizational setting, the social power of the parties based on gender, race, color, national origin, sexual orientation, and other relevant characteristics, and the context of the workplace. One important consideration is, as is obvious in *E.E.O.C. v. Prospect Airport Services*, the reaction of the employer and other employees to the alleged victim's complaints. Because the employer is liable for the workplace environment, its own behavior and that of other employees subsequent to the initial sexually harassing behaviors are relevant to the context and question of the power held by the alleged victim. If the defendant can prove by a preponderance of the evidence that the alleged perpetrator had motives other than sex or gender, and the plaintiff cannot rebut this proof, illegal discrimination has not occurred because of sex.

This chapter demonstrates that courts have been confused about the "because of sex" requirement in Title VII harassment cases. Most notably, courts have treated same-sex and other-sex harassment cases differently. This differential treatment relies on a strong underlying belief that sexual desire is the source of sexual harassment and on an adoption of heteronormativity. But this implicit belief is not accurate. Masculinities theory demonstrates that there are varied reasons, in different contexts and settings, that explain that sex- or gender-based harassing behavior occurs because of sex. The courts should make themselves aware of the social science research supporting these explanations and, as a result, create a presumption that once sex- or gender-based behavior creates a hostile working environment, the behavior occurs because of sex. This chapter explains the presumption and how an employer can prove its affirmative defense. Courts are particularly uncomfortable with the "because of sex" analysis in male-on-male harassment because of the common belief that male-on-male harassment is hazing and/or "roughhousing" and therefore does not occur because of sex. Nonetheless, masculinities theory can trace hazing and roughhousing to sex and gender, and it is important for courts to understand this motivation so that men, as well as women, can enjoy Title VII's protection. Resorting to expertise on masculinities theory should help courts understand the origins of motivations for certain behaviors alleged to occur because of sex. With this understanding, Jonathan Martin's case for sex- or gender-based harassment would succeed.

4

A Question of Standards

Reasonable Men?

Reasonable Men and Sexual Harassment

Even if the court agrees that the behavior directed at Jonathan Martin occurred because of sex, Martin must still convince the court that the harassment was sufficiently severe or pervasive to alter the terms or conditions of his employment. This is both a subjective and an objective test. The behavior must have subjectively polluted Jonathan Martin's work environment. And, it must be sufficiently severe or pervasive to create a hostile working environment for a reasonable person under the circumstances at the Miami Dolphins (*Harris v. Forklift Systems, Inc.* 1993).

The courts do not require significant proof to satisfy the subjective standard. Martin told his parents on a number of occasions that he was upset by his treatment; he later walked off the job and committed himself to a mental institution. Given these facts, it is likely that Martin will not have difficulty meeting the proof requirements imposed by the subjective test. In contrast, courts exact high standards when it comes to objective proof of severity or pervasiveness. These standards are particularly confusing when the alleged victims are men, whether the alleged harassers are women or other men.

When a man is the victim of a woman who sexually harasses him, courts downplay the harm caused by the sexual harassment. In fact, courts seem to believe that the man is lucky or, even if not, that it is not manly to complain about a woman's harassment of him (*E.E.O.C. v. Prospect Airport Services, Inc.* 2010). When a man is a victim of harassment by another man or, in the more common case, a group of men, the courts often dismiss the behavior as normal roughhousing among men that does not meet the standard of severity or pervasiveness (*E.E.O.C. v. Harbert-Yeargin, Inc.* 2001).

This chapter discusses both scenarios: the proper standard for proving severity or pervasiveness where the man is a victim of a woman's sexual advances, and the proper standard where the man is a victim of harassment by a group of other men.[1] Masculinities research can help courts answer the thorny questions about the standard in both instances. In fact, masculinities research can uncover hidden biases and invisible gender issues that the courts often do not perceive. The first example—where a woman harasses a man at work—comes from *E.E.O.C. v. Prospect Airport Services, Inc.* (2007). The second, where a group of men harasses a man, is the hypothetical case based on what we know about Jonathan Martin's complaints. Before moving to a thorough discussion of those examples, however, in the next subsection I offer a short history of the reasonable person standard.

History of the "Reasonable Person" Standard and Current Jurisprudence

Although the Supreme Court has not directly addressed the question of whether the proper objective standard is the "reasonable person," the "reasonable victim," or the "reasonable woman" standard, the Court has used the term "reasonable person" in determining whether the victim meets the objective requirement of severity or pervasiveness. In a few circuits, courts have used the reasonable *woman* standard. When the victim is a man or a person of color, the Ninth Circuit has adapted the standard to be the "reasonable person with the same identifying characteristics," the "reasonable man," or the "reasonable Latino man" standard.

The law in the United States uses the reasonable person standard in a variety of disciplines, including constitutional law, negligence, criminal law, commercial law, and employment discrimination (Chamallas 2010; Moran 2010; Wang 2010). Depending on the area and the particular case, the standard plays different roles. In negligence and criminal law, for example, it determines the culpability of the defendant, including the availability of a justification or defense (Moran 2010). In Title VII law, it has a different purpose: it examines the *plaintiff's* story in light of community norms to determine whether the defendant's (or its agent's) alleged behavior creates a hostile working environment. A plaintiff in these cases must prove that he or she subjectively experienced a hostile working environment and that the gender- or sex-based behavior was sufficiently severe or pervasive to alter the terms or conditions of employment of a reasonable person (*Harris v. Forklift Systems, Inc.* 1993; *Meritor Saving Bank v. Vinson* 1986).

Thus, the reasonable person (or woman or victim) standard in hostile work environment law plays a perspectival rather than a culpability-determining function (Moran 2010). Unlike in negligence law, where the reasonable person standard measures whether the defendant acted tortiously by breaching its duty of care to the plaintiff, in employment discrimination hostile work environment law, the reasonable person standard analyzes whether the *victim's* reaction to the environment was reasonable. This standard indirectly establishes whether the defendant's alleged behavior is culpable, but the primary focus is on the alleged victim's perception of the behavior, and whether a reasonable person under the circumstances would have a similar reaction. While reasonableness of the plaintiff's behavior in responding to the defendant's alleged harassment is considered at a later stage in the litigation (along with the reasonableness of the employer's behavior), if the defendant employer asserts an affirmative defense in a case of supervisor harassment of a subordinate, it is not this examination of the plaintiff that occurs at this stage. Instead, at the prima facie stage, the question is whether a reasonable person (or woman or victim) would view the behavior as creating a hostile work environment itself, not whether the plaintiff could have corrected or avoided the environment had she reported it to her employer (*Burlington Industries, Inc. v. Ellerth* 1998; *Faragher v. City of Boca Raton* 1998).

As noted above, there is some variation in the circuits regarding whether to use the reasonable person or reasonable woman standard in determining whether the behavior is sufficiently severe or pervasive. After the Supreme Court recognized sexual harassment as a form of discrimination under Title VII in *Meritor Savings Bank v. Vinson*, lower courts used the reasonable *person* standard to measure whether a hostile working environment occurred. Both cultural and radical feminists objected to the reasonable *person* measure in hostile working environment cases (Abrams 1995), however, because in their view, the reasonable person standard was, in reality, based on what a reasonable *man* would consider offensive (ibid.; Cahn 1992).

Cultural feminists argued that the standard did not take into account the biological and social differences of women and men; radical feminists concluded that the use of a male norm ignored the power advantages that men had over women (Abrams 1995). These concerns led many feminists to support a reasonable *woman* standard, which the Ninth Circuit adopted in *Ellison v. Brady* (1991). A number of other courts followed, including the First, Second, and Third Circuits (*Gray v. Genlyte Group, Inc.* 2002; *Torres v. Pisano* 1997; *Hurley v. Atlantic City Police Dept.* 1999).

Feminists soon became dissatisfied, however, with the new reasonable woman test; they argued that the reasonable woman standard essentializes women by not taking into account the differences among women based on race, class, national origin, sexual orientation, and other identity factors (Moran 2003; Cahn 1992). Some feminists also condemned the standard because they believed that it reinforces the view that women are marginal workers by assuming that women are different from, and inferior to, men (Bernstein 1997). Others argued that while using a gendered standard may give some victories to women, the reasonable woman standard is problematic because it leaves intact a system of male privilege (Wildman 2000). Another believed that the reasonableness aspect of the test itself preserves male power, and adding women to the test did not resolve the tendency of the test to confirm the status quo (Ehrenreich 1990).

All of these debates assumed male perpetrators and female victims, but cases of male victims would soon arise. Subsequently, in *Oncale v. Sundowner Offshore Services, Inc.*, the Supreme Court held that male (and, presumably, female) victims of same-sex harassment have a cause of action under Title VII if they prove that the harassment is unwelcome, severe, or pervasive and occurs "because of sex" (*Oncale v. Sundowner Offshore Services, Inc.* 1998). Scholars and courts have paid almost no attention, however, to the situation of a male victim of a female coworker's sexual advances.

As noted in chapter 3, a recent Ninth Circuit female-on-male harassment case, *E.E.O.C. v. Prospect Airport Services, Inc.* (2010), raises important issues concerning the standard for female-on-male harassment and, for that matter, male-on-female and same-sex harassment. In *Prospect Airport Services*, Rudolpho Lamas alleged that a female coworker, Sylvia Munoz, sexually harassed him over a number of months, and that their employer did virtually nothing to stop it. He filed a charge with the

EEOC, which brought suit in federal court on his behalf. In response to the defendant's motion for summary judgment, the federal district court commented that most men would welcome this type of behavior and granted summary judgment to the defendant employer (ibid.). The Ninth Circuit panel reversed, chiding the lower court for its attitude toward the male defendant (ibid.).

While it apparently makes sense to consider the identity characteristics of the victim in assessing whether a reasonable victim would find the harassing behavior severe or pervasive, it also seems odd to hold individual male victims to a higher standard than that applied to individual female victims. The reasonable woman standard was established to assure that courts and juries would not impose male sensibilities (or the lack thereof) on female employees who are alleged victims of sexual harassment in the workplace (*Ellison v. Brady* 1991). When the Ninth Circuit adopted the reasonable woman standard in *Ellison v. Brady*, and other courts followed, courts and commentators assumed that sexual harassment victims were exclusively women. For this reason, no one who advocated for the reasonable woman standard had anticipated the standard would apply to future male victims (Moran 2010). Especially because of this failure of forethought, courts should not reflexively apply a "reasonable man standard"—arguably the counterpart to the "reasonable woman" standard where the victim is a female—to a male victim without considering the potential repercussions of doing so.

A major concern about applying a reasonable man standard to male victims is that the law would establish a preferred standard of masculinity that may harm men, women, and society in general. Most likely, the standard would mimic the concept of "hegemonic masculinity," the most powerful ideal form of masculinity in society (Kimmel 2004, 184). This ideal form of masculinity is often unachievable and would therefore judge too harshly those men who may be most vulnerable to other-sex and same-sex harassment: men who do not live up to male gender stereotypes (McGinley 2007). For example, in Jonathan Martin's hypothetical case, the court might conclude, as many of the commentators have done, that Jonathan Martin should have put up with the alleged harassment because a reasonable man would have concluded that it was not sufficiently severe or pervasive to alter his working conditions. This conclusion would hold Martin to the standard of the hegemonic male football player—tough and unflappable. However, masculinities re-search demonstrates that aggressive and competitive masculine norms harm men and women who are compared to the male standard (ibid.).

By the same token, the reasonable woman standard has serious draw-backs. When courts assess harassment of women, they assume that there is only one possible reasonable response from women. There is no ques-tion, however, that different women, depending on the myriad axes of their identities, their experiences, and the contexts of the situations, have varying responses to the same harassing behavior. *Many of these responses are reasonable.*

Prospect Airport Services raises a number of other questions: whether it is possible to have a fair standard that applies uniformly to male-on-female, female-on-male, and same-sex harassment; whether an *objective* standard should consider identities and experiences of the alleged victims together with context of the work situation; and whether the standard ap-plied in these cases makes a difference to the outcome. *Prospect Airport Services* allows us to consider all of these queries. Because *Prospect Air-port Services* features the atypical situation of a man alleging that a female coworker's behavior created a sexually hostile work environment, it is an excellent vehicle for reexamining the standard for determining whether a hostile working environment exists under Title VII.

It permits a lens shift to reconsider sexual harassment law, a law ordi-narily applied to protect women, as it relates to male victims. The meth-odology of the lens shift offers a fresh view of the stereotypes underlying the behaviors of men and women in the workplace and reveals the gen-dered notions incorporated in the judges' opinions and in the legal standards themselves. This new perspective provides valuable insights that clarify the law's effects on male and female victims of other-sex and same-sex harassment, and can lead to the proposal of new theories, jus-tifications for, and interpretations of the law (Dowd 2010).

Shifting the Lens on Severity or Pervasiveness

Example One: Female-on-Male Coworker Harassment

Rudolpho Lamas began work as a passenger service assistant for Pros-pect Airport Services at McCarran International Airport in Las Vegas, Nevada, in April 2002, and was soon promoted to lead passenger service assistant. His job was to assist passengers with disabilities by pushing them in wheelchairs to the gates. Lamas, a religious man and a recent widower, testified that soon after he began the job, a married female coworker, Sylvia Munoz, began to make sexual advances toward him. (*E.E.O.C. v. Prospect Airport Services, Inc.* 2010).

From the beginning, Lamas told Munoz that he was not interested, and he asked her to stop her advances. He also reported his discomfort on many occasions to supervisory personnel at Prospect Airport Services, including the assistant general manager and the general manager. His supervisors made limited efforts to stop Munoz's advances, but to no avail. Munoz began to harass Lamas every day, and had coworkers deliver messages asking Lamas for dates. Because of his failure to respond, coworkers speculated about Lamas's sexual orientation and teased him by asking if he was gay. Lamas felt "constant pressure" as a result of Munoz's and his other coworkers' antics (ibid., 995). Lamas began to see a psychologist about his distress, and his work performance declined. Finally, in June 2003, Prospect Airport Services fired Lamas, citing his poor attitude and unwillingness to give quality customer service.

Lamas filed a charge with the EEOC alleging that defendant Prospect Airport Services had tolerated a sexually hostile work environment, in violation of Title VII of the 1964 Civil Rights Act, and the agency brought the case on its own behalf. After discovery, Prospect Airport Services filed a motion for summary judgment, and the federal district court granted the motion. It concluded that the behavior failed to create a hostile work environment as a matter of law.

The trial court, in essence, used the reasonable man standard, but assumed that the reasonable man is the aggressive heterosexual hegemonic male. It stated that Lamas "admits that most men in his circumstances would have welcomed" the woman's advances and ruled that a reasonable jury could not conclude that a reasonable person with the same "fundamental characteristics" as the plaintiff would find the harassment sufficiently severe or pervasive to alter the terms or conditions of Lamas's employment (*E.E.O.C. v. Prospect Airport Services, Inc.* 2007, 6).

On appeal, a panel of the Ninth Circuit reversed the trial court's grant of summary judgment to Prospect Airport Services (*E.E.O.C. v. Prospect Airport Services, Inc.* 2010). The Ninth Circuit criticized the lower court's stereotypes and assumptions about men who face sexual harassment at work. The court concluded that female and male sexual harassment victims should be treated equally, and that stereotypes that men desire women to make sexual advances to them have no place in analyzing sexual harassment law (ibid.)

The court noted that not all romantic proposals are illegal sexual harassment, and that merely offensive conduct is not sufficient to create a hostile working environment. It concluded that Munoz's advances were not severe, but stated that "the required level of severity or seriousness varies inversely with the pervasiveness or frequency of the conduct" (*E.E.O.C. v. Prospect Airport Services, Inc.* 2010, 1000). Because of the repeated advances, combined with the employer's failure to stop the conduct, the court concluded that Lamas had presented sufficient evidence to go to the jury on the question of severity or pervasiveness. While it overturned the lower court's grant of summary judgment to the defendant, the court of appeals never addressed whether the standard should be reasonable person, reasonable woman, reasonable man, or reasonable victim, and did not discuss the benefits of or problems with using a reasonable man standard.

MULTIDIMENSIONAL MASCULINITIES: METHODOLOGY AND SUBSTANCE APPLIED

Multidimensional masculinities theory may help explain Rudolpho Lamas's reaction to Sylvia Munoz and his other coworkers' harassment. Masculinities theorists explain that although men are powerful as a group, individual men often feel powerless and vulnerable as a result of the pressure placed on them for their perceived failures to live up to the hegemonic ideal of masculinity. As a result of Munoz's advances and Lamas's lack of interest in engaging in a sexual relationship with her, other coworkers ridiculed Lamas and questioned his sexuality. Lamas testified that he felt helpless and began crying frequently. Mr. Lamas's response is unusual in that he admitted his vulnerability to himself, his managers, and a psychologist by telling them about Munoz's advances and his negative reactions to them. His employers and the lower court compounded these feelings of vulnerability by downplaying the importance of his complaints. These feelings of vulnerability result from the necessity to prove one's masculinity continuously, and the fear and shame resulting from a belief that one is not a "real man."

But Lamas also belongs to a number of identity groups that, along with the context of the workplace, probably affected his response and the behavior of others. Lamas is a dark-skinned, Hispanic, fundamentalist Christian man who, at the time of the harassing behavior, had been recently widowed. Lamas was lonely and sad, and he did not want to hurt anyone by repeatedly complaining to management (*E.E.O.C. v. Prospect Airport Services, Inc.* 2010). The failure of management to stop Munoz's harassment actually made the harassment significantly more severe. It appears that management did not take Lamas seriously because he is a man. This is obvious from his manager's statement that Lamas should celebrate the harassment. Management's inaction apparently led to the more pervasive harassment of Lamas by his other coworkers, who openly questioned his masculinity and sexual orientation on numerous occasions. Masculinities theory explains the vulnerability of individual men who do not live up to masculine ideals, and can instruct the courts as to why this behavior was sufficiently severe or pervasive to alter Lamas's terms or conditions of employment.

REASONABLE MAN? WOMAN? PERSON? A REASONABLE RESPONSE
The Ninth Circuit, in *Ellison v. Brady*, adopted the reasonable *woman (or victim)* standard, concluding, "If we only examined whether a reasonable person would engage in allegedly harassing conduct, we would run the risk of reinforcing the prevailing level of discrimination. Harassers could continue to harass merely because a particular discriminatory practice was common, and victims of harassment would have no remedy" (*Ellison v. Brady* 1991, 878). Soon thereafter, the U.S. Supreme Court used the reasonable *person* standard, without explanation, in *Harris v. Forklift Systems, Inc.* (1993). While the issue of the proper standard was before the *Harris* Court in amicus briefs, the Court did not refer to the amicus briefs or explain whether it was rejecting the reasonable woman standard. It merely used the term "reasonable person" in passing. After *Harris*, courts have continued to use a variety of standards.

Legal scholar Mayo Moran argues that in the context of sexual harassment, the reasonable person standard, as adjusted to consider at least some of the individual characteristics of the victim, plays a "corrective" function (Moran 2010, 1237). Because most judges are economically privileged and tend not to have experienced sexual harassment from the perspective of the victim, a reasonable woman (or victim) standard, Moran argues, makes the judge think twice about his initial reactions (ibid.).

Moran notes that the problem with the reasonable person standard, without taking individual characteristics into account, is that it defines a privileged person, rather than a disadvantaged one (Moran 2010). Both Moran and Kathryn Abrams see the reasonable woman (or victim) standard as offering an opportunity to educate the judge and the jury about what it is like for women in the workplace (ibid., 1264; Abrams 1995). To the extent that the law should use the standard to play a corrective function with judges who are themselves privileged, it is necessary to look at individual characteristics in determining what the reasonable person is.

While I agree with Moran and Abrams that fact finders should consider individual characteristics, I have two concerns about their analysis. First, while their proposals take into account identity characteristics and context, they suggest that there is only one reasonable response to a particular combination of characteristics and context. Second, because they discuss the typical situation of the reasonable woman, their discussion tends to ignore how their proposal would affect male victims of other-sex harassment and all same-sex victims. Only if we can find a workable standard for all types of victims will women, the most common victims of sexual harassment, be fully protected.

Masculinities theories may be useful in helping judges and juries understand why men are vulnerable to harassment by coworkers or supervisors. Male and some female coworkers harass gender-nonconforming men for their failure to live up to masculinity norms (Stockdale et al. 2004). These masculinity norms hurt the men who are judged by the norms, but they often also exclude women from the workplace or result in their harassment. Moreover, harassment based on masculinity norms is often invisible (ibid.).

Thus, if judges attempt to use their own "common sense" or to allow the juries to use "common sense" without permitting expert social framework testimony concerning gender norms, they may actually reinforce the very gender norms that cause the harassment. Judges should permit expert testimony to explain to the fact finders how groups enforce gender norms at work for purposes of giving a background to the judge and jury. Where applicable, experts should also testify about how this background evidence relates to the workplace in question in the litigation. There is some disagreement about whether experts should be permitted to apply general principles of their disciplines to the specific fact questions in the case before them. I deal with this debate extensively in chapter 9. But here, suffice it to say that at the very least, plaintiffs' experts should be permitted to testify about their discipline and expertise as background for the jury. And, there seems to be no debate that they may testify about "applied" social framework evidence (or "social facts," as some call them) to the extent that they have conducted research and experiments on the workplace itself or a similar workplace. Experts should not opine about the ultimate finding of fact—whether the employer discriminated against the plaintiff or not—but may give the jury information so that it may make that determination (Mitchell, Walker, and Monahan 2011).

Courts need to understand that social science research will help the court determine whether there is a genuine issue of material fact in order to decide whether to grant summary judgment. The expert testimony will probably complicate the interpretation of behaviors that are important to Title VII law. The result is that courts should grant summary judgment in these context-specific types of cases much less frequently than they currently do and that expert social science testimony will reveal the factual issues (Schneider 2007). There is also a need to permit the case go to discovery and to decline to grant motions to dismiss for lack of plausibility in many of the cases when a court is faced with a motion to dismiss.

CONTEXT MATTERS

In cases decided after *Harris v. Forklift Systems, Inc.*, the Supreme Court has hinted at a broader standard and advocates the consideration of context, a context that may include the victim's identity (*Ash v. Tyson Foods, Inc.* 2006; *Burlington Northern & Santa Fe Railroad Co. v. White* 2006; *Oncale v. Sundowner Offshore Services, Inc.* 1998). This acknowledgment that "context matters" suggests that the Court's "reasonable person" standard in *Harris* may permit consideration of the victim's identity as one factor among many in determining whether the victim's reaction was reasonable. Certainly, the Court encourages an understanding of context, which multidimensional masculinities theory would also encourage.

For example, in *Oncale*, the Court expressly notes the importance of context in determining whether the behavior is actionable (*Oncale v. Sundowner Offshore Services, Inc.* 1998). The Court acknowledged that the same behavior, given the context and the identity of the potential victim, may have different legal effect. The Court states, "The real social impact of workplace behavior often depends on a constellation of surrounding circumstances, expectations, and relationships which are not fully captured by a simple recitation of the words used or the physical acts performed" (ibid., 81–82). It encourages courts and juries to use "common sense" and an "appropriate sensitivity to social context" to distinguish between legal and illegal behavior (ibid.).

The Court also advocates the consideration of context in a case alleging that the employer retaliated against the employee for complaining about sex discrimination. In *Burlington Northern & Santa Fe Railway Co. v. White*, the Court defines what behavior amounts to a sufficient adverse employment action to constitute retaliation; here again, the Court adopts a context-rich approach (2006). It announces that an adverse employment action exists if "a reasonable employee would have found the challenged action materially adverse, which in this context means it well might have 'dissuaded a reasonable worker from making or supporting a charge of discrimination'" (ibid., 68). The test is an objective one: how a reasonable person would react. But, the Court notes that "context matters" and gives a number of examples to illustrate its point (ibid., 69). At least one of those examples encourages the fact finder to consider the subjective situations of the individual plaintiffs involved. For example, the Court suggests that a schedule change would be materially adverse to a young mother with children, and may well constitute retaliation (ibid.). This conclusion relies on the victim's identity as well as the context of her situation.

In a third recent case, *Ash v. Tyson Foods, Inc.*, the Supreme Court again emphasized the importance of context (*Ash v. Tyson Foods, Inc.* 2006). The Court disagreed with the lower court's conclusion that as a matter of law, use of the term "boy" alone, without the qualifier "black" or "white," to refer to two adult black men who were not promoted was insufficient evidence to go to the jury on the question of racial animus. The Supreme Court stated, "The speaker's meaning will depend on various factors including context, inflection, tone of voice, local custom, and historical usage" (ibid., 456).

These cases suggest that the Supreme Court would encourage a more nuanced approach to determining whether an alleged sexual harassment victim's reaction to harassing behavior was reasonable. One concern, however, is the Court's statement that fact finders should use their common sense to decide these cases. While juries ordinarily use common sense to make decisions, use of common sense in an area where social gender norms are involved may lead to discriminatory results. Social norms can lead to erroneous assumptions and misunderstandings concerning motivations behind employees' behaviors and the reactions they produce in other employees. This may be particularly true where the person judged is a member of a less powerful or outsider group (Robinson 2008).

Research shows that when men allege sexual harassment, views of its severity vary according to the identity of the harasser, the type of harassment, and the gender of the person observing the alleged harassment. For example, while psychological studies show that male participants generally perceive female-on-male sexual harassment as less harassing than male-on-female sexual harassment, female participants perceive both types of harassment as equal (Katz, Hannon, and Whitten 1996). Moreover, studies show that male participants view different types of male-on-male harassment differently (Stockdale et al. 2004). They consider negative, hostile harassing behaviors by men directed at other men as less serious than sexual advances by other men. These hostile behaviors, like those experienced by Jonathan Martin, are coined "rejection-based" sexual harassment (ibid., 159). In contrast, male participants find sexual advances by men toward other men ("approach-based male-on-male harassment") as more harassing and serious than hostile behaviors (ibid., 159). Even if a judge exercises common sense in response to a motion to dismiss or for summary judgment or when serving as the fact finder in a case, the judge, too, will probably respond to influences embedded in his or her subconscious (Gertner and Hart 2012). Thus, it is important that judicial education include concepts of masculinity and how they affect human behavior.

Multidimensional masculinities theory endorses the use of varying lenses to view the situation and understand the dynamics. Multidimensionality theory, like intersectionality, urges an anti-essentialist view of identity and recognizes that multiple strands of our identity interact to form the person, and that the individual's experiences vary as the context varies. Use of multidimensional masculinities theory should be explicit in the courtroom. Judges should encourage juries to consider context, but warn them that their first, unthinking response may be discriminatory. Expert testimony on implicit bias and masculinities theory can provide the basis for the judge's instruction. Social gender norms are very strongly held and often invisible to those who accept the norms as natural. The judge should permit expert testimony of social framework evidence, either "pure" or "applied," so that the jury can make an informed decision (Weiss 2011; Mitchell, Walker, and Monahan 2011; Hart and Secunda 2009).

E.E.O.C. v. Prospect Airport Services, Inc. demonstrates the problem with using a "reasonable woman" or "reasonable man" standard. Both standards rely on stereotypical views of how women and men should react in response to a potentially harassing environment. The law, however, should not enforce a stereotyped gender regime by labeling particular male or female behavior "reasonable" on the basis of how the behavior conforms to societal gender norms. There is a wide array of reasonable reactions to the same behaviors in the workplaces. While biological sex and gender may to some extent affect an employee's reaction to behaviors in the workplace, other contextual factors such as organizational power, social power, workplace dynamics, and an individual victim's vulnerabilities may determine whether the individual's response is a reasonable one.

Prospect Airport Services provides a good example. A "typical" male coworker might not have had the trouble with Sandra Munoz's behavior that Rudolpho Lamas had. Even if most men may not have welcomed the behavior, it is likely that most men would not have been intimidated by Sandra Munoz's advances. If bothered by Munoz's advances, a "typical" man would probably have stopped the behavior by responding in a forceful manner. Rudolpho Lamas, however, was unable successfully to rebuff Munoz's advances. Even though Lamas told Munoz to stop a number of times, she did not heed his plea.

Understanding the context of Lamas's home life, his Christian faith, and workplace dynamics would help explain Lamas's reaction to the jury. Lamas attributed his discomfort with Munoz's behavior to his fundamentalist religion and his status as a recent widower. This information helps explain why Munoz's behavior was particularly difficult for Lamas, but the EEOC could have developed more evidence surrounding Lamas's identity and the context of the workplace dynamics. After Lamas refused to involve himself with Munoz, a number of coworkers began to pressure him to go out with Munoz and began to question his masculinity and his sexual orientation. Lamas's coworkers' teasing and his supervisors' reaction to Lamas may have resulted from beliefs that Lamas did not live up to masculine stereotypes. In other words, they may have believed that Lamas should have handled the situation himself, enjoyed Munoz's advances, or shut up because only nonmasculine men will complain about sexual harassment by female coworkers. Another possible contextual reason for Munoz's ability to harass Lamas is racial. Lamas, a dark-skinned Latino male, may have had less power socially than Munoz, a light-skinned Latina, and Munoz's and others' attitudes toward Lamas may have related in part to his color.

Prospect Airport Services demonstrates that the problem with the standard lies in its conclusion that there is only one reasonable reaction to a set of harassing circumstances. The standard should not measure a "reasonable man" or a "reasonable woman" or even a "reasonable person." Rather, it should consider the context of the situation, including identity factors of the victim, the fluid organizational and social power differentials, and the various personal vulnerabilities of the victims to determine whether the victim's response to the harassment was reasonable. This should not be an onerous test. Once the victim's response is deemed potentially reasonable given the contextual and identity factors at play, the focus should be on the *employer's* response to the harassing behavior. Here, again, *Prospect Airport Services* is instructive. The fact finder should consider not only that Lamas was a man but also that he was a fundamentalist Christian who found Munoz's behavior particularly threatening, and that he was a recent widower who was still mourning his dead wife. But an understanding of the facts in *Prospect Airport Services* reveals more. It appears that the injury to Rudolpho Lamas occurred not only at the hands of his female coworker, Sylvia

Munoz, but also as a result of his employer's refusal to stop the behavior, combined with his fellow coworkers' questioning of his failure to live up to their standards of masculinity.

The courts have traditionally analyzed whether a hostile work environment exists before analyzing the separate question of whether the employer is liable for the environment, but in this case, this approach seems inadequate. In fact, the employer's refusal to step in and stop both Munoz's and the coworkers' harassing behavior, and its attitude that Lamas should not take the behavior seriously, actually enhanced the severity of the behavior.

In essence, the employer's behavior was an important part of the hostile work environment itself. This behavior, therefore, is part and parcel of the context of the situation that the fact finder should consider in determining whether Lamas's working environment was hostile. In this case, the fact finder should consider the employer's reaction in determining whether the behavior is sufficiently severe or pervasive to alter the terms or conditions of the employee's employment. Here, perhaps because the employer believed that sexual harassment by a female coworker of a male coworker was less serious than the more common harassment by a male of a female coworker, the employer failed to act, and even ridiculed Lamas's reports of sexual harassment. His supervisor told him that he should be singing, "I'm too sexy for my shirt" (*E.E.O.C. v. Prospect Airport Services, Inc.* 2010, 995; Right Said Fred 1992), and did not take Lamas's report seriously. This behavior, combined with the employer's failure to stop the harassment by Munoz and by fellow coworkers who questioned Lamas's sexual orientation, added to the severity and the pervasiveness of the problem.

Example Two: Male-on-Male Harassment

Jonathan Martin's case serves as a good example of sex-, gender-, or race-based harassment in an all-male environment. Unlike the physical harassment endured by Joseph Oncale on the all-male oil rig, Jonathan Martin suffered repeated verbal harassment by his male coworkers, some of which was explicitly racial in character and some of which implicitly denigrated him for being insufficiently masculine. His teammates claimed that they engaged in the behavior in order to toughen

Martin up and to get under his skin. The behavior included crude and damaging sexual references by teammates Incognito and Pouncey about Martin's mother and sister; claims that his teammates were going to "run a train on your sister" and "fuck her without a condom and cum in her cunt"; remarks that she is a "squirter," that "I'm going to bang the shit out of her and spit on her and treat her like shit," and that "your sister has a wolf-puss. A fat, hairy pussy" (Wells 2014, 9). They made graphic gestures simulating sex with Martin's sister, and one of his teammates claimed he wanted to have sex with Martin's sister and mother simultaneously (ibid.). Two of Martin's black teammates ridiculed Martin for not being "black enough" (ibid., 31).

Incognito left Martin a voicemail in which he called Martin a "half-nigger piece of shit" and stated that he would kill Martin (ibid., 10). He also regularly referred to Martin in the locker room as "my bitch" and a "stinky Pakistani" and, along with two other teammates, regularly called Martin a "cunt," "pussy," and "faggot," in a cutting tone and with an intent to humiliate him (ibid., 12–13). And they did humiliate Martin. He complained frequently to his parents about his treatment and his inability to stand up for himself, and, ultimately, when he could take it no longer, Martin walked out on the team and entered an in-patient mental health facility (ibid.).

This behavior is not only racially charged but also gender based. If Martin's case were to come before the court, there would be a defense that the behavior either did not occur because of sex or race or that it is normal hazing that is common in NFL locker rooms and is therefore not sufficiently severe or pervasive to meet Title VII's requirements. The defendant would also probably argue that Martin welcomed the behavior by participating in the joking or by not complaining about it.

Even though Martin did not always forcefully let his teammates know that he did not appreciate the manner in which they were treating him, and at times he participated in joking in the locker room, the behavior that was directed at him was far more serious than his behavior, and his failure to complain to management is consistent with the behavior of other victims (ibid.). Thus, it appears that there is at least a fact question as to whether Martin welcomed the behavior.

While the racial comments appear more explicit than the gendered ones, there is no question that Martin's teammates targeted him for his failed racial power *and* his failed masculinity. He was "not black" enough, because he was an upper-middle-class black man who did not live up to stereotypes of angry black men. They also called him a "cunt," a derogatory reference to a woman's genitals. An expert in masculinities theory could explain the multidimensional aspects of these types of comments. When in groups in all-male, masculine workplaces, men often engage in race-, gender-, and class-based behavior similar to that present in the NFL locker room. The perpetrators engage in bullying and harassment to demonstrate their own masculinity and toughness to the group and to assure that they will escape the harassing behavior themselves. They compete with one another to prove their masculinity to each other, by picking on a vulnerable teammate. Moreover, they aim to protect the masculinity of the team by harassing the weak link on the team to make him conform to their views of proper masculine behavior. It is therefore because of Martin's race and gender that he endured this behavior.

The defendant would defend on the issue of severity or pervasiveness by attempting to isolate the race-based comments from the gender-based comments. Although there is probably sufficient commentary about both race and gender to create a hostile working environment on each count, such a strategy is designed to dilute the plaintiff's potential cause of action, enabling the defendant to argue that there is insufficient evidence of both race and gender harassment. But it is important to note that there was only one environment experienced by Martin and, as a victim, he cannot separate his race from his gender. It would therefore be mistaken for a court to divide the case into two separate causes of action—race and gender—and to exclude the evidence from each cause of action from the other case.

I disagree with the Wells Report's conclusion about racial motivation and find its failure to address gender motivation troubling. It appears that the report is reluctant to attribute the statements about "not acting black enough" to racial animus because one biracial and one black teammate made the statements. The report notes that although the statements "seem to reflect a problematic attitude toward racial identity and socioeconomic differences that reinforce crude racial stereotypes," they do not seem to demonstrate racial animus (ibid., 31). Moreover, after discussing violent jokes that Incognito made about using a rifle that is "perfect for shooting black people," the report concludes that although such jokes are "reprehensible and arguably reflect deep-seated racial hostility . . . the evidence is sufficiently muddled" that it is difficult to conclude that the comments were "necessarily motivated by racial animus" (ibid., 32).

The report also fails to address the possibility of gender- or sex-based harassment. A masculinities analysis would have benefited its authors. Moreover, Title VII does not require a showing of racial or gender-based animus. Instead, the plaintiff must demonstrate that the behavior occurred "because of race" or "because of sex" or both. Even if Martin's teammates were not harassing him because they hated blacks or black men or men who did not conform to their stereotype of what a man should be, the employer would still be liable if, with the help of masculinities research, Martin can show that the behavior occurred because he was black (or perceived to be a failed black) and/or because he was a man (or perceived to be a failed man). The violent race- and sex-based harassing behavior directed at Martin should be at least sufficient to withstand a summary judgment motion, especially with the help of a masculinities expert who can attest to common behaviors and motivations for those behaviors in all-male workplaces.

A Reasonable Response

In determining the proper objective standard for a hostile working environment, it is important to assure that courts do not use men as a measuring stick of how a reasonable person would react and that courts do not engage in stereotyping in determining how men or women should or do react to a harassing environment. To avoid these problems, the law should allow fact finders to consider variations in the context of the workplace, take into account different lived experiences of the victims, and consider power differentials at work and in society. But, most important, a new standard should recognize that there is a range of reasonable responses to the same set of behaviors. The standard, rather than considering what a reasonable person, reasonable woman, or reasonable victim would have thought, should look at whether the plaintiff's response was *a reasonable one*, given a number of factors. This is a totality-of-the-circumstances test. It is important for judges and juries to understand that the factors listed below are not elements and that not all factors need to be present for a hostile working environment to exist.

In determining whether the plaintiff's response was reasonable, there should be a two-part test, as there currently is (*Harris v. Forklift Systems, Inc.* 1993). The first question, which goes to the subjective element, would remain the same: whether the behavior created a hostile work environment for the plaintiff as a subjective matter (ibid.). If the answer to this question is yes, the second question is whether the plaintiff's reaction was a reasonable one, taking into account the workplace dynamics, the harassing behaviors, and the plaintiff's identity, experiences, and position at the workplace.

Under the law as it currently stands, when engaging in this second query, fact finders focus only on the conduct itself. They consider the following:

- frequency of conduct;
- severity of conduct;
- whether the conduct is physically threatening or humiliating or a mere offensive utterance; and
- whether the conduct unreasonably interfered with the plaintiff's work (ibid.).

These are all important factors that help determine how severe or pervasive the conduct is, but they disregard the context of the workplace, the way power operates, and the victim's identity and experiences. Under the new proposed standard, the fact finder should also consider

- the personal identity of the plaintiff;
- circumstances at work or outside of work that make the alleged victim vulnerable to harassment;
- relative power/powerlessness of the harasser or harassers based on position at work and/or social power;
- whether the individual alleging harassment is a social outsider;
- workplace dynamics; and
- workplace context.

This test has a number of advantages. First, it is flexible enough not only to permit a uniform standard for all types of harassment, no matter who the perpetrators and the victims are, but also to allow consideration of variable factors in particular cases that shed light on whether an objectively hostile work environment existed. Second, the proposal has the benefit of retaining the objective test but also permitting the consideration of important surrounding circumstances in determining whether a hostile working environment existed.

If we were to apply this test to the facts known about Jonathan Martin's harassment, we would conclude that there is at least a question of fact as to whether the harassment by Richie Incognito and other players was sufficiently severe or pervasive to alter the terms or conditions of Martin's employment. The Wells Report indicates that the conduct occurred frequently over more than a one-year period, and while most of it was verbal harassment, many of the comments were quite severe—racial slurs and explicit sexual comments about Martin's sister and mother. The conduct may not have been physically threatening, but it appears to have affected Martin's ability to work in the environment. A fact finder would also consider Martin's personal identity—his upper-middle-class background and education, circumstances surrounding his prior bouts with depression, and the fact that his teammates, because of their group effort and Martin's rookie status, possessed significantly more power than Martin did. Martin was a big guy, but so were his teammates, and he experienced a sense of powerlessness as a result of his mistreatment.

A fact finder should also consider the odd relationship that Martin had with Incognito, a friendship that Martin could not trust to be emotionally safe, and the timing of Martin's reaction. It happened at the beginning of his second year at the Miami Dolphins, when he expected that all of the rookie hazing was behind him. Instead, Incognito called him a "nigger" and told him that he owned him. Considering all of these factors, it seems clear in the Martin case that there would at least be a question of fact for the jury regarding whether Martin's reaction was a reasonable one.[2]

Given inconclusive research on whether the reasonable woman standard makes a difference, and the lack of empirical research on my proposed standard, it is unclear whether a new "reasonable response" standard would have a significant effect on the results in sexual harassment cases, but the new approach should at the very least have a corrective effect on the judges. Because my proposed standard emphasizes that there are numerous reasonable responses, it would take the focus off the reasonableness of the particular victim's reaction and place it more on the employer's response. Moreover, because the proposal encourages a more contextualized approach, it would encourage judges to use humility in relying on their own "common sense" and would lead to admission of expert testimony providing social framework evidence. It should also encourage employers who are creating policies and investigating sexual harassment complaints to understand that their policies and investigation processes should anticipate that there is more than one reasonable response to a particular set of behaviors. Finally, it will provide an opportunity for further research into a more complex understanding of how judges and juries interact and how those interactions affect results in the context of a hostile work environment claim.

In sum, *E.E.O.C. v. Prospect Airport Services, Inc.*, combined with an understanding of multidimensional masculinities theory, permits us to reconsider both the underlying theory of sex discrimination in a hostile work environment case and the proper standard for determining whether a hostile work environment exists. Using multidimensional masculinities theory to shift the lens in sexual harassment cases encourages development of a better theory to support Title VII sexual harassment law, whether the perpetrators and the victims are men or women. Essential to a theory of illegal sex discrimination in a hostile work environment case is the use of organizational and/or social power to create a sex- or gender-based hostile work environment. A multidimensional masculinities approach permits development of a new, more universal standard to determine objective and subjective reasonableness, a standard that takes into account gender, race, and other identity characteristics of the victim, and the victim's personal vulnerabilities in the context of organizational and social power. The fact finder should also consider the employer's response to the victim's complaints in determining whether a hostile work environment existed because of the plaintiff's sex. Clearly, the employer's response plays an important role in the implementation of organizational power to the ends of creating a hostile working environment.

But Rudolpho Lamas's case tells us even more. After shifting the lens to ask "the man question," we need once more to shift back to examine the woman question. That is, masculinities theory is particularly useful in illuminating our blind spots. It permits us to consider varying possibilities where vulnerable men receive unequal treatment. It also allows us to consider why groups of men (or men and women) may engage in behavior that scapegoats less masculine men.

Shifting the lens and applying a multidimensional view helps us understand why women continue to suffer serious workplace harassment. If men and/or women cannot tolerate a workforce where some men are not masculine in the traditional sense, there will be no room in those jobs for women as equals either. Worshipping hegemonic forms of masculinity has a flip side: besides harming men who do not live up to the ideal, masculinity worship denigrates working women (Case 1995).

PART III

Sharpening Disparate Treatment and Disparate Impact Claims

Part II discussed the use of multidimensional masculinities theory to aid courts in evaluating hostile work environment claims. This part discusses the use of multidimensional masculinities theory to illuminate disparate treatment and disparate impact claims under Title VII. The courts have made clear that Title VII is not a remedy for socially unacceptable behavior unless it is motivated by the plaintiff's membership in one of the protected classes or a neutral policy has a disparate effect on members of a protected class. Courts have consistently protested that they do not act as "super personnel committees" and that Title VII is not a "general civility code."

In other words, Title VII does not prohibit bad behavior or bullying in a workplace that is not related to the victim's membership in a protected class. As a result, the courts' efforts focus on distinguishing bullying or legal discrimination from illegal discrimination, and the law of Title VII is inextricably intertwined with a number of complicated court-created proof structures to determine whether the discrimination occurred because of the alleged victim's race, color, national origin, sex, or religion.

Chapters 5 through 8 examine the most common structures used to prove violations of Title VII, identify the problems in the courts' application of these structures, and discuss how masculinities research can aid in interpreting and proving Title VII violations under the disparate treatment and disparate impact theories of discrimination. Chapter 5 explains the development and the methods of proving disparate treatment and disparate impact proof mechanisms under Title VII. Chapter 6 addresses proving intent—a particularly thorny question arising in disparate treatment cases. Chapters 7 and 8 analyze how an understanding of masculinities theory can aid in the interpretation of disparate treatment and disparate impact claims under Title VII and other antidiscrimination statutes.

5

The Law of Disparate Treatment and Impact

Distinguishing Disparate Treatment and Disparate Impact

Title VII of the 1964 Civil Rights Act makes it illegal for an employer to discriminate against an applicant or an employee "because of" the individual's race, color, religion, sex, or national origin. There is no mention of intent in the liability section of the statute, but the original remedies section states that a judge may grant relief to a complainant "if the court finds that the respondent has intentionally engaged in or is intentionally engaging in an unlawful employment practice charged in the complaint" (42 U.S.C. § 2000e-5(g)(1)). While it is not clear from these provisions that the statute requires proof of intent to discriminate rather than intentional conduct, the courts early on required a showing of discriminatory intent in disparate treatment cases.

Activists and EEOC lawyers recognized soon after passage of the Act, however, that requiring an intent to discriminate would limit the statute's usefulness in combating racial inequalities in the workplace (Eskridge 1994). They brought cases alleging that neutral employment policies that have disparate effects on the plaintiffs because of their race were illegal under Title VII. One of those cases was *Griggs v. Duke Power Co.*, which the U.S. Supreme Court decided in 1971. In *Griggs*, black employees demonstrated that high school diploma and standardized test requirements for transfer to "inside" operating jobs in the defendant's power plant had a disparate impact on black employees in the company. The Supreme Court unanimously adopted the disparate impact theory of discrimination, and held that the black employees had established a violation of Title VII because the employer could not prove that the test and diploma requirements had a "demonstrable relationship to successful performance of the jobs for which [they were] used" (*Griggs v. Duke Power Co.* 1971, 431). The Court declared that the "touchstone is business necessity" and assigned the employer with the burden of proving that "any given requirement must have a manifest relationship to the employment in question" (ibid., 431–32). *Griggs* made it clear that Title VII plaintiffs could prevail using disparate impact theory even absent a showing of discriminatory intent.

Disparate impact theory, however, would not apply to all Title VII cases. Only two years after *Griggs*, the Supreme Court decided *McDonnell Douglas Corp. v. Green*, where the Court distinguished *Griggs* and established the test for proving disparate treatment in individual cases through the use of the indirect proof method (*McDonnell Douglas Corp. v. Green* 1973). Unlike the plaintiff in *Griggs*, the plaintiff in *McDonnell Douglas* did not argue that a particular neutral policy created a disparate impact on employees. Rather, he alleged that the employer failed to rehire him because of his race. The *McDonnell Douglas* proof method permits the plaintiff to prove intentional discrimination through the use of a three-step approach, which is described more fully below.

Since *Griggs* and *McDonnell Douglas*, the Supreme Court and lower courts have emphasized the distinction between the disparate treatment and disparate impact theories of proving discrimination under Title VII. The characteristic that distinguishes disparate treatment from disparate impact is proof of the employer's intent. Suits brought under Title VII using the disparate treatment theory require a showing of the employer's discriminatory intent. Those alleging disparate impact claims, which attack an employer's neutral policy that has an adverse effect on members of the protected classes, do not.

The Evolution of Employment Discrimination Law

Title VII is an evolving statute. It relies a great deal on the Court's interpretation. But, when Congress perceives the Court to have overstepped its power, it has intervened and overturned Supreme Court cases by amending the statute. During the fifty years since the passage of the 1964 Civil Rights Act, Congress has amended the statute a number of times. The first major amendment added public employers as possible defendants in 1972. Next, the Pregnancy Discrimination Act of 1978 (PDA) amended the Act to overturn a conservative Supreme Court case that held that employers who discriminated on the basis of pregnancy did not discriminate because of sex (*General Electric Co. v. Gilbert* 1976). The PDA amended the definition of discrimination "because of sex" to include pregnancy and pregnancy-related conditions, thereby making it illegal to discriminate on the basis of pregnancy.

Perhaps the most significant amendments, however, appeared in the 1991 Civil Rights Act, in response to conservative Supreme Court opinions issued during the 1989 term. For our purposes, the most important changes in the 1991 Act include (1) an amendment stemming from the Court's prior treatment of the so-called mixed-motives cases; (2) a provision in the statute for the first time creating a disparate impact cause of action (even though it had existed by way of judicial decision as early as 1971); (3) a provision granting the parties a right to a jury trial in disparate treatment cases; and (4) the addition of compensatory and punitive damages to the already existing equitable remedies of back pay, reinstatement, injunctive relief, and declaratory relief in a disparate treatment case.

Proof Methodologies in Disparate Treatment Cases

Much of employment discrimination law revolves around the proof methodologies the Supreme Court has assigned to different types of cases. As noted above, courts characterize cases as disparate treatment or disparate impact, but even within the disparate treatment intentional discrimination category, the courts have traditionally defined different types of cases largely by the methods of proof used. These include the so-called single- and mixed-motives cases, proof by direct method, indirect proof method, individual cases, and pattern and practice cases. At least to date, plaintiffs alleging the so-called single-motive cases under Title VII have had to prove that their membership in a protected class was a "but for" cause of the adverse employment action. I use the phrase "so-called single-motive cases" because it has become apparent over the years that there is no such thing as a single-motive case. People engage in behavior for a variety of complex motives, and the single-motive moniker is inaccurate. Nonetheless, in these cases, the plaintiff alleges a discriminatory motive for the adverse employment action and the employer brings forth evidence that it had a legitimate nondiscriminatory reason for the action. In these cases, but-for causation means that but for the plaintiff's membership in a protected class, he or she would not have suffered an adverse employment action. As stated by the

Supreme Court, "but for" proof means that age (or race, sex, etc.) "actually played a role . . . and had a determinative influence on the outcome" (*Hazen Paper Co. v. Biggins* 1993, 610).

Direct Proof: Individual Case/"Single Motive"

Soon after the 1964 Civil Rights Act passed, employers were fairly unsophisticated regarding employment discrimination. Early case law reflects this reality. Plaintiffs often proved employment discrimination by direct evidence. An employer who told a female job applicant that "girls can't be salesmen" as he denied her job application exposed his company to a sex discrimination lawsuit. Likewise, an employer who told an older employee that "old people work too slowly" as he fired the employee created the possibility of a lawsuit under the Age Discrimination in Employment Act (ADEA) (29 U.S.C.A. § 621). These are the easy cases that appeared right after the passage of the Civil Rights Act (and the 1967 passage of the ADEA); plaintiffs proved discrimination directly by placing into evidence the defendants' or their agents' admissions.

While occasionally the easy cases still come along, employers have become much more sophisticated. Generally, they know that they cannot fire someone or refuse to hire or promote her because of her race, color, sex, national origin, religion, age, or disability. And, in many states and localities, it is illegal to discriminate on the basis of the employee's or applicant's sexual orientation and/or gender identity. Increased employer sophistication means that, to some extent, discrimination is less likely, but the discrimination that exists is more hidden and difficult to prove. Certainly, a direct proof method does not suffice where the employee's best evidence is circumstantial.

Indirect Method of Proof: Individual Case/Single Motive

Although the Supreme Court did not view all discrimination cases as falling within the *Griggs* disparate impact analysis, it recognized, in the early 1970s, the need in a disparate treatment case to create a method of proof that would allow plaintiffs with circumstantial evidence to survive defendants' procedural motions to dismiss, for summary judgment, and for directed verdicts. Thus, the Court created a proof methodology that allowed a plaintiff to shift the burden of production to the defendant upon a minimal showing. Once the plaintiff made that showing, it was up to the defendant to produce evidence of a legitimate, nondiscriminatory reason for its employment action. In *McDonnell Douglas Corp. v. Green*, the Supreme Court created the now-familiar *McDonnell Douglas* proof methodology. In a hiring (or rehiring) case, the Court held that the plaintiff proves a prima facie case by establishing that (1) he is a member of a protected class; (2) he is qualified for the position; (3) he applied for the position and was rejected; and (4) the position either remained open or the employer hired someone who was not a member of the plaintiff's protected class. Once the plaintiff establishes the prima facie case, the burden of *production* shifts to the defendant to articulate a legitimate, nondiscriminatory reason for failing to hire the plaintiff. Once the defendant meets its burden of production, the burden of production shifts back to the plaintiff and merges with the burden of *persuasion*, which requires the plaintiff to prove that the defendant's articulated nondiscriminatory reason is a pretext for discrimination. The plaintiff can prove pretext by demonstrating that the employer's articulated reason for failing to hire the plaintiff is either not true or not the real reason for the failure to hire.

Soon courts adapted this proof methodology to cases other than failure-to-hire cases; all types of adverse employment actions, such as firings and failures to promote, could employ the *McDonnell Douglas* method with some tweaking. For example, an employee alleging that the employer fired her because of her race can demonstrate that (1) she is a member of a protected class; (2) she is qualified for the position—in some circuits, she was doing her job in a manner that met the employer's reasonable expectations; (3) she was fired; and (4) other employees similarly situated who were not of her race (sex, etc.) were not fired. A number of courts have replaced the fourth requirement with proof that is sufficient to create an inference of discrimination (*Johnson v. Ready Mixed Concrete Co.* 2005; *Habib v. NationsBank* 2001; *Whitley v. Peer Review Systems, Inc.* 2000). The prima facie case would then shift the burdens in the same manner as in the failure-to-hire cases. Moreover, the courts applied this methodology to suits brought under the ADEA, 42 U.S.C. §1981, which prohibits race discrimination in contracting, and the Americans with Disabilities Act (ADA), when it was enacted in 1990.

The rationale for the *McDonnell Douglas* methodology is that the prima facie case eliminates the two most prevalent reasons for failing to hire someone: that there are no job openings and that the applicant is unqualified. Once these two factors are eliminated and the plaintiff demonstrates that he or she is a member of a protected class and that others who are not members of the protected class were treated more favorably, an inference arises that the adverse employment action occurred because of the plaintiff's membership in a protected class (*International Brotherhood of Teamsters v. United States* 1977). This inference justifies shifting the burden of production and requires the employer to articulate a legitimate nondiscriminatory reason for its action (ibid., 360). This articulation, then, narrows the inquiry to the question of whether the employer's articulated reason is a pretext for discrimination.

Key to proving a case through the indirect method is the ability to demonstrate pretext by offering evidence that others who were similarly situated, and who did not belong to the plaintiff's protected group, were treated better. These other employees are known as comparators. However, courts began to quibble with how close a fit should exist between the comparator and the plaintiff (Lidge 2002; *Johnson v. Ready Mixed Concrete Co.* 2005; *Holbrook v. Reno* 1999; *Neuren v. Adduci, Mastriani, Meeks & Schill* 1995).

Through the years, the *McDonnell Douglas* methodology, which courts applied to discrimination claims brought under Title VII, the ADA, and the ADEA, changed slightly depending on the type of case and the circuit (*Stella v. Mineta* 2002). A number of cases interpreting the *McDonnell Douglas* method made their way to the Supreme Court. The most important were *St. Mary's Honor Center v. Hicks* (a race discrimination case) and *Reeves v. Sanderson Plumbing Products, Inc.* (an age discrimination case).

In *St. Mary's Honor Center v. Hicks*, the Supreme Court held that if the fact finder finds that the plaintiff proved that the employer's legitimate nondiscriminatory reason is pretextual, it may, *but is not obliged to*, conclude that illegal discrimination occurred. In other words, the plaintiff must prove that the defendant's false reason is a pretext *for discrimination* (*St. Mary's Honor Center v. Hicks* 1993). Thus, a demonstration that the employer's articulated reason is untrue does not, in and of itself, *automatically* lead to a finding of discrimination.

Ordinarily, however, according to *Reeves v. Sanderson Plumbing Products Inc.*, an ADEA case that the courts have applied to Title VII cases, proof of a prima facie case plus a finding that the employer's articulated reason for the employment action is pretextual is *sufficient* for a jury to conclude that illegal discrimination occurred (*Reeves v. Sanderson Plumbing Products, Inc.* 2000). If there is sufficient evidence for a jury to conclude that the defendant's articulated reason for the adverse employment action is pretextual, usually the judge should deny a defendant's motion for summary judgment and allow a trial so the fact finder can decide the case. Moreover, the Supreme Court held in *Reeves* that in determining whether the evidence was sufficient, the lower court should consider all the evidence supporting the prima facie case as well as evidence of pretext (ibid.).

Individual/Mixed Motives

Another category of disparate treatment involves what has commonly been called mixed-motives cases. In these cases, the plaintiff has sufficient evidence to prove that the protected characteristic is a motivating factor in bringing about the adverse employment action, but the employer alleges and proves that it was also motivated by a nondiscriminatory reason. The classic case is *Price Waterhouse v. Hopkins*, where the plaintiff proved that the defendant was motivated by her sex in denying her partnership in the firm, but the employer also proved that the plaintiff was unduly harsh and aggressive in her interpersonal relationships in the office (1989). The case has a long history of procedural turns, ultimately culminating in a congressional amendment to the 1991 Act and in another Supreme Court case, *Desert Palace Inc. v. Costa*, which interprets the amendment (2003). When *Price Waterhouse* reached the U.S. Supreme Court (before the 1991 congressional amendment), a majority of the Court agreed that Title VII cases that present mixed motives, one legal and one discriminatory, use a different proof method than the cases proved under the *McDonnell Douglas* method. But the justices disagreed about the proper standard for proving a mixed-motives case. The 1991 Civil Rights Act overturned portions of *Price Waterhouse* and established the standard for proving a mixed-motives case.

The law of mixed motives today appears in the 1991 amendment, as interpreted later by the Supreme Court in *Desert Palace Inc. v. Costa*. The 1991 amendment on mixed-motives cases appears in two parts. It establishes that a plaintiff can prevail by demonstrating that the employer's action was in part motivated by discrimination. Title VII states in pertinent part,

> Except as otherwise provided in this title, an unlawful employment practice is established when the complaining party demonstrates that race, color, religion, sex, or national origin was a motivating factor for any employment practice even though other factors also motivated the practice. (Title VII, 42 U.S.C. 2000e-2(m))

Once the plaintiff demonstrates that a protected characteristic motivated the employer's behavior, the plaintiff has proved her case. However, the employer may limit the plaintiff's remedies to declaratory and injunctive relief and attorney's fees and costs if it proves by a preponderance of the evidence that it would have taken the same employment action regardless of the plaintiff's membership in a protected class. The Act states,

> On a claim in which an individual proves a violation under section 703(m) and a respondent demonstrates that the respondent would have taken the same action in the absence of the impermissible motivating factor, the court—may grant declaratory relief, injunctive relief . . . and attorney's fees and costs . . . and . . . shall not award damages or issue an order requiring any admission, reinstatement, hiring, promotion or payment. . . . (Title VII, 42 U.S.C. 2000e-5(g) (2) (B))

After passage of the 1991 amendments, many courts permitted plaintiffs to use this methodology only if the plaintiffs proved through direct evidence that the protected characteristic motivated the employer in making the adverse employment decision. In *Desert Palace Inc. v. Costa*, however, the Supreme Court concluded that because the language of the Act did not limit the type of evidence needed to prove a mixed-motives case, plaintiffs can prove the "motivating factor" using *direct or circumstantial* evidence or a mixture of the two. The result in *Desert*

Palace raised questions about whether *McDonnell Douglas* is still good law. The motivating-factor test of the 1991 amendments seems to require less proof than the but-for test of the *McDonnell Douglas* methodology. Moreover, it is not realistic to assume that any employer has only a single motive when taking an adverse employment action against an employee or applicant. Good lawyers can characterize almost any case as a mixed-motives case.

While many academics have written about the potential demise of *McDonnell Douglas*, courts still use both tests (Harper 2010; Zimmer 2004; Corbett 2003). They appear to permit the plaintiff to determine what type of case he is bringing and, therefore, to determine which test is applicable (Standardized Civil Jury Instructions for the Ninth Circuit; Standardized Civil Jury Instructions for the Third Circuit). Initially, when the 1991 Act added the motivating-factor test, many scholars believed that it would be more beneficial for plaintiffs to use the mixed-motives test because it requires only a "motivating factor" rather than a "but for" test.

But the choice of whether to ask for a "motivating factor" or a "but for" instruction from the judge is more complicated. Many plaintiffs' attorneys today do not advocate asking for a mixed-motives instruction because doing so gives the defendants a "second bite at the apple" and may encourage the jury to "split the baby" (Selmi 2014; Sherwyn, Heis, and Eigen 2014; Engelhart 2011; Cummins 2007; Mollica 2005; Zimmer 2004; *Ponce v. Billington* 2012). In other words, the "motivating factor" test permits the jury to find the defendant liable, but then allows the defendant to severely limit the plaintiff's remedies. The "but for" test has no provision that permits the defendant to limit the plaintiff's remedies. Once the plaintiff proves "but for" causation, he or she wins the lawsuit, and is entitled to the remedies provided by the statute, including back pay and damages. What is truly mystifying about the courts' distinction between proof of "single motive" cases using the "but for" test and proof of "mixed motives" using the "motivating factor" test is that in tort law "but for" cause is not necessarily the sole cause of the injury. To equate "but for," therefore, with a single motive is inaccurate. In any event, the important practical result is that courts continue to use both tests in determining whether a plaintiff has made out her case.

Systemic Disparate Treatment: Pattern and Practice/ Class Actions

Where there is a pattern and practice of discriminatory employment decisions, the EEOC can bring a pattern and practice case—the equivalent of a class action—alleging that discrimination is the employer's "standard operating procedure" (*International Brotherhood of Teamsters v. United States* 1977, 336). In the alternative, a private attorney can bring a class action alleging a pattern and practice of discriminatory decision making. *Teamsters* established the legal requirements for proving a pattern and practice case (ibid.). In *Teamsters*, the government alleged that T.I.M.E.–D.C. engaged in a pattern and practice of racially discriminatory hiring practices against blacks and Latinos. Specifically, the plaintiff alleged that men of color were not hired for or promoted into the better-paid line driver positions, even though there were blacks and Latinos working in the lower-paid city driver positions who presumably were available for promotion to line driver jobs (ibid., 329). The Court held that the government must prove that racial discrimination was the company's "standard operating procedure—the regular rather than the unusual practice" (ibid., 336).

To meet this proof standard, the government offered snapshot statistics of the percentages of blacks, Latinos, and whites in line driver positions and compared them to the percentages of blacks, Latinos, and whites in the general population from which the company drew its employees. The Court reasoned that the general population comparison was effective in determining whether there was underrepresentation of blacks and Latinos in the line driver positions because the job required no special qualifications other than a driver's license, and all members of the general population were presumed to be qualified for the position. The evidence demonstrated that in March 1971, only .4 percent of the line drivers were black and all of the black line drivers had been hired after the complaint was filed; only .3 percent of the line drivers were Latino (ibid., 337). In contrast, blacks and Latinos were overrepresented relative to their white counterparts in the lower-paying city operations and serviceman jobs. Historically, the company had hired only one black line driver before 1969. In contrast, the neighborhoods where the trucking company operated had a large percentage of minorities, and the pool of potential line drivers in the minority population was significantly higher than the percentage of those hired. The Supreme Court recognized a long period where there were no black line drivers—"the inexorable zero" (ibid., 342, n. 23).

The government also presented anecdotal evidence from black and Latino city drivers who had sought line driver positions but were either denied or ignored. A number faced discriminatory comments when they asked about the positions. The Supreme Court held that the statistical and anecdotal evidence combined constituted sufficient evidence of a pattern and practice of race discrimination, given that the defendant made little effort to rebut the plaintiff's statistics. Statistics are probative in pattern and practice cases but there is no obligation to balance one's workforce. Rather, statistics may create an inference of intentional discrimination. The theory is that, "absent explanation, it is ordinarily to be expected that nondiscriminatory hiring practices will in time result in a work force more or less representative of the racial and ethnic composition of the population in the community from which employees are hired" (ibid., 340, n. 20).

In *Hazelwood School District*, the Court held that for a job with special qualifications such as a school teacher's position, the proper comparison is made to the qualified pool, not the general population (*Hazelwood School District v. United States* 1997). In *Bazemore*, the Court approved the use of multiple regression analysis to determine whether particular variables such as race or gender have a statistically significant influence on the hiring results (*Bazemore v. Friday* 1986). If so, and absent the defendant's proof that the statistics are in error, the plaintiff will prevail if it can demonstrate sufficient statistical significance (*United States v. City of New York* 2010; *Bradley v. City of Lynn* 2006; *Watson v. Fort Worth Bank & Trust* 1988). While the Supreme Court has emphasized that there are no rigid proof formulas (*Watson v. Fort Worth Bank & Trust* 1988), generally, the courts require two or three standard deviations between the expected numbers of minority employees and the actual numbers (Information on Impact, 29 C.F.R. § 1607.4; *Howe v. City of Akron* 2013; *Tabor v. Hilti, Inc.* 2013; *Bradley v. City of Lynn* 2006).

But the recent case of *Wal-Mart Stores, Inc. v. Dukes* places in question the Supreme Court's jurisprudence in systemic disparate treatment cases, a jurisprudence that had developed over a thirty-five-year period.

In *Wal-Mart*, the Ninth Circuit certified a nationwide class of 1.5 million current and former female workers at Wal-Mart who alleged that they had suffered sex discrimination in pay and promotions. The women alleged that the company had developed a corporate culture of sexism and had permitted lower-level management employees excessive discretion that they exercised disproportionately in men's favor. The plaintiffs produced pay and promotion statistics that demonstrated significant pay disparities and underrepresentation of women in management, compared to their representation in the qualified pools.

The underlying statistics were strong. Although women filled 70 percent of hourly jobs, only 33 percent of members of management were women. The higher up one looked in the company, the fewer women occupied management positions. Women had lower salaries than men in every region, and the salary gap widened over time even for women and men who were hired into the same job at the same time (*Wal-Mart Stores, Inc. v. Dukes* 2011, Ginsburg, J., dissenting). Nonetheless, the majority opinion never mentioned these specific statistics. The plaintiffs also produced anecdotal evidence describing 120 incidences of sex discrimination, as well as expert testimony of Dr. William Bielby, a sociologist who testified that the corporate culture at Wal-Mart made the company vulnerable to sex discrimination. Despite these statistics and expert testimony, the Supreme Court overturned the lower court's certification of the class.

Although the issue in *Wal-Mart* was whether the lower court improperly certified the class of plaintiffs, the Court's majority opinion discussed the underlying substance of the pattern and practice case brought by the plaintiffs. The majority noted that it was necessary to go beyond the pleadings and to engage in a "rigorous analysis" that "overlap[s] with the merits of the plaintiff's [sic] underlying claim" (ibid., 2551). The Court reaffirmed the standards set forth in the pattern and practice cases, noting in a footnote that the plaintiff must show that discrimination is the "standard operating procedure" and that once this standard is met, the evidence creates a rebuttable inference that all class members are victims, an inference that justifies prospective injunctive relief (ibid.). Despite this reaffirmation, the Court concluded that to meet the commonality requirement of the class action Rule 23(a)(2), the plaintiffs must demonstrate either that the class members were all subject to a biased testing procedure (which was not the case in Wal-Mart) or that there is significant evidence that the employer operated under a general policy of discrimination (ibid., 2553).

The Court concluded that the plaintiffs' statistical, anecdotal, and sociological evidence were insufficient to demonstrate that the employer operated under a general policy of discrimination. First, the Court emphasized that Wal-Mart has a general written policy of nondiscrimination. Next, it rejected Dr. Bielby's "social framework" evidence because Dr. Bielby could not state what percentage of the decisions was caused by stereotyping. Next, the Court stated that the statistical evidence was insufficient for class-wide proof because there was no evidence of specific practices that caused the disparity between pay and promotions of men and women. This statement seemed to confuse systemic disparate treatment and disparate impact. Although in disparate impact cases, the courts and Congress have concluded that it is ordinarily necessary to prove that specific employment practices caused the disparate impact, systemic disparate treatment cases have not historically required a showing that a specific practice caused the disparity. Instead, as noted above, the Court ruled in *Teamsters* that a combination of the statistics and the anecdotal evidence was sufficient to raise a rebuttable inference of intentional discrimination (*International Brotherhood of Teamsters v. United States* 1977).

Finally, the Court stated in *Wal-Mart* that in such a large class, the anecdotal evidence of 120 incidences of discrimination was insufficient. It noted that in *Teamsters* there were forty instances of discrimination proved, which amounted to one example for every eight class members. In *Wal-Mart*, however, the 120 affidavits represented only one instance of discrimination for every 12,500 class members, and the affidavits came from only some of the stores and were predominantly from only a few states (*Wal-Mart Stores, Inc. v. Dukes* 2011).

It is too early to know how the Court's language in *Wal-Mart* will affect systemic disparate treatment law (*United States v. City of New York* 2011). It is possible that the unwieldy size of the plaintiff class and the scope of the litigation influenced the Court. All justices agreed, for example, that the plaintiffs had not adequately dealt with the question of how the defendants would have an opportunity to rebut the plaintiffs' claim on an individual basis once the plaintiffs proved that sex discrimination was the "standard operating procedure." Ordinarily, in pattern and practice cases, the defendants have individual hearings to rebut the individual plaintiff's claims that they suffered illegal discrimination and deserve monetary relief. The plaintiffs in *Wal-Mart*, because the proposed class was so large, had suggested a sample set of plaintiffs and a formula derived of average damages to be applied to the entire class. This process, however, the Court noted, would deprive the defendant of the opportunity to litigate its statutory defenses to individual claims (*Wal-Mart Stores, Inc. v. Dukes* 2011). Thus, the size of the class and the difficulty of assuring fairness to the defendants may have influenced much of the Court's language with reference to the pattern and practice case. The Court might not have similar concerns in a pattern and practice suit where the plaintiff class is smaller.

Nonetheless, there is some risk that *Wal-Mart* will significantly curtail plaintiffs' rights in pattern and practice cases, whether the classes are small or large. The Court did not limit its language in *Wal-Mart* to the size of the plaintiffs' class, and it seemed to require for the first time in a pattern and practice case that the plaintiffs prove that specific employment practices caused the disparity. Thus, there is a possibility that *Wal-Mart* presages a change in the law and that the proof that was sufficient in *Teamsters* for a plaintiff's victory may be insufficient in future pattern and practice cases after *Wal-Mart*. One New York federal court stated that *Wal-Mart* "reduced to rubble more than forty years of precedent in the Courts of Appeals" (*United States v. City of New York* 2011, 33).

Moreover, some believe that *Wal-Mart* may have closed the door to the type of "social framework" evidence presented by Dr. Bielby. It is still likely that general social framework evidence will be admissible to give the jury social science background information, however. But there is a question whether Dr. Bielby or another expert would be permitted to comment on the facts in the case before the court (Mitchell, Walker, and Monahan 2011).

Finally, and related to the social framework evidence, is the question of unconscious discrimination or implicit bias. Because of a surge in social science evidence that many discriminatory employment decisions occur as a result of unconscious or implicit processes, many plaintiffs' attorneys have become interested in arguing that evidence of implicit bias should be sufficient to create a disparate treatment cause of action. Certainly, Justice O'Connor recognized in the plurality decision in *Watson v. Forth Worth Bank & Trust* that unconscious bias may be a potential cause of discriminatory actions, and she stated that subjective decision-making processes may lead to disparate impact discrimination as a result. She wrote, "even if one assumed that any such discrimination can be adequately policed through disparate treatment analysis, the problem of subconscious stereotypes and prejudices would remain" (*Watson v. Fort Worth Bank & Trust* 1988, 990).

But *Wal-Mart* also raised the possibility that if an employer is aware that the statistics are lopsided, there may be a potential systemic disparate treatment cause of action. Nonetheless, although the Court's majority in *Wal-Mart* did not overtly reject the concept of implicit bias or unconscious discrimination to argue that discretionary practices result in intentional discrimination, it certainly did not embrace the concept either. Moreover, the open disparagement of "social framework" evidence means that it is likely that social scientists in the future may serve as experts, but not for the purpose of commenting on the evidence in the case before the court (Doneff 2014; Hernández 2014; Lieder 2014; Rosenman and Newman 2014; Amalfe 2013; King and Wilder 2012; Pedersen 2012; Weiss 2011; Wencelblat 2011).

In sum, *Wal-Mart's* effect on the use of implicit bias to prove intentional discrimination is unclear, and the opinion may be damaging to the prospects of theories of implicit bias. Nonetheless, implicit bias is still a concern of lawyers, legal academics, and judges, and expert testimony that explains implicit bias to the jury in discrimination cases should be admissible. Implicit bias is important to understanding that the defendant engaged in biased decision making related to the plaintiffs' membership in a protected class. Masculinities theory, which explains that issues of gender may be invisible to onlookers, goes hand in hand with proof of implicit bias research because it provides an explanation for how gender-based considerations may have motivated the employer's actions, even though at first instance a discriminatory motivation is not obvious.

Disparate Impact

While individuals may bring disparate impact causes of action, a group or class of individuals normally brings disparate impact cases. The class alleges that a particular policy or practice used by the employer creates a disparate impact on a protected group. As noted above, *Griggs v. Duke Power Co.* established the disparate impact cause of action. In *Griggs* and its progeny, the Court held that a neutral policy that created a disparate impact on a protected group was illegal discrimination unless the employer proved that the policy or practice was a business necessity and job related. Even if the employer met this burden, the plaintiffs would still prevail if they demonstrated that less discriminatory alternatives existed (*Albemarle Paper Co. v. Moody* 1975).

Between 1971, when *Griggs* was decided, and 1989, when the Court decided *Wards Cove Packing v. Atonio*, the law of disparate impact was fairly stable, but in *Wards Cove*, the Court overturned established law. It held that the burden of persuasion never shifts to the defendant and that the plaintiffs must prove that there is no employer justification for the policy (*Wards Cove Packing Co. Inc. v. Atonio* 1989). In response, Congress passed the 1991 Civil Rights Act, which restored the original burdens of proof, but it also adopted the *Wards Cove* requirement that the plaintiffs prove that a specific employment practice used by the employer caused the disparate impact, unless the plaintiff can prove that it would be unable to separate specific processes from the entire employment structure.

Disparate Impact under Title VII: History and Theory of Disparate Impact Law

From Griggs to the 1991 Civil Rights Act

As noted above, in 1971, the U.S. Supreme Court unanimously adopted the disparate impact theory of discrimination in *Griggs v. Duke Power Co.* (1971). Lawyers representing the plaintiffs and the Supreme Court saw the violation as occurring under 42 U.S.C. §. 2000e-2 (a)(2) of the statute, which prohibits limiting, segregating, or classifying employees in a way that would deprive them of employment opportunities based on their race, sex, color, national origin, or religion.

In *Griggs*, black employees demonstrated that high school diploma and standardized test requirements for transfer to "inside" operating jobs in defendant's power plant had a disparate impact on black advancement in the company. The employer could not prove that the requirements had a "demonstrable relationship to successful performance of the jobs for which [they were] used" (ibid., 431). Therefore, the Court held that the black employees had established a violation of Title VII. The Court declared that the "touchstone is business necessity" and assigned the employer with the burden of proving that "any given requirement must have a manifest relationship to the employment in question" (ibid., 431–32).

When Congress amended Title VII in 1972 to add public institutions as possible defendants, it did not overrule the *Griggs* ruling. Many scholars saw this failure as an indication that Congress had adopted the Supreme Court's view that disparate impact was a viable theory of recovery under Title VII.

After 1972, the Court decided a number of disparate impact cases, clarifying and, at times, muddying the *Griggs* ruling. In *Dothard v. Rawlinson*, the Supreme Court applied disparate impact theory to practices causing discriminatory effects based on sex, and struck down height and weight requirements for prison guards in Alabama (*Dothard v. Rawlinson* 1977). In *Watson v. Fort Worth Bank & Trust,* the Supreme Court held that plaintiffs may challenge *subjective* employment practices in hiring and promotions by using the disparate impact cause of action (1988). Despite the majority's expansion of disparate impact theory to subjective employment practices, a plurality of the Court in *Watson* laid the groundwork for a major change to the burden of persuasion. Before *Watson*, courts and commentators generally agreed that once a plaintiff proved that an employment practice caused a disparate impact, the burden of persuasion shifted to the employer to demonstrate that the practice was job related and necessary to the business (*Connecticut v. Teal* 1982; *Dothard v. Rawlinson* 1977). The plurality in *Watson*, however, argued that the plaintiffs should retain the burden of persuasion throughout and advocated for a significant reduction in the quality of evidence that the employer would need to produce. Before *Watson*, courts required the employer to prove business necessity; after *Watson*, the plurality would require employers merely to produce evidence of a business justification (*Watson v. Fort Worth Bank & Trust* 1988). In 1989, the *Watson* plurality's formulation gained a majority of the Court's support in *Wards Cove Packing Co., Inc. v. Atonio* (1989).

Wards Cove changed three important aspects of the law. First, it held that employees may not prove disparate impact by comparing statistics of two groups of employees within an employer's workforce when those jobs had fundamentally different qualification requirements. Rather, it was necessary to compare those in the job with those in the qualified labor pool, including those inside and outside of the employer's workforce. Second, the Court held that the employees had to prove that a specific employment practice caused the disparate impact. Finally, following the plurality in *Watson*, the Court imposed the burden of persuasion on the plaintiff throughout and reduced the defendant's rebuttal requirement to business justification (ibid.).

There was substantial opposition to *Wards Cove* and to other Supreme Court opinions decided in 1989 that moved the interpretation of civil rights significantly to the right (McGinley 1993). As a result, Congress enacted the 1991 Civil Rights Act, which the president signed.

Proving Disparate Impact after the 1991 Act

PROPER COMPARISON POOL—QUALIFIED LABOR POOL

The 1991 Civil Rights Act clarified a number of issues concerning the disparate impact cause of action, but left others unresolved. It states in relevant portion:

(A) An unlawful employment practice based on disparate impact is established under this title only if—
(i) a complaining party demonstrates that a respondent uses a particular employment practice that causes a disparate impact on the basis of race, color, religion, sex, or national origin and the respondent fails to demonstrate that the challenged practice is job related for the position in question and consistent with business necessity; or
(ii) the complaining party makes the demonstration described in paragraph (C) with respect to an alternative employment practice and the respondent refuses to adopt such alternative employment practice. (42 U.S.C. § 2000e-2(k)(1)(A))

There is general agreement that after the 1991 Act, a plaintiff ordinarily may prove disparate impact through statistics by comparing the proportion of members of the protected class in the *qualified* labor pool with the proportion of members of the protected class in the employer's workforce. This concept was well established by the Supreme Court in a 1977 systemic disparate treatment case, *Hazelwood School District v. United States*, and clearly applies to disparate impact cases after the 1991 Civil Rights Act as well (*Hazelwood School District v. United States* 1977). The legislative history demonstrates little or no disagreement over the basic issue of comparing the employer's workforce with the qualified labor pool.

Nonetheless, statistical proof may not be necessary or even convincing in cases brought under Section (a)(1) of 42 U.S.C. § 2000e-2 where the plaintiffs argue that the terms or conditions of employment create a disparate impact on protected groups. Examples of this type of disparate impact case include challenges to English-only rules by Latinos, to dirty portable bathroom facilities allegedly having an unequal impact on women, to 150-pound weight-lifting requirements having a disparate impact on pregnant women, and to leave requirements having an unequal impact on pregnant women, among others (*Garcia v. Woman's Hospital of Texas* 1996; *Garcia v. Spun Speak Co.* 1993; *Scherr v. Woodland School Community Consolidated District No. 50* 1988) *E.E.O.C. v. J. C. Penney Co.* 1988; *Colby v. J.C. Penney Co.* 1987; *Lynch v. Freeman* 1987; *Wambheim v. J.C. Penny Co.* 1983).

There is another caveat to the general principle that plaintiffs should use statistics to compare the employer's workforce to the qualified labor pool. When the plaintiff alleges that a particular qualification creates a disparate impact, the appropriate "qualified" labor pool cannot be limited to those possessing the challenged qualification, or it would be impossible for the plaintiff to prove that the qualification itself causes the disparate impact. In *Griggs*, for example, the plaintiffs alleged that high school diploma and intelligence test requirements created a disparate impact on blacks for operating positions at the defendant's plant (*Griggs v. Duke Power Co.* 1971). To determine whether there was a disparate impact on blacks imposed by these requirements, the Court looked at the difference in high school graduation rates between whites and blacks in North Carolina, and evidence of a much higher pass rate for whites than for blacks on the required employment test (ibid.). It did not compare those in the employer's workforce with blacks possessing a high school diploma and/or passing test scores.

Likewise, after the passage of the 1991 Act, the plaintiffs in *Anderson v. Zubieta*, American citizens of Panamanian and Hispanic descent working in the Panama Canal Zone, alleged that the practice of paying workers less if they became citizens after a particular date had a disparate impact based on national origin (*Anderson v. Zubieta* 1999). Because the plaintiffs alleged that the timing of the citizenship requirement caused the disparate impact, the U.S. Court of Appeals for the District of Columbia Circuit refused to include early citizenship in the definition of the qualified labor pool. To do so would "effectively define disparate impact analysis out of existence" (ibid., 342).

PARTICULAR EMPLOYMENT PRACTICES AND CAUSATION— SUBJECTIVE PRACTICES

According to the 1991 amendments, the plaintiff has the burden of proving that a particular employment practice causes the disparate impact or that "the elements of a respondent's decision making process are not capable of separation for analysis." In the event that the process is not capable of separation, the entire process will be treated as one employment practice (42 U.S.C. § 2000e-2(k)(1)(B)(i)).

BURDENS OF PERSUASION AND PRODUCTION

The 1991 Civil Rights Act clearly overrules the *Wards Cove* allocation of the burdens of production and persuasion. The Act shifts the burden of persuasion—not merely the burden of production—to the defendant once the plaintiff has proven that the employer's practice(s) cause(s) a disparate impact on a protected group. The 1991 Act also amends the definition of exactly what the employer has to prove to rebut a showing of disparate impact. First, the plaintiff has the burden of proving a prima facie case by a preponderance of the evidence. Once this proof is made, the burden shifts to the defendant to prove that the challenged practice is "job related for the position in question and consistent with business necessity" (42 U.S.C § 2000e (m); 42 U.S.C. § 2000e-2 (k)(1)(A)(i)). Members of Congress had difficulty reaching agreement on exactly what the defendant has to prove upon the plaintiff's showing of a disparate impact, and there is varying interpretation of the meaning of the 1991 Act. Some argue that "job-related" is a very general term that does not apply to the performance of the particular job. This interpretation seems to stretch reality. While it is clear that the Democrats did not get all the language they would have preferred in the Act, they did shift to the employer the burden to prove that the neutral practice is job related and consistent with business necessity. In fact, Congress reached a compromise that included a decision to allow some ambiguities to remain for the courts to resolve.

LESS DISCRIMINATORY ALTERNATIVE EMPLOYMENT PRACTICES
Although the 1991 Act makes it appear that plaintiffs may prove alternative employment practices *instead of* proving that a disparate impact exists (42 U.S.C. § 2000e-2 (k)(1)(A)(ii)), courts and commentators have uniformly interpreted this section to follow the three-step burden of production and persuasion that existed before *Watson* and *Wards Cove* were decided (*E.E.O.C. v. Beauty Enterprises, Inc.* 2005; *Robinson v. Metro-N. Commuter Rail Road Co.* 2001; *Albemarle Paper Co. v. Moody* 1975). In those cases, after the defendant proves that the employment practice is job related and/or a business necessity, the burden shifts back to the plaintiff to prove that an alternative employment practice exists that would have a less discriminatory effect on the protected group (ibid.). The 1991 Act requires that the plaintiff demonstrate that a less discriminatory alternative was available and that the employer refused to adopt it.

RICCI V. DESTEFANO
Since the passage of the 1991 Act, the U.S. Supreme Court has decided *Ricci v. DeStefano* (2009). In *Ricci*, a disparate treatment case that includes important language concerning disparate impact causes of action, one Hispanic and seventeen white New Haven firefighters sued the city under Title VII, alleging that the city's failure to certify the results of promotional exams because of the race (predominantly white) of the successful exam takers was illegal intentional race discrimination. The city defended its failure to certify the results of the exams by offering evidence that the exam had a disparate impact on African Americans and Hispanics. The Supreme Court analyzed the case as a battle between two conflicting theories under Title VII: disparate treatment and disparate impact. It held that the city was liable for intentionally throwing out the exam results because of the race of the successful candidates. The

Court concluded that a city under these circumstances could success-fully defend against a disparate treatment claim for refusing to use the test results only if it had a strong basis in evidence that it would lose a disparate impact suit if the unsuccessful minority candidates brought one. In *Ricci*, the Court held that a strong basis in evidence was lack-ing (ibid.). In reaching this conclusion, the Court emphasized that New Haven had hired an expert consultant to design the test, who, in turn, got significant feedback from firefighters who were members of racial minorities. Thus, the Court concluded that the test was job related.

The Court also emphasized that the city had created "legitimate ex-pectations" in the (overwhelmingly white) firefighters who studied hard and were successful in the test. Finally, the Court noted that it would be legitimate to take race into account while creating the assessment, but if the department created expectations by giving and scoring a job-related test, it was illegal to throw out the test results because of the race of suc-cessful test takers (ibid.). In essence, the Court created a disincentive to throwing out a test based on uneven results and a mild incentive for employers carefully to consider the possible ramifications of giving the test or of using a different assessment mechanism before administering the test. Because of *Ricci*, it is more difficult but not impossible to throw out results that the employer believes create an illegal disparate impact, but an employer will be far more likely to achieve a diverse promotional pool if it is very careful in establishing the evaluation techniques and promotion standards with an interest in creating a diverse pool of quali-fied candidates before engaging in the testing.

As we shall see in the upcoming chapters, masculinities theory is helpful to prove both disparate treatment claims and disparate impact claims. Next, chapter 6 discusses the importance of the intent require-ment in disparate treatment causes of action while chapter 7 analyzes masculinities theory and its role in proving stereotyping disparate treat-ment claims. Chapter 8 discusses the use of masculinities theory to in-terpret disparate impact claims.

6

Intent in Disparate Treatment Litigation

Disparate Treatment: Defining Intent

Masculinities theory observes that because masculinity and femininity are considered the norm, masculine structures, performances, and practices are so common that they are actually invisible to most observers. Concepts of masculinity are intertwined with the definition of work. In fact, men who engage in masculine practices and performances often define their behaviors as doing work (Martin 2001). In her study of gender practices in for-profit corporations, sociologist Patricia Yancey Martin dealt with only the behaviors of men who did not consciously harm their female colleagues. Nonetheless, the women who worked with the male colleagues suffered harm as a result of the men's masculine practices (ibid.). This research raises serious issues regarding employment discrimination in the workplace against women and gender-nonconforming men. It also creates concern about how the plaintiff should define and prove intentional discrimination in a Title VII case. Disparate treatment cases require the plaintiff to prove that the employer or its agent intentionally discriminated against the plaintiff because of the plaintiff's membership in a protected class.

But what does intent mean in this context? What should it mean? And, can it incorporate the understandings of masculinity research? There is no question that an employer illegally discriminates against an employee or applicant if the employer takes an adverse employment action against the employee because the employer dislikes members of the protected class to which the employee or applicant belongs. For example, it is clear that a black man who owns a business illegally discriminates by refusing to hire Asian applicants because he does not like Asians. If the employer is open about these views and his reason for refusing to hire Asian applicants, the Asian plaintiffs will establish discriminatory intent in a Title VII action. This is the easy case.

There are two reasons why establishing intent can be much more difficult. First, as we shall see below, research by social psychologists and other social scientists demonstrates a significant shift in the type of discrimination that occurs in this country. Unlike in earlier times, there is substantial societal disapproval of racism. While this disapprobation has lessened overt racism in the country, it has also caused racial attitudes to move from conscious or explicit bias to unconscious or implicit bias. These subtle manifestations create significant proof problems in disparate treatment cases. The question arises whether discriminatory intent under Title VII should prohibit adverse employment actions caused by the implicit or unconscious biases of the employer.

Second, even where the employer experiences conscious or explicit bias toward particular groups, employers have become much more savvy about antidiscrimination law, and are often aware of and/or able to cover up the fact that employment decisions resulted from their own conscious biases. In this case, employers can hide their true motives, and the question of whether the adverse employment decision was motivated by discriminatory attitudes becomes an issue of proof.

In either case—whether we recognize adverse employment actions resulting from unconscious bias as illegal discrimination, or whether an employer who harbors conscious bias hides his true reasons for the adverse employment action—determining the existence of discriminatory intent in a disparate treatment case is inextricably intertwined with the question of proof. Proving discrimination becomes even more complicated because the employer is often represented by a number of supervisors or other agents who are engaged in judging the employee's work product. The courts have struggled with whose intent matters. In *Staub v. Proctor Hospital*, the Supreme Court held that in a case brought under the Uniform Services Employment and Reemployment Rights Act (USERRA), an antidiscrimination act designed to protect members of the armed services, even if the decision maker in an employee firing had no discriminatory intent, the employer may be liable if a supervisor, intending to discriminate on the basis of the plaintiff's protected characteristic, recommended to the ultimate decision maker that the employee be fired, and the decision maker followed that recommendation (38 U.S.C. § 4311; *Staub v. Proctor Hospital* 2011).

Scholars, judges, and practitioners have struggled with the concept of defining intent for purposes of disparate treatment. One possible interpretation is that intent means a purpose-to-harm the applicant or employee because of race, color, sex, national origin, or religion. A second plausible interpretation is that the intent requirement exists merely as a causation requirement. According to this view, the purpose of the intent requirement is to assure that the person's membership in the protected class played a substantial motivating role in the employment decision. This view would hold the employer liable for adverse employment acts stemming from hidden or implicit biases, or "unconscious discrimination," in addition to explicit bias.

A third position that falls somewhere in between these two polar opposites would not require a purpose-to-harm or discriminatory animus, but would require proof that the applicant's or employee's protected characteristic consciously motivated the employment decision. Under this view, even though the employer does not have a discriminatory animus toward the individual because of his or her membership in the protected class, the employer knowingly makes the employment decision, aware that it results, at least in part, from the person's class membership. For example, an employer who harbors no discriminatory animus against women but decides not to hire women as truck drivers because he believes it would be dangerous for them to drive cross-country at night would be liable under this view. Despite the employer's good motive and absence of discriminatory animus toward women, the employer is liable because he is aware of his stereotypes about women and nonetheless acts upon them in making his employment decision. Given the history of patriarchal attitudes toward women in this country and their effect on women's employment opportunity, the courts have ruled that the statute does not permit even a good faith patriarchal motive as a defense to a Title VII suit.

Purpose-to-Harm Definition

These three views of intent all reflect different understandings of the meaning of discrimination. Under the first view, the "purpose-to-harm" definition of intent, the focus is on the employer: discrimination results from the bad acts and motives of the individual employer or its agent. The wrong itself does not exist without animus even though the applicant or employee may have lost the job because of his race or her sex. This view may be most consistent with that of the legislators who enacted Title VII (Dirksen Congressional Center 2006). The passage of the Civil Rights Act of 1964 occurred in response to segregated facilities that caused racial unrest in the South and other parts of the country (ibid.). Congress was concerned primarily with overt racial discrimination as a result of the history of race relations in the country at the time (ibid.). Moreover, the purpose-to-harm approach replicates the views held by social scientists in the early and mid-twentieth century regarding the nature and origins of prejudice (Bodenhausen 1993; Stoessner and Mackie 1993). At the time, psychologists believed that stereotyping and discrimination resulted from the affect (or emotion) of the person holding the stereotype toward members of a particular out-group (Bodenhausen 1993). Discriminatory behavior, according to this view, resulted from conscious negative attitudes or emotions held by the discriminator (ibid.; Stoessner and Mackie 1993).

Causation Definition

The second or "causation" definition of intent focuses more on the victims as individuals and as members of groups that have historically suffered discrimination. It is less interested in proving that the discriminator is evil or harbors evil motives. The wrong is that a person has lost a job or an employment opportunity because of membership in a protected class. Proof of the causal link between protected class membership and an adverse employment decision is sufficient for a violation.

Under this definition, it does not matter whether the employer harbors discriminatory animus or even whether he or she made the decision based on overt stereotypes. The key issue is whether there is proof that the victims lost their job opportunities *because of* membership in a protected class. This causation concept of intentional discrimination is sufficiently broad to acknowledge that group processes and dynamics within workplaces can cause discriminatory results even if there is no particular actor who intentionally discriminates. Susan Sturm and Tristin Green, among other legal scholars, have demonstrated that group dynamics can lead to adverse consequences based on gender and race even absent bad actors or individuals within the group who harbor discriminatory biases (Green 2003; Sturm 2001). As this chapter demonstrates below, the causation definition of intent is also more consistent with contemporary research of social scientists.

Causation-Plus Definition

The third view, which I will call the "causation-plus" definition of intent, lies somewhere in between. Like the purpose-to-harm intent, causation-plus intent focuses on the individual employee or manager who makes the employment decision, but causation-plus intent does not require that the individual harbor discriminatory animus toward protected groups. It is sufficient to prove a violation of Title VII if the employer is consciously motivated by the plaintiff's protected status when it makes the adverse employment decision. Under the causation-plus view, the employer is liable if it or its agent knowingly fires or refuses to hire employees or applicants because the employer *consciously* harbors stereotypes about a protected group or because of the discriminatory preferences of customers.

For example, under this view, a school district would be liable for intentional discrimination if a principal decided to hire a woman rather than a man as a kindergarten teacher because of the principal's consciously held views that women are more loving and better suited to working with young children than men. But the employer would not be liable for the action of its managers based on a protected characteristic if neither the manager nor the employer was aware that the act resulted from implicit biases. If, for example, the principal of the school interviewing the female and male applicants for the kindergarten teaching position hired the female teacher because he believed that she would be a more loving teacher, there would be no liability even though the principal's belief resulted from stereotypes or implicit bias in favor of women as kindergarten teachers that caused him to assess the female applicant, even erroneously, as more loving. Under causation-plus intent, the employer is not liable under a disparate treatment theory for employment practices that cause adverse employment actions based on protected characteristics unless the employer is aware of the causal connection between the discriminatory stereotypes and the employment practices.

Most judges and lawyers who are experts in the field would opine that the law of intent, as interpreted by the courts, is closest to the causation-plus definition. Employers need not have discriminatory animus toward members of a protected group in order to prove intentional discrimination. Moreover, the Supreme Court recognized in *Price Waterhouse v. Hopkins* that proof that the decision maker considered stereotypes in denying a woman a promotion to partnership is sufficient for a finding of intentional sex discrimination (*Price Waterhouse v. Hopkins* 1989).

But employers may not always be conscious of the implicit biases or stereotypes that drive their decision-making processes. Social science literature demonstrates that even the most liberal among us may respond in race-based and sex-based ways when prompted. Often, courts and lay people are unaware that their responses result from automatic cognitive processes (Banaji and Greenwald 2013). This research presents a challenge to the law. In choosing which definition of intent to apply to the law of employment discrimination, we should consider a variety of issues: (1) the policies behind the law and the purposes of the law; (2) whether social science supports a rethinking of the law's contemporary definition of discrimination; (3) whether the policies and purposes of the law are best served by recognizing implicit bias; (4) whether it is possible to prove that implicit bias caused the individual's adverse employment action; and (5) whether employers can avoid making employment decisions based on implicit bias. We will return to these questions after we evaluate the social science research on implicit bias in the next subsection.

The Social Science View of Discrimination

Soon after passage of Title VII, psychologists began to focus on cognition rather than affect as the cause of attitudes held by members of one group toward another (Hamilton and Mackie 1993).[1] Cognitive theory posits that human beings create categories to process information efficiently. Cognitive processing causes stereotyping of individuals who are members of out-groups. Out-groups include any group that is not dominant. Black people, people of Asian ancestry, people who don't believe in democracy (in the United States), and so on, can form an out-group. Once formed, stereotypes are entrenched and cause individuals to filter information through the given stereotype. Thus, stereotypes, acquired in unconscious or subliminal fashion, account for processing of information in inaccurate or biased ways (ibid.). Psychologists recognize today, however, that prejudice and the resulting discrimination do not result from either affect or cognitive processing alone (Hamilton and Trolier 1986). Instead, they result from a complex interaction of motivational, cognitive, and cultural factors (ibid.). Social scientists are confident about one conclusion: stereotypes often result from unconscious or subliminal processes.

While few judges would acknowledge that Title VII reaches or should reach unconscious discrimination, there is significant social science research that race and gender bias is "invisible, deep and pervasive" in this country, and that bias is probably responsible for discriminatory practices (Bartlett 2009). Many studies of social psychologists over the past forty years suggest that even though our society acknowledges the evils of race and sex discrimination, a large percentage of people who otherwise believe that they do not discriminate have biased attitudes and behave in biased fashion without awareness of their implicit attitudes and stereotypes (Banaji and Greenwald 2013; Greenwald et al. 2009; Greenwald and Krieger 2006; Kang 2005; McGinley 2000; Greenwald and Banaji 1995).

These studies demonstrate that cognition, affect (emotion), and motivation are connected to race and gender bias. Cognitive bias results from the normal operation of the human brain. Our brains tend to divide people and things into categories to organize our responses to stimuli. Cognitive processing is important to human beings because it helps them make life-saving quick decisions, but when it operates to further stereotypes, it tends to entrench power. That is the case because humans are social beings who automatically prefer insiders to outsiders (Fiske 2005).

There are many measures of implicit bias in the workplace. One of the most popular tests with social psychologists is the Implicit Association Test (IAT), which measures implicit (unconscious) bias. The subject is given a questionnaire to answer. The questionnaire measures explicit (conscious) bias. The same subject then takes the IAT, which measures automatic reaction time to photographs of persons of different races, linked to adjectives that are positive or negative. In the Race

IAT, for example, a comparison of the results on the questionnaire and those of the IAT demonstrates that individuals who show little or no explicit (conscious) bias on the questionnaire often show significant implicit or unconscious bias in favor of whites on the IAT (Greenwald and Krieger 2006). These studies have also demonstrated that the IAT implicit measures have significantly greater predictive validity than the explicit questionnaires do (ibid.; Greenwald et al. 2009; Nosek, Banaji, and Greenwald 2002). That is, the IAT results on race issues predict behavior of the individual more accurately than the results of the explicit questionnaire do. The difference reflects a change in societal attitudes toward racial discrimination and racism since the early part of the twentieth century. Generally, society disapproves of racism and racial discrimination, and that disapproval is reflected on the questionnaires. Interestingly, research suggests that there is a greater taboo against racist behavior than against similarly offensive behavior that is sexist or antigay (Czopp and Monteith 2003). Of course, given the speed with which gay rights have been accepted, these research results may change rapidly.

Scientists have also used technology to study brain activity to determine unconscious responses based on race or outsider status. Cognitive psychologists use functional magnetic resource imaging (fMRI) as well as electroencephalography (EEG) and magneto-encephalography (MEG) to measure neural activity in different parts of the brain (Harris and Fiske 2009; Tovino 2007). In conjunction with this technology, they administer tests that determine whether subjects believe that they have racial biases (Eberhardt 2005; Cunningham et al. 2004). The tests measuring explicit (conscious) bias generally demonstrate that white subjects believe that they have little or no bias, while at the same time the tests measuring implicit (unconscious) bias show that they harbor more positive attitudes toward whites than blacks (ibid.).

Social scientists doing the research claim that fMRI has permitted social scientists to view these unconscious reactions and to measure them in human brain activity (Phelps and Thomas 2003; Phelps et al. 2000). Over the past decade and a half, Alan Hart, Elizabeth Phelps, and their colleagues have conducted experiments in which white subjects view pictures of black persons while the fMRI maps changes in the oxygenation of the blood in the amygdala (Phelps and Thomas 2003; Hart et al.

2000; Phelps et al. 2000). The amygdala is a small structure in the medial temporal lobe of the brain that is known for measuring emotional learning and memory (Tovino 2007). Results from these studies demonstrate that white subjects' brain activity is activated differently in the amygdala depending on whether the photograph is of a white or a black object. Thus, Phelps concludes that the photographs of different social groups evoke different reactions in the amygdala and that these different reactions occur as a result of unconscious processes (Phelps et al. 2000). Another study by Elizabeth Phelps demonstrates that when whites view a photograph of a black man who is unknown to the viewer, the variation in the amygdala occurs. When white subjects view a photograph of a well-known and respected black object like Michael Jordan or Martin Luther King, the white subjects do not have the same amygdala variation as they do when they view unknown black people (ibid.). Other experiments demonstrate that other parts of the brain tend to moderate the response of the amygdala (Cunningham et al. 2004).

Perhaps for our purposes the most interesting article about cognitive processing and implicit biases was authored by a number of law professors, social scientists, and one sitting federal judge. In *Implicit Bias in the Courtroom*, Professor Jerry Kang and his coauthors demonstrate through reports of dozens of social science experiments and years of results on the IAT that many, if not most, people have implicit biases that go well beyond their explicit biases. This means that many people believe that they are not biased and consciously and explicitly express a belief in equality (Kang et al. 2012) but, when they are tested, reveal implicit biases even though they do not express explicit biases (ibid.).

In fact, studies suggest that biases may affect human behavior, and people who are the surest that they are not biased are more likely to make biased decisions. The studies seem to demonstrate that people often unconsciously resort to stereotypes when judging people, and then justify their decisions by altering the selection standards post hoc so that their decisions conform to their stereotypes (ibid.).

Even if one questions the IAT as proof of implicit bias, there is a substantial body of research demonstrating implicit and explicit biases "based on a century of cognitive psychology" (Fiske and Borgida 2011). This literature establishes that at least some bias is experienced in the unconscious and is caused by social factors.

Despite this work by psychologists, sociologists, and neuroscientists, and articles by a number of legal scholars who have introduced the courts to the social science data, the idea of unconscious motive, per se, has not gained traction with the federal courts (Gertner and Hart 2012; Hart 2005; McGinley 2000; Krieger 1995; Oppenheimer 1993). In fact, Judge Nancy Gertner and Professor Melissa Hart argue that federal judges' implicit biases affect their decision making in Title VII cases, an effect that leads to inappropriate grants of motions to dismiss and summary judgments to defendants (Gertner and Hart 2012). Plaintiffs bringing Title VII suits may suffer doubly: first, from the implicit biases enacted in the workplace and, second, from judges' erroneous "commonsense" understandings of behavior that enshrine their own implicit biases in the law (ibid.). Nor have the courts embraced the concept of structural discrimination proposed by Susan Sturm and Tristin Green, who rely on organizational behavioral experts to explain how structures at work can allow unconscious processes to combine to produce discriminatory results (Green 2003; Sturm 2001).

The Law's Reaction to Societal Changes and Social Science Research

Since it was first enacted in 1964, Title VII has evolved with the changing nature and understanding of discrimination in society. Through judicial interpretation and legislative amendment, Title VII now includes a disparate impact cause of action, mechanisms that permit a showing of intentional discrimination through circumstantial evidence, and causes of action for harassment and hostile work environments based on protected characteristics. The Supreme Court has held that prohibitions against sexual harassment apply to same-sex harassing behaviors. And, the Court has interpreted the term "sex" in Title VII to include gender. Thus, it is now illegal, at least in many circumstances, to make adverse employment decisions because an applicant or employee does not live up to societal gender stereotypes. Furthermore, a number of lower courts have applied the sex-stereotyping doctrine to forbid discrimination based on stereotyping against transgender employees in the workforce (*Glenn v. Brumby* 2009; *Schroer v. Billington* 2008; *Smith v.*

City of Salem 2004). These understandings go well beyond the original understanding of Congress, which enacted the statute. Justice Scalia notes, however, that where a statute is unambiguous, its application "'in situations not expressly anticipated by Congress does not demonstrate ambiguity. It demonstrates breadth'" (*Pennsylvania Department of Corrections v. Veskey* 1998, 212, quoting *Sedima, S.P.R.L. v. Imrex Co., Inc.* 1985, 499).

The definition of intent under Title VII has undergone similar evolution since the statute was enacted in 1964, but the courts have not yet totally embraced the social science research demonstrating that discriminatory behavior can result from implicit bias. The Supreme Court has on occasion recognized the operation of stereotypes and unconscious bias, but it has not openly adopted the causation definition of intent. In *Price Waterhouse*, the stereotyping case, there was evidence that the partners made decisions based on their stereotyped views of women and how the plaintiff did not conform to these views. It is not clear, however, whether the partners who voted against Ann Hopkins harbored ill will or discriminatory animus toward women in the workplace. Even absent this proof of a purpose-to-harm, the Court held that there was sufficient evidence that gender played a substantial (or motivating) factor in the employment decision. This showing of intent was sufficient for liability (*Price Waterhouse v. Hopkins* 1989).

Curiously, even though not acknowledged by most courts, the law already permits a finding of disparate treatment where the defendant engages in unconscious bias. This may occur in individual cases where the plaintiff proves discriminatory intent through the indirect method established in the *McDonnell Douglas/Reeves* line of cases and in systemic disparate treatment cases like *International Brotherhood of Teamsters v. United States*, where the plaintiffs use statistics combined with individual anecdotal evidence to establish that the defendant's operating procedure was intentionally discriminatory (*Reeves v. Sanderson Plumbing Products, Inc.* 2000; *International Brotherhood of Teamsters v. United States* 1977; *McDonnell Douglas Corp. v Green* 1973). It may also occur in the cases covered by the motivating-factor test because the Court has made clear that proof of discrimination using this test does not require a demonstration of direct evidence of a discriminatory motive (*Desert Palace Inc. v. Costa* 2003).

In the *McDonnell Douglas/Reeves* line of cases, an individual proves discriminatory intent by circumstantial evidence through the indirect method. She establishes a prima facie case by demonstrating that she is a member of a protected class who suffered an adverse employment action under circumstances that raised an inference of discrimination. In the failure-to-hire and failure-to-promote cases, the plaintiff can establish the inference by introducing evidence that there was a job opening for which the plaintiff is qualified and that the defendant hired someone outside of the protected class or left the job open while refusing to hire the plaintiff. In discharge cases, the plaintiff can raise the inference of discrimination with evidence that others who were not members of the protected class received more favorable treatment after engaging in similar behavior or work.

Proof of a prima facie case raises an inference of discrimination and shifts the burden to the defendant to produce evidence that it made the employment decision based on a legitimate nondiscriminatory reason. Once the defendant responds with this proof, the burden of production shifts back to the plaintiff and merges with the plaintiff's ultimate burden to prove that the defendant's articulated reason is a pretext for discrimination. The plaintiff makes this proof through direct and/or circumstantial evidence. As the Court states,

> Proof that the defendant's explanation is unworthy of credence is one form of circumstantial evidence that is probative of intentional discrimination, and it may be quite persuasive. In appropriate circumstances, the trier of fact can reasonably infer from the falsity of the explanation that the employer is dissembling to cover up a discriminatory purpose. Such an inference is consistent with the general principle of evidence law that the fact finder is entitled to consider a party's dishonesty about a material fact as "affirmative evidence of guilt." Moreover, once the employer's justification has been eliminated, discrimination may well be the most likely alternative explanation, especially since the employer is in the best position to put forth the actual reason for its decision. Thus, a plaintiff's prima facie case, combined with sufficient evidence to find that the employer's asserted justification is false, may permit the trier of fact to conclude that the employer unlawfully discriminated. (*Reeves v. Sanderson Plumbing Products, Inc.* 2000, 135)

Because the court instructs the jury to consider all evidence that suggests that the employer's articulated reason is pretextual, the plaintiff can offer a wide variety of types of evidence, including statistics on the presence of other members of the protected class in the workforce, comparator evidence of differential treatment of other employees who are not members of the protected class, and statements made by decision makers that suggest discriminatory attitudes toward protected groups. While the Supreme Court explains the proof of pretext as a means of disproving the employer's dishonest reason for accounting for the adverse employment action, the *McDonnell Douglas/Reeves* pretext method actually permits a finding of discrimination absent the employer's dishonesty. Given the broad range of evidence, the jury may find that the employer's reason is pretextual where the employer was actually unaware of its implicit biases that caused the adverse decision.[2] Similarly, statistical and anecdotal evidence sufficient under *Teamsters* to prove pattern and practice cases also permits findings of discrimination based on implicit, rather than explicit, bias.[3]

Judges have reacted to the *McDonnell Douglas/Reeves* proof mechanism by adopting a number of judicially created doctrines that limit the possibility of a plaintiff's recovery. The "stray remarks" doctrine, the "same-actor" defense, and the "honest belief" doctrine all make it more difficult for plaintiffs to prove discrimination because of limitations on admissibility of evidence or presumptions or inferences that arise from certain types of evidence.[4] Moreover, recently in *Wal-Mart v. Dukes*, the Supreme Court expressed serious reservations about the testimony of the plaintiffs' expert, Dr. William Bielby, who used social science evidence to testify that unregulated discretion of supervisors causes biased decision making against women in the workplace (*Wal-Mart Stores, Inc. v. Dukes* 2011). It is fair to say, then, that despite the increasingly strong evidence of the importance of implicit bias in decision making, the courts have failed to incorporate this evidence into their application of legal principles. In fact, Judge Nancy Gertner and Professor Melissa Hart assert that federal judges, like all people, harbor biases and prejudices, but are blind to their existence and application in their work: "The biases—implicit and otherwise—of judges reviewing discrimination claims may well play as much a role in the story of employment discrimination litigation as the biases that triggered the lawsuit" (Gertner and Hart 2012, 94).

Legal Scholars' Views

A number of legal scholars agree that proof of causation is sufficient under current law to hold employers liable for hidden bias. Kate Bartlett, for example, explains that both proponents and opponents of Title VII understood that the law would reach hidden bias (Bartlett 2009). She also argues that the stereotyping doctrine that arose from *Price Waterhouse* holds some employers liable on the basis of unconsciously held stereotypes (ibid.). When Congress codified the "mixed motives" proof mechanism in the 1991 Civil Rights Act and adopted the "motivating factor" test from *Price Waterhouse*, Bartlett asserts, it explicitly adopted a causation requirement rather than an intent requirement (ibid., 1925). She bolsters her argument with the Court's subsequent decision in *Desert Palace, Inc. v. Costa*, where the Court concluded that under the new provisions of the 1991 Civil Rights Act, a plaintiff may use circumstantial as well as direct evidence of discrimination in order to prevail (Bartlett 2009).

Professor Bartlett's observation that Title VII can capture hidden bias is accurate. But, while the courts recognize evidence of stereotyping in determining whether the employer's discrimination occurred because of the plaintiff's membership in the protected class, they have not explicitly embraced the notion of unconscious intent or hidden bias as sufficient to prove a discriminatory treatment case. At least when it comes to disparate treatment causes of action that require intent, the courts still appear to distinguish between the causation and the causation-plus views of intent, adopting the latter but not the former.

Purpose of the Act

The question becomes whether courts should openly interpret Title VII to permit a showing of pure causation as sufficient to establish discriminatory intent in a disparate treatment case. Research by legal scholar Jerry Kang and others suggests that they should, but the answer to this question may depend on the purposes and policies of the Act, the availability of proof, and whether employers have meaningful opportunities to prevent discrimination caused by unconscious processes.

The primary purpose of the Act was to assure equal employment opportunity for a group of individuals who historically had been denied such opportunities because of their membership in the protected classes. This purpose would support the causation definition of intent—a finding of discrimination so long as the employee can prove that her protected characteristic motivated the adverse employment decision, regardless of whether the employer was consciously aware that implicit bias led to the adverse employment action. In other words, an employer's good faith belief that it is not discriminating on the basis of the employee's protected characteristic may not be sufficient to exonerate the employer. Rather than focus on the employer's conscious reason for the decision, the causation view of intent looks to the real reason for the employer's behavior. The policies of the Act—to ensure equal employment opportunity—are furthered by a broader definition of intent.

There is some concern, however, that employers' businesses may be stifled by a broader definition of intent. The question becomes whether employers will be able to prevent their managers and other employees from discriminating and thereby to avoid liability. This issue raises serious concern. An explicit recognition of implicit bias as an illegal source of discrimination should, however, create an incentive for employers to train managers to question their own assumptions.

Many legal scholars believe that there are resources that employers can use in the workplace to eliminate and prevent discrimination. Susan Sturm discusses how companies have implemented internal procedures that strive to uncover and fix the problems of discriminatory practices in the workplace (Sturm 2001). Sturm explains that Deloitte and Touche, America's third-largest accounting, tax, and management consulting firm, implemented a Women's Initiative that increased women's advancement in the company (ibid.). The firm accomplished this by creating "ongoing, participatory task forces with responsibility for determining the nature and cause of a gender gap in promotion and turnover, making recommendations to change the conditions underlying these patterns, developing systems to address those problems and to make future patterns transparent, and monitoring the results" (ibid., 492).

The chairman of the company discovered that although Deloitte had been hiring women at a rate of about 50 percent for more than ten years, the rate of promotion for women was approximately 10 percent. This shocking gender gap result made hiring and training professionals an important priority (ibid.).

Moreover, although social scientists previously believed that implicit and cognitive biases were inalterable, recent social science research suggests that cognitive biases are much more malleable than previously thought (Blair 2002; Rudman, Ashmore, and Gary 2001). Some possible means of eliminating bias in the workplace include bias literacy or counterprejudicial training (Carnes et al. 2012; Calanchini et al. 2013), use of strategies (called "implementation intentions") that engage reflexive or automatic (not conscious) forms of control (Mendoza, Gollwitzer, and Amodio 2010; Stewart and Payne 2008), use of comparative thinking with a focus on differences among people (Corcoran, Hundhammer, and Mussweiler 2009), mental imagery (Blair, Ma, and Lenton 2001), perceptual other-race training (learning how to distinguish faces of persons from another race) (Lebrecht et al. 2009), and exposure to members of the class of those suffering from prejudice who do not meet common stereotypes (Dasgupta and Asgari 2004). This research suggests that programs can be (and some have been) created to help employers train their supervisors to avoid implicit biases in decision making. But, it is important that employers use reputable companies whose training is research based because the research also demonstrates that if training is carried on improperly, it may actually increase prejudice (Legault, Gutsell, and Inzlicht 2011).

The National Center for State Courts has published a report that reviewed the scientific research and suggested strategies for courts to help attenuate bias present in the court system (NCSC 2012). The NCSC-recommended strategies include

- raising awareness of implicit bias;
- seeking to identify and consciously acknowledge real group and individual differences (in other words, eschewing the "color-blind" approach);
- routinely checking thought processes and decisions for possible bias;
- identifying distractions and sources of stress in decision-making environments and eliminating or reducing them;
- identifying sources of ambiguity in decision making contexts and establishing more concrete standards before making a decision;
- instituting feedback mechanisms; and
- increasing exposure to stigmatized group members and counterstereotypes and reducing exposure to stereotypes. (ibid., 5–19)

Masculinities and Implicit Bias

What is the importance of the definition of intent for masculinities in employment? Masculine structures and practices, because they confirm our stereotypes about how men and women are and should be, are often invisible in society and in the workplace. In essence, implicit biases about how men and women should perform their gender often affect the way employers react to men and women on the job. Society in general and managers in particular often consider gender itself a "woman's issue." Therefore, when issues of masculinity arise, no one sees them.

An example of the invisibility of masculine structures is the typical doctor's office. Most doctors' offices have one or two male doctors with a bevy of women working as nurses, physician's assistants, receptionist, secretaries, and file clerks supporting the male doctors. Even when the doctor is herself a woman, the support staff is invariably female. While there may be nothing wrong with these setups, if one understands gender, they are startling. The jobs are clearly segregated by gender, with the best-paid, most respectable professional positions occupied predominantly by men and the lower-paid support positions occupied, almost invariably, by women. Another example is staff who cut the prime rib at the table of a national restaurant chain. The carvers are invariably men, while the wait staff who take the customers' orders is nearly always female. Most people would not even notice this occupational segregation, but consider your reaction if you had knee replacement surgery scheduled and when you entered the surgical suite all of the surgeons were women and all of the nurses and aides were men. Would you notice? I suspect you would. We all would.

These examples demonstrate that employers may slot men and women into particular jobs on the basis of their gender even if they do so unconsciously. In fact, the jobs themselves become gendered, and women or men are attracted to them or considered qualified for them in large part because of their gender. Some employers may make conscious decisions on the basis of gender or sex stereotypes. But others may have no awareness at all that they are selecting employees according to gender (Heilman 2012). Because gendered expectations appear to be normal and natural, employers and others do not even perceive the workplace as gendered.

Moreover, there are various examples of invisible masculine practices that harm women who are supposedly in equal positions to the men. Sociologist Patricia Yancey Martin published the results of her study of seventeen for-profit organizations in *"Mobilizing Masculinities": Women's Experiences of Men at Work*; her research included observations and extensive open-ended interviews of workers in operational or managerial settings from 1992 to 1995. Her article displayed only those stories of women who believed that men *did not consciously intend to harm them*. Unfortunately, however, the men did harm the women by "mobilizing masculinities" in various ways.

For example, men in a predominantly male research organization expected the only female Ph.D. working with approximately one hundred men to perform wifely tasks such as answering the telephone for them, listening to their personal problems, and sympathizing with them. Although these masculinities do not seem particularly egregious, these microaggressions were implicit job expectations that were based on the female Ph.D.'s gender, and she was harmed because the counseling that she engaged in cost her extensive work time and diminished her self-esteem as a scientist. In another setting, a male salesman described his vow never to meet his female hosts for dinner the evening before an out-of-town meeting even though he always met with male counterparts to plan the next day's events. Even though he realized that his decision not to dine out with women created informal networks with the men that he denied the women, he refused to change his practice. This decision was based on the stereotype that women are seductresses to be avoided, and it harmed women who did not have informal relationships with him (Martin 2001).

These are just a few examples that show that a purpose-to-harm and even a causation-plus approach to intent may not sufficiently protect men and women from harmful stereotypes that define and limit their work opportunities. Only with a causation definition of intent that recognizes implicit biases can we be sure that gender will not determine or limit work opportunities. The next chapter deals with how awareness of masculinities theory can help judges and juries determine whether intentional discrimination has occurred in situations often considered natural and nondiscriminatory.

7

Establishing Disparate Treatment through Masculinities

Masculinities theory can explain why sex stereotyping against women and men at work constitutes disparate treatment. In some stereotyping cases, the defendant will have conscious awareness of his stereotypes and that he is acting upon them (causation-plus model of intent). In others, the defendant will act upon unconscious stereotypes (causation model of intent). In either situation, it is consistent with the purposes of Title VII to recognize these behaviors as illegal discrimination because the victim suffers because of his membership in a protected class, and there is evidence that employers can train managers to eliminate decision making based on implicit bias.[1]

Sex Stereotyping as Disparate Treatment

As noted in chapter 2, the Supreme Court first articulated the stereotyping doctrine in *Price Waterhouse v. Hopkins* and concluded that evidence of sex stereotyping was sufficient to prove that sex was a motivating factor in the refusal to promote Ann Hopkins. Justice O'Connor concurred, decrying the use of stereotyping in employment and treating it as if it were direct evidence of conscious discriminatory intent:

> It is as if Ann Hopkins were sitting in the hall outside the room where partnership decisions were being made. As the partners filed in to consider her candidacy, she heard several of them make sexist remarks in discussing her suitability for partnership. As the decision makers exited the room, she was told by one of those privy to the decision making process that her gender was a major reason for the rejection of her partnership bid. (*Price Waterhouse v. Hopkins* 1989, 272)

Masculinities research demonstrates that workplaces are structured around gender and saturated with practices that are based on stereotypes of the proper roles of men and women. To the extent that these practices and structures limit a plaintiff's career prospects within the firm or in other ways alter the terms and conditions of a plaintiff's employment and cannot be justified by the BFOQ defense,[2] these structures and practices should be actionable under Title VII. Limiting a woman's or a man's career possibilities, and structuring work assignments and expectations on stereotypes of whether the job is "female" or "male" are invidious practices that can be invisible but nonetheless very harmful to women and some men.

Masculinities Theory: Stereotypes and Disparate Treatment

Masculine Woman as "Aggressive Bitch"

Many studies note the presence of the "double bind" for women who are attempting to operate in traditional male jobs. Particularly, studies show that women are judged differentially when they hold leadership positions (Valian 1998; Foschi, Lai, and Sigerson 1994; Butler and Geis 1990; Heilman et al. 1989). Very assertive women are viewed especially negatively for the same behavior that, if seen in men, is considered positive (Fletcher 2001; Lorber 1994; Eagly, Makhijani, and Klonsky 1992). Joyce Fletcher studied female engineers who were expected to act relationally—to be feminine and good listeners. Ironically, the same men who expected women to act relationally devalued women for acting in a relational style (Fletcher 2001). Cecilia Ridgeway attributes this reaction to female leaders to "status beliefs." Status beliefs are shared cultural beliefs concerning the competence of one group vis-à-vis another. Assumptions about the ranking of one group over another are legitimated by presumptions of differences in competencies among people in different groups. Ridgeway notes,

> When gender status beliefs are effectively salient in a situation, as they are in mixed-sex and gender-relevant contexts, they create implicit performance expectations for women compared to similar men that shape men's and women's willingness to speak up and assert themselves, the attention and evaluation their performances receive, the ability attributed to them on the basis of their performance, the influence they achieve, and consequently, the likelihood that they emerge as leaders. When women

do assert themselves to exercise authority outside traditionally female domains, as they must do to be high-status leaders in our society, gender status beliefs create legitimacy reactions that impose negative sanctions on them for violating the expected status order and reduce their ability to gain compliance with their objectives. (Ridgeway 2001, 637–38)

In *Price Waterhouse*, the partners considered Ann Hopkins too aggressive, lacking in interpersonal skills, and abrasive. The Court noted that some of the partners reacted negatively to Hopkins's personality because she was a woman (*Price Waterhouse v. Hopkins* 1989). For example, one partner described her as "macho" while another stated that she "overcompensated for being a woman" (ibid., 235). Another partner told Hopkins to take a charm school course; others criticized her use of profanity. Still another said that the male partners disliked Hopkins's use of profanity only because she was a woman (ibid.). While Hopkins's mentor advised her to walk, talk, and dress in a more feminine style, another partner noted that Hopkins, who used to be a "somewhat masculine" and "tough-talking" manager, had matured into a "much more appealing lady [partner] . . . candidate" (ibid.). Dr. Susan Fiske, a well-known social psychologist, testified that because Hopkins was the only woman considered for partner and the evaluations were subjective, the sharp critical remarks—even those that were gender neutral—were most likely influenced by sex stereotyping (ibid., 236).

Like Ann Hopkins, the female lawyers in Dr. Jennifer Pierce's study of paralegals and lawyers in a law firm and a major corporation suffered because of sex stereotyping. Male colleagues criticized female litigators in an aggressive profession for not being tough enough to do the job (Pierce 1995). In contrast, aggressive female litigators were labeled "shrill" or "unladylike" (ibid., 113). These women were expected to behave in a manner that conforms to concepts of feminine behavior while simultaneously performing the job well, a job that, as it is configured, requires the performance of masculinities. Ridgeway found that when women leaders adopt assertive, self-directed, or autocratic styles, they are judged more harshly than men who use the same style (Ridgeway 2001).

As the Court ruled in *Price Waterhouse*, making adverse employment decisions because a woman does not conform to stereotypically female behavior or patterns of dress is discrimination because of sex. Before the

Supreme Court, the defendants argued that Dr. Fiske's testimony should be excluded, but the Supreme Court called her testimony "icing on Hopkins' cake" (*Price Waterhouse v. Hopkins* 1989, 256). It was evident to the Court that the partners judged Ann Hopkins on the basis of their stereotypes of what a woman should be. Therefore, Dr. Fiske's testimony may not have been necessary. But, what happens where the courts themselves are blind to the stereotypes and their effects on managers and the judges themselves? It is here where the intervention of expert testimony should occur.

Masculinities theory, for example, further demonstrates that many women suffer by trying to live up to the ideal of the masculinized job of aggressive, competitive litigator or business dealer. This fact should lead to examination of the assumptions underlying these jobs and of whether the criteria of aggressiveness and hypercompetitiveness are truly related to the job in question and necessary to the business. Because an employer may argue that these criteria can be characterized as gender neutral, plaintiffs may want to challenge that classification by using the disparate impact cause of action. Chapter 8 examines this issue by use of the disparate impact theory of discrimination. But a particular employer may use stereotypes to make decisions about individual employees, and, as in *Price Waterhouse*, doing so may also constitute intentional disparate treatment.

Woman as Caregiver

Women at work experience differential treatment based on the stereotype of a woman as caregiver (Martin 2003; Kerfoot and Knights 1998; Pierce 1995). In fact, many jobs become "feminized" because they require skills that are modeled after the stereotypical notion of woman as mother or wife and caregiver. Managers and coworkers punish women who do not conform to the stereotype of women as caregivers by harassing them or by making adverse employment decisions against them. Even when performing the same job, men are not ordinarily required to exhibit the same amount of caregiving. To the extent that women are expected to exhibit caretaking but men in the same job are not required to do so, this is differential treatment. And, if there is an adverse job action or severe or pervasive harassment of women who do not engage in the expected caregiving, masculinities theory will support a cause of action for sex discrimination under Title VII. Experts in masculinities can make this differential visible to courts and juries.

Deborah Kerfoot and David Knights, for example, recognize that expecting women to act as caregivers offers "comfort" to many men and few women (Kerfoot and Knights 1998, 8–9). Masculinity derives in large part from an "identity that generates and sustains feminine dependence and, along with it, support for a masculine self that is continuously feeling threatened and vulnerable as a consequence of the failure, potential or otherwise, to maintain control" (ibid.). The authors note that the masculinity that predominates in management tends to displace intimacy and to reward the emotionless, rational manager. This suppression of intimacy, however, does not replace emotion. Instead, it can lead to a build-up of emotions that are often expressed at work in a "virulent and violent" form, such as rage (ibid., 9).

When this emotion is expressed, the masculine manager appeals to the dependent female caregivers, who are expected to soothe, comfort, and empathize in order to "restore emotional stability to a masculinity that is damaged by this deviation from rational control" (ibid.). These caregivers are often subordinates such as secretaries, assistants, clerical workers, and other support staff. Their role is to assess the mood swings of the manager and to act as buffers or gatekeepers between the manager and others, smoothing relationships and relieving stress (ibid.). This role of a subordinate as a "soother" who mediates conflicts and protects the manager from stress caused by others, answers telephones, takes messages, and reschedules meetings requires an employee who acts passively and who willingly sacrifices her own emotional needs to further those of the manager and of the organization. Kerfoot and Knights observe that this role is the model of the "ideal feminine womanhood." While not all women act in this passive way, Kerfoot and Knights observe that passivity pervades the expectations of women and silences women's authority (ibid.).

In *Gender Trials*, Jennifer Pierce observed that male lawyers expect female paralegals to listen to their complaints about their cases, to soothe their tempers, and to smooth their ruffled feathers. They expect female paralegals to absorb the male lawyers' aggressive behavior and criticism without complaining (Pierce 1995). If the female paralegals fail at this mission, the lawyers sanction them (ibid.).

The emotional labor required of the female paralegals includes care-taking and deference to the attorneys' expertise (ibid.). Neither deference nor caretaking is reciprocal. Emotional labor, similar to the work a wife traditionally performs for her husband, creates stress in the individual paralegal. She must manage her feelings of frustration and resentment at her unequal treatment and assumptions that she is stupid, even though she may know more than the beginning lawyer for whom she works (ibid.). While paralegals may interrupt busy attorneys only as the law-yers choose, lawyers frequently interrupt female paralegals, causing stress concerning the paralegal's time management. The paralegal is "invisible" (ibid., 96–98). Attorneys regularly ignore their presence when they do not need them to do work for them, an attitude that paralegals resent.

Pierce notes that paralegals' job evaluations depend in large part on their demeanor and ability to treat others pleasantly even in very stress-ful situations (ibid.). Besides alleviating the anxieties of attorneys, wit-nesses, and clients, the paralegal must express gratitude for the attorney to others and act as the interpreter of the attorney's moods and feelings (ibid.). Similarly, other researchers have noted that women are expected to be "nice" and often work in "circumstances that prohibit expressions of anger" (Rogers and Garrett 2002).

Male paralegals in Pierce's study received different, and better, treat-ment than their female counterparts. They had more responsibility, and outsiders and clients often mistook them for attorneys (Pierce 1995). They had greater access to power and authority than the female para-legals, and lawyers in the firm presumed them to be on their way to law school. In contrast, clients mistook female paralegals for secretaries, and in some instances, lawyers asked them to type documents for them. While male paralegals performed emotional labor, it was of a different sort than that expected of the women. Instead of expecting the male paralegals to soothe them, the attorneys engaged the male paralegals as political advisors or to acquire from them gossip or political informa-tion (ibid.).

Even women in high-powered jobs must perform emotional labor for their male counterparts. In "Mobilizing Masculinities": Women's Experiences of Men at Work, Patricia Yancey Martin describes Sara, a Ph.D., the only woman working with approximately one hundred men. Although by title Sara was not her male colleagues' subordinate, they expected her to perform the emotional role of "mother" and "sounding board." The men talked to her about their wives, children, families, and personal lives, requested her sympathy, and asked her to explain their wives' behavior to them. This "counseling" cost Sara extensive work time. Even though Sara graduated with a Ph.D. from an elite university, and did cutting-edge patent work, the men's treatment of her as a "woman" rather than a "true scientist" diminished Sara's self-esteem (Martin 2001).

Martin's and Pierce's observations of male-female interactions in organizations support the theory posited by Kerfoot and Knights. Pierce's research identifies the masculinization and feminization of traditional jobs in the workplace (Pierce 1995). The jobs of attorneys, especially those of litigators, are characterized by ideals of masculine behavior identified by Kerfoot and Knights as aggression, competitiveness, and repression of emotion. The repression leads to outbursts of anger; the jobs of their subordinates, the paralegals, are feminized. As traditional wives and mothers would do, female paralegals defer to and take care of their male attorneys. The structure of the relationship at work, therefore, reflects the socially accepted structure of the roles of men and women in the traditional family. Men working in the "feminized" paralegal jobs can transcend their job titles.

Male paralegals are not expected to act as caregivers to the extent that the women are. Moreover, they benefit from hegemonic masculinity: others regularly mistake them for lawyers, and lawyers in the firm invite male paralegals to join them at informal gatherings.

Judging women's job performance more harshly than men's in the same job because of the women's failure to act in the stereotypically female manner is differential treatment because of their sex. To the extent that an employer refuses to hire, fails to promote, or fires a woman because of her inability or unwillingness to perform emotional labor that is not required of men in the same job, the employer discriminates against her because of her sex. A woman placed in this position should be able to prove, through the use of the *McDonnell Douglas,* or the "motivating factor" test, that the employer violated Title VII (*McDonnell Douglas Corp. v. Green* 1973; 42 U.S.C. § 2000e-2(m)).

Courts need to be sensitized to the issues. A woman can prove her prima facie case by demonstrating that she is a woman, was qualified for the position, applied, and was not hired or promoted, or was fired from the job, and either that men holding the same job have fewer and different requirements of emotional labor or that other women who were willing to perform the emotional labor were hired, retained, or promoted. An employer would probably attempt to use the woman's "inability to get along with others" as a legitimate nondiscriminatory reason for its adverse employment decision. The plaintiff's response, armed with expert evidence of masculinities present at work, is that the employer's reason is pretextual because it is based on sex: men in the same jobs are not judged by the same criteria. To prove that sex is a "motivating factor" in the female employee's adverse employment action, she can show that the employer expected her to conform to sex stereotypes and that she was adversely affected because of her failure to do so (*Price Waterhouse v. Hopkins* 1989).

Even in a workplace where there are no men in the particular job and caregiving is required, the plaintiff should offer masculinities research to demonstrate that specific job criteria are based on sex stereotyping. Once this premise is established, evaluations of one's job performance are based on sex. For example, a secretary who is penalized for failing to take care of her boss in stereotypically feminine ways such as by bringing him coffee, buying gifts for his wife, or soothing his anger, should offer expert evidence of masculinities theory to demonstrate that making employment decisions on the basis of these factors is discrimination because of sex unless the employer can prove that these criteria are bona fide occupational qualifications.

There is no question that there are certain jobs for which caretaking is a legitimate criterion. For example, an employer has the right to expect a soothing, caring personality from a kindergarten teacher or a nurse. To avoid violating Title VII, however, an employer should apply this expectation equally to women and men in the workplace. Moreover, an employer who refuses to hire a man as nurse or kindergarten teacher because of the employer's stereotype that women are more caring and soothing illegally discriminates against the male applicant because the employer uses sex stereotyping to determine that the male applicant cannot meet the expectations of the job. Conversely, an employer who does not employ a male applicant as a kindergarten teacher because the applicant is too effeminate also violates Title VII. The subsection below,

"Stereotypes of Men," further discusses the case of Ariel Ayanna, a male attorney mentioned in chapter 1, who alleged that he was fired from his job because of his caretaking responsibilities and his views about fathers' engagement with their families. The *Ayanna* case provides an example of how stereotypes of men as breadwinners and not caretakers may harm men who seek to be more involved fathers.

Woman as Siren

A third stereotype is that of woman as dangerous temptress. Patricia Martin's field research produced Tom, a middle-aged manager and a married self-professed Christian who vowed to himself for thirty years that he would never dine alone with a woman other than his wife (Martin 2003, 348). Tom traveled often for his job; when he arrived at his destination, he would meet his "host" for dinner to plan the next day's meetings, unless the "host" was a woman (ibid.). Finally, after thirty years of this practice, Tom realized that his behavior discriminated against the women who were his "hosts" because he created an informal network with the men but did not get to know the women well (ibid.). Despite this realization, Tom did not change his policy. Professor Martin notes that this policy "frames women as sexual beings, as signs of sexuality, as a temptation to engage in sex" (ibid., 349). When Tom became aware of the discriminatory nature of this policy and still continued to practice it, he was performing his masculine gender fully aware that doing so might harm his company. Instead, the institution of gender determined his behavior.

Tom's story demonstrates that women suffer professionally from the stereotype of woman as dangerous sex symbol. This stereotype, combined with the *informalism* that excludes women from important relationships, creates serious barriers to women's advancement at work, contributing in large part to women's inability to move up the career ladder. Certainly, the use of a sex stereotype such as "woman as siren" to make decisions concerning hiring, promotion, or firing is illegal under Title VII as disparate treatment because of sex.

But some courts do not see that discriminating against women because they are attractive is discrimination based on sex. In *Nelson v. Knight*, a dentist fired his dental assistant who had worked for him for over ten years because he found her too attractive and his wife was worried that he would have an affair with the assistant. The Iowa Supreme Court concluded that the plaintiff, Melissa Nelson, did not have a cause of action for sex discrimination based on the firing. It was not her sex but her attractiveness and her friendly relationship with her boss, the court concluded, that led to her discharge (*Nelson v. Knight DDS, P.C.* 2013). Expert testimony from masculinities theorists can help judges and juries realize that the decision a manager makes to avoid contact with or to fire a lower-level employee because she is sexually attractive is illegal discrimination because of sex and may perpetuate and amplify inequalities between women and men at work.

Stereotypes of Men: Man as Breadwinner, Not Caregiver

Men, too, suffer from the stereotypes attributed to them at work. Traditionally, society expects a man to be the breadwinner—to earn sufficient money to support his family— and to leave his family's emotional and personal needs to the children's mother. Masculinities researchers challenge the view that men are biologically programmed to be the breadwinners and to have less involvement with their families. Rather, this role results from society's teaching of boys from the time they are young that they will be responsible for their families' finances, and that they should hide their emotions. These attitudes can affect the treatment of men at work who attempt to counter the stereotype. One way of countering the masculine stereotype is for a man to spend time on caregiving. Men who care for their children and reduce their work hours because of family needs earn significantly lower wages, as compared to men who reduce their hours for other reasons. While men who care for family members and reduce their hours suffer a wage penalty of 25 percent, other men who work fewer hours suffer only a 5 percent wage penalty (Cunningham-Parmeter 2013). According to Keith Cunningham-Parmeter,

> [T]he caregiving man has an even higher hurdle to overcome. For, at its
> core, his nonconformity represents a fundamental threat to masculine
> power and established gender hierarchies. Whereas macho mothers re-
> inforce the masculinization of work and tender mothers reinforce the

feminization of domestic life, caregiving men challenge the gendered nature of both spheres. In this way, they raise an exceedingly uncomfortable
question: why should either realm be gendered at all? In order to avoid
this question, the rules of manhood call upon every worker to "out man"
the other, while feminizing and punishing men who refuse to compete.
(Cunningham-Parmeter 2013, 299)

A good example of a man who alleged he was punished for caregiving
appears in a case that arose from the firing of a male law firm associate.
In *Ayanna v. Dechert LLP*, the plaintiff, a white male associate at the defendant law firm in its Boston office, was fired after working at the firm
for two years and three months (Complaint and Jury Demand intro,
Ayanna v. Dechert LLP 2010). Ayanna's complaint alleged retaliation for
exercising his rights under the Family Medical Leave Act (FMLA) and
sex discrimination under the Massachusetts employment discrimination law, which is similar to Title VII (Massachusetts General Laws Annotated § 151B).

Law firms are hierarchical institutions where a dominant form of hegemonic masculinity prevails. Law firm culture is both masculine and
antiquated, making it difficult for women and persons of color but also
challenging men to engage in masculine competitive behaviors that
harm some men and many women. The dominant type of masculinity—
hegemonic masculinity—is the norm in law firms.

"The Anglo-American legal adversarial system values qualities such
as individualism, autonomy, and competition" (Macerollo 2008, 121).
Because men were historically the only members of the legal profession,
it is not surprising that these qualities, considered by many as masculine, are esteemed in the profession. In fact, one sociologist argues that
public confidence in law in part depends on the "masculine ideals which
have become synonymous with lawyers" (ibid., 121). Moreover, the legal
system depends on a linear career model, one that is available to men
who live a more traditional lifestyle but infrequently available to women
who have families (ibid.).

Female lawyers recognize that there is often an invisible gender bias
in the legal profession. Women continue to believe that they have to be
better than, and more assertive than, their male colleagues in order to
be considered competent lawyers, even though their colleagues dislike

them for being assertive. Furthermore, female lawyers are expected to trivialize instances of sexism, to engage in some sexual banter, and to do work that is delegated to them on the basis of stereotypes (ibid.).

Masculine performances identified by David Collinson and Jeff Hearn that are discussed in chapter 1—*authoritarianism, paternalism, entrepreneurialism, informalism,* and *careerism* (Collinson and Hearn 1994)—either alone or in concert, are common in law firms. They co-exist with societal notions of men as breadwinners, a masculine norm that places pressure on men to support their families financially and to rely on a wife as caretaker of the children and the home. They create an environment that makes it difficult for women to achieve because, at least in upper-middle-class families, women are still predominantly the caregivers.

The contemporary law firm is even more gender regimented because of the extreme business pressures that exist. Richard Collier describes the gendered structure of large law firms:

> [T]he ideal legal professional in City law firms continues to be gauged in terms of a three-fold spatial, economic, and corporeal nexus—that is, in terms of ideas of bodily presence/visibility/performance, of economic production (the amount of money generated). . . . This ideal worker is constituted via reference to still powerful and resonant gendered divisions, practices and cultures—in particular, ideas around embodiment, sexuality, authority and power that are commonly associated with (hegemonic) masculinity. Further, this subject is marked by an overarching organizational commitment to the law firm that—when "work" and "life" clash—is seen as inevitably taking precedence over what Martha Fineman terms the "inevitable dependencies" and vulnerabilities associated with family life. (Collier 2013, 426–27)

Besides practices that seem to value a certain type of masculinity— the hegemonic masculinity—practices and attitudes in large law firms are also linked to the reproduction of the "hegemony of men," that is, to the power of men as a group over women as a group (ibid., 427–28). Collier notes that attitudes prevalent in law firms about "heterosexuality, reproduction, child care, men's authority, male weakness, and vulnerability" are influenced by biological notions of masculinity and femininity and "inform assumptions about the kind of individual who will, and will not, succeed in such a firm" (ibid., 427). These attitudes reflect a gendered acceptance of the "inherently competitive nature of a career in large law firms" (ibid.).

The increase of female lawyers in the profession has not led to feminization in large law firms and other corporate entities in the fields of global finance and business (ibid.). Rather, there is an increasing gendered polarization within the legal workforce, with a rise of a hypercompetitive business culture. This culture results from a process of "gender segmentation" in which "men's resistance to change as a defense mechanism for an embattled profession, leads to continued male domination. Crucially, this is done in such a way that male lawyers can seek to maintain their status and rewards while still formally aligning with gender neutral, progressive equality policies" (ibid., 428). In fact, there may be "a regressive retrenchment and masculinization of the law" that "paradoxically, runs alongside the rise of equality and flexible working agendas and the growing recognition of the importance of fathers" (ibid., 429).

These processes are even more complicated than they appear. Norms are changing for masculinity and fatherhood, and normative ideas about masculinity change over a man's lifetime (ibid.). All of this occurs at the same time that law appears to be moving away from the old-fashioned (and perhaps sexist, but more gentle) idea of lawyers as "gentlemen" (ibid., 432). Today, many lawyers perform "transnational business masculinities": a "new form of masculinity" has emerged that is characterized by "egocentrism, conditional loyalties (even to the corporation), and a declining sense of responsibility for others (except for the purposes of image-making)" (ibid.). Whereas in the past lawyers saw law as public service, today it is entrepreneurial and hypercompetitive (ibid.).

But there is a contradiction: as lawyers become more entrepreneurial and hypercompetitive and remasculinize the law, new norms of masculinity have arisen that emphasize the hands-on father and an acceptance of the discourse of gender equality (ibid.). Even the hypercompetitive law firms accept and engage in this discourse, but there is significant pressure on male lawyers not to work flexible schedules and not to take long paternity leaves (Thornton and Bagust 2007; Williams et al. 2007). Moreover, in large law firms there is a great disparity between the percentages of male and female lawyers working part-time (Selmi 2007). In 2011, only 6.2 percent of lawyers worked part-time, and the overwhelming majority—70 percent—were women (NALP 2015).

The complaint in *Ayanna* tells the story of a young father of two children whose wife suffered from mental illness that, at times, meant that Ayanna needed to care for her and their children (Amended Complaint and Jury Demand, *Ayanna v. Dechert LLP* 2012). Ayanna alleged that the firm retaliated against him for taking FMLA leave to care for his wife and children, and that the firm discriminated against him because of his sex because he failed to fit the firm's stereotype of how a male lawyer should behave (ibid.). That stereotype, he alleged, was of a hard-driving lawyer who leaves childcare and other family responsibilities to his wife. He also alleged that female associates with family responsibilities were treated differently and better than he was. According to the complaint, women in the Financial Services Group, where Ayanna worked, were permitted to leave the office and/or rearrange their schedules in order to take care of family obligations, to work from home, and to return to work later in the evening. Unlike Ayanna, the complaint alleges, the women were not derided for taking care of family responsibilities (ibid.).

Ayanna makes a novel sex discrimination claim, alleging that the firm had a "macho" culture and that it discriminated against him for his failure to meet the stereotype of macho lawyer (ibid., par. 11). According to the complaint, Dechert's masculine culture "equate[s] masculinity with relegating caretaking to women and working long hours in the office" (ibid., intro.). The macho culture "praises and encourages male associates and partners to fulfill the stereotypical male role of ceding family responsibilities to women" (ibid., par. 11). The complaint alleges that "caregiving is for wives of male attorneys and tolerated only for female attorneys. The firm culture does not require female attorneys to conform to the 'macho' stereotype" (ibid.).

Because Ayanna was an equal coparent and he rejected the "macho" stereotype, the complaint alleges, Ayanna advocated for more equitable treatment of attorneys who cared for their children (ibid.).

There are a number of complicating questions in this fact pattern, and without the benefit of a trial it would be difficult to determine whether Ayanna's allegations are accurate. But the evidence of record appears to create genuine issues of material fact as to whether the firm fired Ayanna for his failure to live up to masculine stereotypes, and in retaliation for his taking FMLA leave. Dechert filed a motion for summary judgment and argued that the sole reason for Ayanna's firing was his low billable hours (Defendant Dechert LLP's Memorandum, *Ayanna v. Dechert LLP* 2012).

The allegations in the complaint were supported, however, by Ayanna's deposition testimony. As to the sex stereotyping, Ayanna testified that he was treated differently from women who had family responsibilities, and he named a number of female associates who received better treatment (Ayanna Deposition, *Ayanna v. Dechert LLP* 2012). Moreover, Ayanna testified that on a number of occasions other male associates discussed how much they worked, bragged that they saw very little of their wives and children, and one even bragged that he had the firm pay for his wife to visit her family in New Orleans with their children so she would leave him alone to work (ibid.). Ayanna also testified that he was present when another associate asserted that the female associates' work product was inferior to that of the male associates. A number of male associates told Ayanna that they were afraid to take much time off when their children were born because they feared retaliation (ibid.).

Furthermore, Ayanna testified that he was known in the firm for having an equal coparenting relationship with his wife, for challenging the parental leave policies as discriminatory, and for wanting to improve the firm's policies. He testified that at a firm meeting in which retention of female associates was discussed, he told the partner that the firm should have policies that are more family friendly. The partner responded, according to Ayanna's deposition, by stating that it was an industry-wide problem and that Dechert could not do anything about it (ibid.). Ayanna also testified that one of the partners rolled his eyes, that others commented on his "leaving early, or advised him to come in early" (ibid., 57–60, 160–63, 166), and that other associates warned him that he should stay in the office after hours so people would know he was working late.

The federal district court granted the summary judgment motion in part and denied it in part (*Ayanna v. Dechert LLP* 2012). The court concluded that, viewing the facts in the light most favorable to Ayanna, there was sufficient evidence to raise a genuine issue of material fact as to whether the defendant's alleged reason for firing Ayanna—low billable hours—was a pretext for retaliation for Ayanna's taking FMLA leave (ibid.). The court concluded, however, that there was insufficient evidence of sex stereotyping and granted the defendant's motion for summary judgment on the sex discrimination claim. The court noted that Ayanna's "broad claims" about a "'macho'" culture at Dechert were not supported by individual instances of discrimination against Ayanna (ibid., 5). Moreover, the court concluded that there was evidence in the record that women, too, had some negative repercussions because of their childcare responsibilities. According to the court, the evidence did not support the conclusion that Ayanna's supervising partner treated Ayanna the way he did because he was a *man* engaging in childcare responsibilities. It was just as likely that his adverse treatment was based on his caregiver status alone (ibid.). The case settled before trial.

Given the testimony in the record, the federal district court should not have granted summary judgment on the allegation of sex discrimination based on stereotyping. The court ignored significant evidence in the record from which a reasonable jury could have concluded that the defendant fired Ayanna at least in part because of his failure to live up to the stereotype of a male lawyer. It appears that the court did not actually understand the sex-stereotyping claim, especially given that the court required Ayanna to prove differential treatment of men and women.

Ayanna's testimony regarding the atmosphere at the law firm and his own treatment reflects masculinities observed by Jeff Hearn and David Collinson in their study of corporate workplaces. Ayanna's testimony clearly describes entrepreneurialism and careerism, as well as the hierarchical relationships found in authoritarian workplaces. Ayanna's testimony, if believed by the jury, demonstrates that there is a clear authoritarian relationship between firm partners and associates. The partners rely, it appears, on associates' fear that they will not be promoted to the partnership. Partners demand "face time" at work to demonstrate how obedient, loyal, and hard-working the associate is.

Entrepreneurialism is evident in the ethic that work is more important than family and that associates should not bend to family pressures. According to the testimony, mothers may have some relief from this ethic, but in the end, the firm, as well as the industry, cannot retain female associates perhaps because the ethic that hard work and visibility come before family is too brutal and punishing for many mothers (Ayanna Deposition, *Ayanna v. Dechert LLP* 2012). It is not only hard work that makes the atmosphere entrepreneurial, authoritarian, and masculine. It is also the expectation that the firm owns the associates' time and that the firm expects, even if there is no pressing work to be done, that associates be visible at work, before and after hours, to demonstrate loyalty and submission to the firm.

Careerism, as expressed through competition, is also evident. Male associates speak of the "inferior" work product of their female colleagues; they also compete over who works the longest hours and who spends less time with their families. In this environment, it is a badge of honor, of manly strength, to ignore one's family. This environment is clearly masculine—born in the days when it was a man's job to be the breadwinner and protector. The breadwinner is the "ideal worker" in that he has no outside needs or responsibilities (Williams 2001). He has a wife who takes care of every familial need, and his job is to support the family economically. Thus, a man is more masculine and a better father if he makes more money. He is less of a man and even less of a father if he gives more care (Garcia 2012).

Assuming the veracity of Ayanna's complaint and deposition testimony, for most women and for men who do not adhere to these traditional beliefs and lifestyles, work in the law firm may be difficult. These associates have to perform their identities, as Carbado and Gulati describe, in a way that may take an emotional and physical toll (Carbado and Gulati 2013). Men such as Ayanna need to perform their masculinity in the acceptable manner—to be the breadwinner, not the caretaker. If they do not, they risk their jobs. Society expects female associates to be caretakers and considers them to be bad mothers if they ignore their families. The firm will give female associates some leeway to perform their identities in a less masculine way, but women must beware: they are often considered to be not committed to their work once they become mothers, and they pay a price for performing their identities in a "motherly" way (Bornstein 2012). They may risk being placed on the "mommy track" and failing to achieve a promotion to partnership.

In *Ayanna*, the federal district court judge assumed that the masculine characteristics and demands at the law firm are gender neutral. As masculinities scholars note, masculine gender is invisible in a managerial setting (McGinley 2004), as it was to this judge. In effect, masculinities are so prevalent that these gender practices are seen as the definition of work rather than as gendered. Sociologist Patricia Yancey Martin explains that men's superior power in most workplaces grants them the right to deny that they are practicing masculine behaviors and to define those behaviors as work itself (Martin 2003). In other words, when women or gender-nonconforming men are faced with behaviors that enhance men's masculinity and power, and attempt to call men on the behaviors, men often define what they do as work. When the behavior is defined as "work" rather than as masculine behaviors or discrimination, it is nearly impossible, absent an understanding of masculinity studies, to explain why women and gender-nonconforming men suffer from illegal discrimination. As a result, law firms and other male-dominated workplaces tend to reproduce themselves.

Ayanna alleged that his treatment occurred because of gender stereotyping. That is, because he was a man engaged in childcare responsibilities and he took that role seriously, he was treated worse than the female associates with childcare responsibilities who performed their law firm associate responsibilities similarly. The court concluded, however, that there was insufficient evidence to prove that Ayanna was treated differently than the women who engaged in childcare responsibilities, and that there was insufficient evidence that his treatment resulted from his gender rather than his caregiver status (*Ayanna v. Dechert LLP* 2012). In fact, there was sufficient evidence to go to a jury that Ayanna's treatment differed from that of his female colleagues who had children, but, nonetheless, by requiring the comparative proof, the court's holding demonstrates an unduly formalistic understanding of sex stereotyping.

When dealing with illegal stereotyping, the plaintiff merely needs to prove that he or she suffered an adverse action as a result of the employer's stereotypes about the plaintiff. The plaintiff does not have to prove that he or she is treated differently than members of the other sex. Even if the employer treats both women and men badly because of their caregiving responsibilities, the employer could be engaging in sex discrimination against both groups.

If the job is gendered male because the firm perceives that the ideal worker is a male breadwinner who exhibits competitive traits, and has the ability because of his family situation to work unlimited hours, it may illegally discriminate against both men and women who do not exhibit these traits or flexibility. For the man, like Ayanna, the discrimination because of sex may entail sex stereotyping—the idea that Ayanna is not a real man: he is not one of us because he chooses to be a caregiver of his wife and children. For the woman who has caregiving responsibilities, the firm may respond by acting on its own biases that women with small children are not committed to their work. In both cases, the employer is engaging in sex stereotyping. The man does not live up to the firm's sex stereotypes of the ideal male worker, and the woman confirms the firm's sex stereotypes about mothers as workers (Bornstein 2012; *E.E.O.C. Enforcement Guidance* 2007; *Back v. Hastings on Hudson Free School District* 2004). In *Back v. Hastings on Hudson Free School District*, Judge Calabresi for the court stated, "The principle of *Price Waterhouse* . . . applies as much to the supposition that a woman *will* conform to a gender stereotype (and therefore will not, for example, be dedicated to her job), as to the supposition that a woman is unqualified for a position because she does *not* conform to a gender stereotype" (ibid., 119–20, citing to *Price Waterhouse v. Hopkins*, 490 U.S. 228 (1989)).

Both *Back* and *Ayanna* differ somewhat from *Price Waterhouse*. In *Price Waterhouse*, Ann Hopkins was not promoted to the partnership in part because of her failure to conform to feminine sex stereotypes (*Price Waterhouse v. Hopkins* 1989). She was considered too aggressive, and she failed to dress and behave in an acceptably feminine manner.

The employer placed Hopkins in a double bind because the job itself required aggression—one of the very characteristics for which Ann Hopkins was punished. In *Ayanna*, the employer allegedly discriminated against the plaintiff because of his failure to conform to stereotype, but unlike the case in *Price Waterhouse*, Dechert did not place Ayanna in the same double bind. Ann Hopkins simultaneously had to act aggressively to do her job and femininely to gain the partners' acceptance (ibid.). Because these partners considered aggressive behavior and failure to conform to stereotypes masculine, they judged Hopkins as a woman who was not sufficiently feminine, and this prejudice at least partially motivated the partners to vote against Hopkins. Ayanna, in contrast, was expected to follow the male stereotype (which happened to conform to the way the partners viewed the job) of always available, hard-working, and flexible in his hours. Allegedly because he chose to perform his identity and work in a less masculine and more feminine way, the partners decided to fire him. While there is no double bind imposed on Ayanna, he still suffered from adverse treatment based on his failure to adhere to the preferred male stereotype.

Ayanna alleged that the female associates with children were treated better than he was (Amended Complaint and Jury Demand, *Ayanna v. Dechert LLP* 2012). In essence, his allegation was that the law firm gave mothers more leeway in the way that they juggled their caregiving and work responsibilities. Certainly, if Ayanna supported this allegation with evidence at trial of differential treatment, he would have proved that the firm discriminated against him because of his sex. This differential treatment would prove two things. First, it would prove that it was possible to do the job in a different way because the firm tolerated mothers who performed the job in that way. Second, combined with evidence that decision makers in the firm were uncomfortable with his caregiving role, differential treatment would probably be sufficient to demonstrate that Ayanna was fired for failing to live up to the firm's preferred stereotype of how a man should handle fatherhood and work.

Even without this evidence of unequal treatment of male and female caregivers, however, Ayanna might have proven that the firm fired him because he failed to adhere to stereotypes of how a man should act. In other words, the firm's requirement, if proved, that all of its associates, both male and female, be available to work in the office for extremely long hours and be totally flexible about workplace demands is a gendered requirement. As Richard Collier notes, law firms have cultures that demand bodily presence, visibility, and performances of hypermasculinity (Collier 2013). These cultures themselves are masculine and competitive, and the requirement that the job be performed in this manner is itself gendered. In a culture where mothers are still the predominant caregivers of their families, this requirement harms women and particularly mothers. But it also harms fathers who, masculinity scholars recognize, are often forced to choose between fulfilling the breadwinner stereotype and actively participating in their children's upbringing (Cunningham-Parmeter 2013; Dowd 2012).

Masculinities scholarship recognizes that a law firm's demand that its associates be available for unlimited hours is gendered male because it describes the historical and traditional arrangement that middle-class married men have used to further their careers and to support their families. This arrangement—that the husband/father work long hours to support financially the wife/mother and their children, and that the wife/mother work in the home, taking care of all of the non-work-related obligations of the family—permits the father to work unlimited hours without worrying about the well-being of his family. It is also gendered male because it describes a patriarchal relationship in which the husband/father is the head of the household who has the power to govern the family relationships and to make decisions for the family. Law firms and their clients benefit from these patriarchal relationships because if the family is largely dependent upon the father's breadwinning capacity, law firms and their clients can exercise significant power over the associates and can exact from the associates work behaviors that are preferred, but not absolutely necessary to the furtherance of the clients' goals.

In addition, and perhaps more importantly, the law firm practice as defined here is masculine because it furthers a competitive environment in which men seek to prove their masculinity to one another and thereby confirm their own masculinity. One way of doing so is for a man to demonstrate how little sleep he needs, or the small amount of time he spends with his family. These demonstrations are examples of men "doing masculinities"—engaging in masculine practices to prove their worth to themselves and others (Martin 2003, 360–61).

This is not to say that women do not engage in these masculine practices. Some do. But the mere fact that women engage in these practices as well does not negate that the practices are the result of masculine norms, birthed in the traditional relationship between husbands/fathers and their families. To the extent that the firm's culture requires associates to engage in these practices, it creates job qualifications that are gender differentiated. Enforcing these requirements is similar to saying, "No unmanly men need apply. No feminine women need apply."

To the extent that a male associate is unwilling or unable to conform, the employer's decision to terminate him is a gender-based decision because he does not meet the stereotype of how a man should act. To the extent that the firm believes that a woman is unable to conform, the employer's decision to terminate her is also a gender-based decision because it results from the firm's stereotype that mothers will not be able to do the job. Moreover, by enforcing these masculinity-based requirements, the law firm polices the boundaries of masculinity, ensuring that those who make it are "real men," thereby reinforcing the masculine identity of the law firm partners. Enforcing these requirements is about gender in two ways: it assures that only the most masculine men will be successful in the firm, and it confirms that the partners who reinforce the norms are masculine themselves. The few women who make the sacrifices needed for success in this environment are often considered outliers—not real women—so their presence is not necessarily threatening to the male partners.

Title VII forbids discrimination against an employee based on sex or gender (after *Price Waterhouse*) and, to the extent that these are gender-based requirements imposed upon associates of the firm, under Title VII, the employer must demonstrate that meeting these requirements is a bona fide occupational qualification (BFOQ) for the job (Title VII). The BFOQ is an affirmative defense that the sex-based characteristics are "reasonably necessary to the normal operation of the particular business" (ibid.). The Supreme Court has interpreted this provision to apply only in very narrow circumstances (*International Union et al. v. Johnson Controls* 1991). In essence, the employer must prove that its gender-based requirement relates to the "essence" or "central mission" of the employer's business, and is objectively and verifiably necessary to the employee's performance of job tasks and responsibilities (ibid., 201–4).

While there are times when law firm associates must work very long hours to finish the work they have, many of the gendered requirements will not meet the BFOQ test. It is not necessarily true, for example, that associates who work from 9:00 a.m. until 11:00 p.m. are at their best at all times while working. In fact, much of the work time is often wasted because sleep-deprived associates cannot necessarily do their best work. Legal scholar Theresa Beiner's work demonstrates that associates who work without sufficient sleep actually have the mental abilities of a person who is intoxicated (Beiner 2014). Moreover, requirements that an associate demonstrate "face time" or that he forgo a parental leave do not usually relate to the essence or central mission of the firm's business and are not ordinarily necessary to the performance of job tasks or responsibilities.

As this chapter demonstrates, workplaces are saturated with and constructed of gender and class expectations about the proper roles of men and women. In fact, because of the historical patterns of gender-segmented roles, jobs themselves have genders. Because of how engrained these structures are, however, people do not even perceive gender. Judges and juries must be made aware of the gendered structures, expectations, roles, and stereotypes in order to make proper decisions in Title VII cases. Masculinities research can help judges and juries consider whether workplace structures and behaviors discriminate because of sex.

Masculinities research can make many unequal relationships at work visible to judges and juries trying Title VII cases. There are times, however, when it would be difficult to prove that a plaintiff has suffered an adverse employment action as a result of masculinities, because there is no comparator—a "similarly situated" person who is not a member of the protected class who was treated better than she—with whom a plaintiff may compare her job progress (*McDonnell Douglas Corp. v. Green* 1973, 411). Or, in the alternative, certain structures that have a disparate effect on women or men may not be as obviously gendered as those discussed in this chapter.

These plaintiffs, however, may be able to redress the masculinities at work by alleging disparate impact. Under disparate impact theory, a plaintiff may allege that some masculinities are neutral practices that have a disparate effect on members of a protected class—women, for example. Chapter 8 discusses the use of masculinities theory to prove a disparate impact cause of action.

8

Proving Disparate Impact through Masculinities

This chapter examines the use of masculinities theory to prove a disparate impact cause of action under Title VII of the 1964 Civil Rights Act.[1] Disparate impact creates a potential remedy for the negative effects produced by masculine promotion policies, standards, and practices in workplaces (Title VII). As explained in chapter 5, unlike disparate treatment causes of action, disparate impact claims do not require proof of the employer's intent to discriminate *(Ricci v. DeStefano* 2009). Rather, disparate impact law requires the plaintiff to prove that a facially neutral employment practice, which is also neutral as to its intent, causes an adverse disparate effect on a group protected by the statute (ibid.). If the employer cannot demonstrate that the practice is job related and consistent with business necessity, the plaintiff will prevail (ibid.). Even if the employer proves the job-relatedness and business necessity of the challenged practice, the plaintiff can still prevail if she proves that there are less discriminatory alternatives available that the employer refused to adopt (ibid.). Because masculinities are rarely visible or intentionally discriminatory, litigants may successfully use disparate impact to challenge masculine employment structures, hiring and promotion requirements, and practices that create a disparate effect on women and/ or nonconforming men.

Consider the following hypothetical situation: a new chief of police, Jack Strong, takes charge of the department in Barneyville, a rapidly growing medium-sized city that is struggling with poverty and an increasing crime rate. The new mayor, Dan Payner, who recently appointed Strong as chief of police, was elected on a "law and order" platform. Both Payner and Strong understand that Barneyville needs a more professional police department. There will be a number of promotional openings in the police department for lieutenant and captain positions, and they hope to use those promotions to professionalize the force. Strong wants to assure that blacks and Latinos are represented in the new promotions but is wary of liability under Title VII. He knows that in *Ricci v. DeStefano*, the U.S. Supreme Court held the City of New Haven liable to white firefighters (and one Latino firefighter) for intentional race discrimination (disparate treatment) under Title VII for throwing out test results of a promotional exam on which the white firefighters and the one Latino firefighter performed well. The city's fear of a disparate impact lawsuit brought by Latino and black firefighters was insufficient reason for throwing out the test results (*Ricci v. DeStefano* 2009). The Supreme Court ruled that because the city did not have a "strong basis in evidence" to conclude that the minority firefighters had a successful claim under the disparate impact provisions of Title VII, the city violated the Title VII rights of the nonminority firefighters when it discarded the test results on the basis of the racial composition (primarily white) of successful exam takers. This violation constituted intentional race discrimination (disparate treatment) and a violation of Title VII (ibid., 561).

Jack is in a conundrum: he hopes to promote blacks and Latinos in proportion to their representation on the police force, but he is concerned about litigation from white police officers. He believes that black and Latino police officers are necessary to calm antipathies between the police and residents in the predominantly black and Latino neighborhoods in Barneyville, and that many of the black and Latino officers on the force are ready to serve as lieutenants and captains. But he wants to avoid a lawsuit. Jack hires a consultant to work on establishing testing standards for the promotions. The consultant, in order to avoid a disparate impact on applicants of color, recommends a written test that would represent 40 percent of the final promotional score, and creates the test in consultation with a number of groups representing both whites and minorities. For the written test, he creates questions that are related to the specific jobs in Barneyville. He also recommends that the remaining 60 percent of the test include an oral interview and a role-play in which the candidate's command presence is evaluated.

Police departments in other communities have had success promoting qualified police officers of color using these standards. Command presence is the physical manifestation of how an officer leads: appearance, apparent confidence and control of the situation, body movements, eye contact, and tone of voice (Wollert 2012). Barneyville adopts the consultant's recommendations, and the city uses teams of trained evaluators to grade those who have applied for promotions using written tests, oral interviews, and role-plays. Strong is pleased because when the city uses these new evaluation standards, a representative proportion of blacks and Latinos achieves promotions, and deserving white officers are also promoted. He uses the system for a four-year period, and the results are consistent. Apparently, the system is fair.

Until Strong discovers one day that it may not be. A female police officer discusses her concerns with Strong. She points out that the four years of promotion testing produced no female lieutenants or captains, even though there are a number of well-qualified female officers on the force who are ready for promotion. Female candidates did very well on the written portion of the test, but failed the interviews and role-plays at high rates. Women represent 14 percent of the police force but zero percent of the lieutenants and captains.

Strong is crestfallen. He doesn't understand why he had never noticed that women had not earned promotions under the new system, and he is very concerned that the female officers will sue the city. When he consults the city attorney, she informs him that the city may be vulnerable to a Title VII lawsuit alleging that the neutral standard—command presence—created a disparate impact on women who applied for promotions on the force. But Jack finds the city attorney's analysis troubling. He knows that command presence is an accepted standard nationwide for predicting police officer success on the job. In fact, in the police academy, students who receive an unacceptable command presence rating have a 99 percent chance of failing the practical evaluation, whereas those with an acceptable command presence rating have a 99 percent chance of passing the practical evaluation (Wollert 2012).

In other words, command presence has near-perfect predictive value of how a candidate will do in the practical evaluation. Strong and the city attorney eventually agree that there is a reasonable chance that the city would have a successful defense that the command presence standard is job related and consistent with business necessity if the female officers sue the city for sex discrimination. Nonetheless, Strong is troubled by the department's failure to promote promising female officers who have demonstrated their strength in the field, and he agrees to meet with the female officers' lawyers concerning the possibility of changing the evaluation methods for promotion.

There is a series of negotiations between the lawyers representing interested female police officers and the city, but the negotiations break down. During the talks, female police officers' lawyers claim that under *Price Waterhouse v. Hopkins*, negative evaluations of female officers is sex stereotyping that, if used to deny promotions, constitutes illegal intentional sex discrimination (disparate treatment) under Title VII. They argue that the evaluation standards place women in a double bind: they score poorly in the command presence evaluation if they act aggressively and in control because these characteristics are unappealing in women, but they also score poorly if evaluators perceive them to be too feminine. In essence, the command presence job qualification is, or at least is interpreted by the evaluators to be, masculinity itself, but men and women who exhibit traditional masculine traits are treated differently: men are promoted and women are not.

Furthermore, the lawyers argue that, in the alternative, the command presence requirement can also be attacked as a neutral (not facially discriminatory) standard that has a disparate impact on women when they are evaluated subjectively under the standard. The lawyers therefore claim that female applicants for promotions should succeed in a disparate impact suit against the city because command presence, as interpreted by the evaluators, is neither job related nor consistent with business necessity and should therefore not be used as a standard for promoting officers because the standard disparately affects women's promotion prospects. They also argue that even if command presence is job related and consistent with business necessity, there are alternatives that are equally as effective for promoting excellent police officers that would have a less discriminatory effect on women. They ask the city not to use command presence as the standard for further evaluation. In the alternative, if the city intends to keep command presence as a standard, the women's lawyers recommend (1) studying the definition and application of the command presence standard; (2) redefining it to deemphasize traditionally masculine characteristics such as aggression, and to include traditionally feminine characteristics; (3) engaging in targeted training of those selected to evaluate the candidates; and (4) assuring that a significant percent of those evaluators be female police officers from outside of Barneyville. They also recommend that if he decides to retain command presence as a criterion for promotion, Jack create training for male and female police officers interested in promotion on how to adopt and exhibit command presence. Strong refuses to make any changes, and Barneyville once again uses the previous standards for promotional testing that again result in no female promotions.

The female officers bring a disparate impact claim under Title VII against Barneyville. The women allege that the city's use of command presence has had a disparate impact on women. The city may concede the disparate impact but will argue that command presence is the "coin of the realm," that it is unquestionably job related, and that it is necessary to the police department to have lieutenants and captains who possess command presence. It is likely that the court will agree with the city on its defense because of the broad use of command presence in the police academy and, increasingly, in police departments. At this point, the burden of persuasion will shift back to the women to prove that there are less discriminatory, equally effective alternatives for selecting officers for promotion and that the city has refused to adopt them. This is a difficult case because command presence appears to be such an important quality for a leader in the police force (and even for officers on the beat). Masculinities theory may offer some help to the lawyers representing the women and, in turn, to the judge assigned to the case.

Command presence is an example of a neutral standard that can be imbued with gender and have a disparate effect on women's promotional opportunities. This chapter discusses in detail the potential lawsuit against the City of Barneyville and offers other examples of masculinities at work and the social science research that plaintiffs could use to prosecute a disparate impact claim under Title VII. Some other examples of masculinities that exist in the workplace that have a disparate impact based on gender alone (or combined with race, sexual orientation, national origin, or class) include "up or out" promotion tracks for tenure or partnership, hidden curricula in training programs such as those found in some police departments, and aggressiveness or competitiveness as hiring or promotion qualifications. The "hidden curricula" include implicit messages discussed below in training materials and videos that women are inferior to men.

Using Disparate Impact to Challenge Masculinities in the Workplace

Structures Creating Barriers to Advancement and Retention

Masculinities in the workplace include structures that privilege men by designing work around male bodies and lifestyles. These structures create opportunities for men and barriers for women (Connell 2005; Lorber 1994). Many of these structures are invisible because society is so accustomed to them that it assumes their necessity without exploring plausible alternative structures that may have less of an adverse effect on women. The disparate impact cause of action offers an opportunity to make these structures visible and to consider what these alternative structures may be. Particularly problematic for women's careers is the structuring of employment opportunities around the reproductive processes of men (Connell 2005). This structure has a negative effect on women because of biology and social prescriptions. Other problematic policies permit the employer to graft subjective, unconscious views about the proper roles and behavior of men and women onto the job requirements. One example of this subjective practice appears in the application of the promotional standards in the City of Barneyville hypothetical.

City of Barneyville "Command Presence" and Promotion Standards

The plaintiffs will argue that using the standard of command presence is a neutral employment practice that causes a disparate impact on women. This proof will require plaintiffs to produce statistics demonstrating that in the Barneyville Police Department, the use of command presence has a disparate impact on women. Even if there is insufficient evidence in the Barneyville Police Department, the plaintiffs should present national statistics of police and fire departments that use command presence to judge promotional opportunities that create a disparate impact on women's promotional abilities (*Dothard v. Rawlinson* 1977). This proof should satisfy the 1991 Act's requirement that the plaintiff demonstrate that the employer uses a particular employment practice that causes a disparate impact on women and shifts the burden to the city to demonstrate that command presence is job related and consistent with business necessity.

It is highly likely that when presented with evidence that a finding of command presence has a predictive value of 99 percent for passing the practical evaluation in the police academy, and the argument that command presence is important to professionalizing the police force, the court will agree that it is a job-related standard that is necessary to the business of policing.

If the court agrees that the city has met its burden, the burden of persuasion will shift back to the plaintiffs to prove that there is a less discriminatory alternative that is equally effective. This will be a difficult proof to make because experts in the Department of Homeland Security consider command presence to be a highly effective standard (Wollert 2012).

The problem may be the application of the command presence standard rather than the standard itself, given implicit biases of the evaluators. Masculinities research, combined with the research on leadership, may aid the plaintiffs to argue that use of command presence, at least as it has been applied in the past, is a subjective practice that violates Title VII because as it is interpreted and applied, it creates a disparate impact on women. In *Watson*, the Supreme Court approved of using disparate impact to attack subjective practices that create a disparate impact on members of a protected class. Justice O'Connor specifically mentioned in *Watson* that plaintiffs can use disparate impact to challenge the effects of unconscious discrimination *(Watson v. Fort Worth Bank & Trust* 1988).

The plaintiffs could present an expert in masculinities theory to testify that all-male work environments such as police departments are structured around notions of gender. The jobs of police officer, lieutenant, and captain are gendered male. The jobs have masculine gender in that the ideal police officer/lieutenant/captain is strong, tough, fast, able to think on his feet, etc. Because the job is historically a male job—one that protects others—women by their very nature are not considered to be qualified for the position.

Men in police departments may see their position as affirming their masculinity. Having a female police lieutenant/captain may actually threaten the men's self-identities. Leadership studies confirm that women as leaders are not valued and are often judged more harshly than men who engage in the same work performance. This is the case because of the prescriptive status belief that women should act a certain way—passively—a manner of acting that does not describe a leader (McGinley 2009a). On the basis of this testimony, the plaintiffs will argue that because the jobs of police lieutenant and captain are gendered male, it is nearly impossible for the evaluators of the oral interviews to judge women's command presence fairly. If there is empirical research or evidence of experiences in other police departments that have more success in promoting women after training evaluators to eliminate their unconscious biases, training of the evaluators in how to apply the command presence standard may be a less discriminatory alternative. In this case, Barneyville's refusal to adopt this alternative should suffice to meet the plaintiff's proof requirements.

The plaintiffs can also look at the 40/60 percent split between the written and the oral tests as a practice that creates a disparate impact on women. It may be that women do better on the written evaluation than they do on the oral evaluation that is more subjective. The plaintiffs can attack this split (40/60, as opposed to 60/40, for example) as a neutral practice having a disparate impact on women. This may be problematic, however, because fire departments have found that changing this proportion from 60/40 to 40/60 has actually improved the numbers of minorities who pass the promotional exams (*Ricci v. DeStefano* 2009). There may exist a direct conflict between attempting to assure that women get promotions in proportion to their numbers on the force and attempting to assure that minorities receive promotions proportionally. The defendant will argue that the 40/60 split is job related and consistent with business necessity because it provides the most diverse group of qualified officers for the promotion. The plaintiffs will argue, however, that there are less discriminatory (to women) alternatives, and will suggest alternatives.

Finally, the plaintiffs may use masculinities experts to help with their argument that the courts should use the "bottom line" statistics of female promotions rather than look at any of the individual practices or policies that make up the promotional practices. Due to the subjective nature of the oral part of the exam, plaintiffs can argue that the system is incapable of separation. Because being a policeman is traditionally a male job and promotions to supervisory positions have excluded qualified women, the masculinities experts may argue that the whole process is imbued with gender and that it is impossible to separate the different elements of the process. If the plaintiff convinces the court of this argument, the defendant will argue that its promotion process as a whole is job related and consistent with business necessity. If the court accepts this argument, the plaintiff will have to prove less discriminatory alternatives to the system used. Potentially, experts in masculine workplaces and in implicit biases would aid the plaintiff to suggest an alternative evaluation method that would consider not only race but also gender and attempt to avoid the pitfalls of excluding members of particular groups.

Up or Out Promotion Structures

Another example of structures that are vulnerable to disparate impact litigation are "up or out" tenure tracks in academia. These mechanisms place pressure on individuals to work extremely hard and long hours at a time in their lives when, because of biology and social circumstances, it is generally easier for men to do so than for women.

"Up or out" promotion tracks for tenure are gendered structures built around male bodies and lifestyles. Most universities have tenure-earning and non-tenure-earning jobs. Academic tenure-track jobs are more prestigious and better paid than non-tenure-earning jobs, and an employee holding tenure has greater job security than one without it. Ordinarily, the first five or six years of teaching, scholarly publications, and service determine whether the candidate earns tenure. Tenure grants a faculty member the right to continue teaching and researching at the university unless the university establishes good cause for de-tenuring the individual. The purpose of tenure is to protect the individual's academic freedom to teach, research, and freely discuss his or her subject matter, and to provide a "sufficient degree of economic security to make the profession attractive to men and women of ability" (AAUP 2006a). This is a worthy goal because it furthers independent thought, research, and teaching. Additionally, it would be problematic to eliminate the job security afforded by tenure. However, the process of determining who receives tenure is inflexible and biased toward men's bodies and lifestyles (AAUP 2006b).

The disparate effect of tenure tracks on women is amplified by the long years of education and preparation for a tenure-track position, a period when it is inadvisable to take on the responsibilities of bearing and rearing children due to the intensive time commitment involved. Most universities require a Ph.D. and "post-docs," fellowship years after the Ph.D. (Wilson 2005). Given that women are often advised not to have children during graduate school, that the average age of persons earning a Ph.D. is thirty-three or thirty-four (Wolfinger, Goulden, and Mason 2009), that a postdoctoral fellowship takes at least an additional year, and that the tenure track itself lasts approximately six years, the pretenure years coincide roughly with the average professor's life from ages thirty to forty (Mason and Goulden 2004). This age span presents few problems for men or women who do not aspire to have a family. For those who wish to have a family, however, men enjoy a distinct advantage over women, who suffer a serious disadvantage—both socially and biologically.

The female Ph.D. student's education and training, combined with her pretenure years, coincide with prime childbearing age (Shrier and Shrier 2009). As women age, their fertility rates are reduced and their offspring become more vulnerable to genetic disorders. A woman who waits until she accomplishes tenure risks the possibility of never having children or of creating significant risks to her future offspring. Knowing this, some women forgo having children (Mason and Goulden 2004). Other women delay having children during this time period to increase their likelihood of success at their jobs, but risk never having children as a result. Others have children, but at considerable risk to their careers. Those who have children have less time to devote to their research and teaching because of the physical difficulties of pregnancies, childbirth, and postpartum periods, to say nothing of subsequent periods of childcare.

As a matter of biology, men, in contrast, do not suffer the choice between delaying or never having children and suffering from lower productivity. Furthermore, it is considered socially much more acceptable for a mother to take time off to care for a child once he or she is born than it is for a father to do so. These social pressures, combined with concepts of male masculinity that emphasize breadwinning, often place mothers in two-parent homes in a position that requires them to choose between caregiving and careers.

When social factors are added to biological differences in bearing children, the disparate impact on women is great. The placement of a trial period early in a man's career benefits the man who heads a traditional family with a wife or partner who not only bears the children but also rears them. The mother's labor grants the father the opportunity to focus on his career. Women in academia often lack similar support, and therefore suffer a disadvantage that is enhanced by the demanding, inflexible, short time lines of the "up or out" tenure clock (Armenti 2004).

Moreover, society conceives of men as breadwinners, and men construct their masculine identities by competing in the workplace as breadwinners (Collinson 1988). The hard-driving, competitive atmosphere reinforces the masculine self-concept of many men. Society reinforces men's belief that men benefit their families by working extremely hard, even if working long hours causes men to neglect their families (Wallace and Young 2008).

Women are socialized differently than men. Society conceives of women as caregivers. While society rewards a man who spends all his time at work for being a good family man (based on his ability to be a good breadwinner), society views a woman who spends the same amount of time working as harmful to the family rather than supportive of it (Williams 2001).

Moreover, heterosexual mothers with equally as demanding careers as their partners' are expected to spend more time with their families and working in the home (Shrier and Shrier 2009; Wolfinger, Goulden, and Mason 2009; Wolfinger, Mason, and Goulden 2008; Wallace and Young 2008; Mason and Goulden 2004; Hochschild 1989). At the same time, employers often view a woman who struggles to accommodate both the needs of her family and those of her workplace as not committed to work (Armenti 2004; Williams 2001).

In lesbian partnerships and single-parent homes, the "up or out" processes also present a problem. While academia can be more tolerant of nontraditional lifestyles, the tenure-track structure is unforgiving, with a disparate effect on women. The ability to do research at home draws many who have childcare and homecare responsibilities, but the tenure track forces those who have these responsibilities to work on a short and inflexible timetable that clashes with the biological clock of many women.

Evidence of the disparate effects of the tenure process on women is startling. Recent studies demonstrate that men with babies entering their households *within* five years of receiving their Ph.D.s are 38 percent more likely than their female counterparts to receive tenure (Mason and Goulden 2004). Moreover, only one in every three women who takes a tenure-track university job before having children will ever become a mother (ibid.). Women with tenure are twice as likely as their male colleagues to be single twelve years after receiving their Ph.D.s, and women who are married when they begin their academic careers are much more likely to be divorced or separated from their spouses than their male counterparts are (ibid.). These statistics measure both the biological and the social constraints on women who attempt to further a career in academia.

Perhaps more telling is the proliferation of adjunct teaching jobs in academia that are not tenure-track jobs. Academics holding these positions are considered second-class citizens. They have low pay, long hours, and little job security. These positions have increased as the percentage of women entering academia has risen. While 22 percent of female faculty members hold these positions, only 11 percent of male faculty members hold non-tenure-track academic positions (Wolfinger, Goulden, and Mason 2009). Mothers with children under six years old are "disproportionately likely to have adjunct professorships" (ibid., 1612). Research demonstrates that women who leave the tenure track to work in non-tenure-track positions are sometimes hired into tenure-track positions after their children grow up, but many are not (ibid.). The combination of gender and family formation clearly harms a woman's ability to succeed in traditional academic tenure-track positions that have a rigid "up or out" structure.

In an "up or out" situation, courts should permit plaintiffs to use a variety of types of evidence to establish a prima facie case of disparate impact. The law requires that a plaintiff prove that the employer uses a particular employment practice that causes a disparate impact on a protected group. Plaintiffs should attack the short "up or out" track as the particular employment practice that causes the differential between the success rates of men and women at tenure time. As permitted in *Dothard v. Rawlinson*, plaintiffs should present national statistics to prove their case (*Dothard v. Rawlinson* 1977). National statistics will demonstrate a significant difference in success rates in achieving tenure for women and men in academia. The plaintiffs should also present evidence that an inflexible tenure track and a differential between men's and women's success rates exists in the plaintiff's workplace.

They should supplement this evidence with social science testimony that explains why the rigid "up or out" track causes the differential. The social science evidence should demonstrate not only the biological burdens women encounter when bearing children but also the extra social burdens shared by women with children who work outside of the home.

Masculinities expert testimony would educate the judge and jury about the benefits that men as a group receive from "up or out" structures and the harm these structures do to women as a group. This testimony would explain the importance of a man's role as breadwinner to society's judgment of men and the adoption of this view by individual men themselves. This stereotype, translated into a structure in workplaces, is visible in "up or out" tracks and harms women as a group. This evidence should be sufficient for most courts to recognize the burdens that the "up or out" process places on women's careers.

Some respondents will probably argue that the plaintiffs are attempting to hold the university responsible for societal discrimination. In the equal protection cases, the Court has made clear that societal discrimination does not justify a remedy based on a racial classification (*Wygant v. Jackson Board of Education* 1986). Unlike in the affirmative action cases in which a conscious race- or gender-based remedy is requested of the court, however, the "up or out" cases do not seek a gender- or race-based remedy. And, the facts in the "up or out" cases are not significantly different from those in *Griggs*.

In *Griggs*, the Court held the employer responsible for testing mechanisms that screened out black employees who presumably failed the test because of an inferior education due to societal discrimination in imposing poor, segregated schools upon blacks (*Griggs v. Duke Power Co.* 1971). While the employer was responsible, it was not judged morally culpable. The Court saw the disparate impact cause of action as necessary to encourage employers to eliminate non-job-related employer practices that created barriers to blacks as a result of past discrimination against blacks in society. In the case of "up or out" structures, the plaintiffs would ask the courts to strike down a process that, without moral culpability of the employer, builds arbitrary barriers against women who have children or wish to have children.

Proof of a disparate impact on women would shift the burden to the employer to prove either that it did not use an "up or out" system or that it ameliorated it by implementing policies that stopped the tenure clock during a woman's pregnancy and childcaring years. Or, if it used an "up or out" process, the employer would have to prove that the "up or out" process is related to the job in question and consistent with business necessity. Whether a university employer could meet this burden is unclear. The university would probably argue that one of its core missions is research and that it is vital that a faculty member be seriously engaged in research early on in order to promote the faculty member's and the university's reputations. Similarly, good teaching is crucial to the university and the "up or out" process allows the faculty to assure that the individuals engaged in the teaching and research mission of the university are excellent. Finally, the "up or out" track allows the university to assure that the individuals' academic freedom is protected.

Although a court might accept the university's defense, there are good reasons why it would not. The American Association of University Professors recommends that universities and colleges adopt "general policies addressing family responsibilities, including family care leaves and institutional support for child and elder care" and "more specific policies, such as stopping the tenure track, that relate directly to untenured faculty members who are primary or coequal caregivers" (AAUP 2006b, 220). It recommends that universities permit untenured faculty caregivers to stop the tenure clock one year each for the birth or adoption of a child up to a maximum of two years total (ibid.). This recommendation would permit untenured faculty members who have children to continue to work full-time and draw full-time salaries while the tenure clock is stopped.

An increasing number of prestigious universities and colleges have adopted this recommendation and other family-friendly policies (Pribbenow et al. 2010; Wilson 2008; University of Michigan Center for the Education of Women 2007). While tenure may be job related and necessary to the business of academia, the existence of these "stop the clock" policies in many highly ranked institutions demonstrates that the short five- or six-year track may not be necessary or job related.

Even if a court concludes that a short tenure track is job related and is a business necessity, the plaintiff in a disparate impact case has the option of proving that an alternative exists that has a less discriminatory impact on women that will be equally effective in furthering the university's goals of promoting excellence. The plaintiffs can demonstrate that an "up or out" process that includes flexibility for parents (women and men) who have childcare responsibilities would not undermine excellence in teaching and research. They can present evidence of prestigious universities that have adopted the AAUP's recommendation to stop the tenure clock that have not lost prestige or scholarship as a result.

Some universities and colleges apply the "stop-the-tenure-clock" policies more equitably than others. For example, while some schools do not require those stopping the clock to produce additional scholarship during the time period while the clock is stopped, others expect additional scholarship of the candidate, a practice that defeats the purpose of stopping the clock in the first place. Still others review a candidate negatively merely because he or she has stopped the tenure clock (Thornton 2005). Furthermore, in some institutions, the family-friendly policies are allocated only to those women who are perceived to be "the best and the brightest" (Spalter-Roth and Erskine 2005, 19). These practices are not less discriminatory alternatives that should be adopted. Instead, the plaintiff should focus on those universities that apply the policies in equitable manners. Making reference to programs at these universities, especially if there are studies demonstrating that these processes are equally as effective in achieving the university's goal, would be particularly useful.

Training Programs with Hidden Curricula

Masculinities studies may also reveal and recognize as harmful hidden (or not so hidden) messages sent to women in predominantly male blue-collar environments. For example, in *"There Oughta Be a Law against Bitches": Masculinity Lessons in Police Academy Training,* Anastasia Prokos and Irene Padavic describe an ethnographic study of the overt and hidden curricula of a police academy's training program in a midsized city in the United States. While the overt curriculum taught gender equality, the hidden curriculum allowed men to construct their masculine identities in the police academy program by distinguishing themselves from women in the program, treating women as outsiders, exaggerating gender differences, denigrating and objectifying women, and resisting powerful women with authority (Prokos and Padavic 2002). Male instructors and students demonstrated that they considered themselves superior to the women by using gendered language and male-centric examples when describing how to do police work. Male students used the classrooms as male-bonding experiences. The men glorified violence and associated it with masculinity. They exaggerated the differences between men and women and resisted the authority of female instructors.

The authors concluded that the men created informal barriers between themselves and the women to counter the threat to their masculinity of women's entry into a male profession (ibid.). They opined that "[s]ome male resistance stems from women's disruption of male bonding and the equation of masculine men with masculine work" (ibid., 454). Male students and instructors used the women's presence to "aid in their construction of divisions along gender lines" (ibid.). The resistance helped the men sustain the gender status quo (ibid.). The authors concluded that the resistance may have been exaggerated because the male police academy instructors and students' identities align with a type of masculinity that is associated with violence and control. "Control over institutionalized violence is a core component of men's authority in western cultures. Thus, while police culture, like the culture of many other male-dominated occupations, defines itself through masculinity, it is perhaps the association not only with masculinity, but also with violence that leads men to resist women in policing" (ibid., 455).

This study describes an employer practice—the requirement that recruits attend a training program—that is neutral in that it overtly prohibits discrimination, but that actually has a disparate effect on women who attend the training. While the study does not say whether women performed less well than men in the training program or in their employment as cops as a result of the training program, a showing of an adverse effect on hiring or promotional opportunities should not be necessary in order to tackle the program through disparate impact theory. Although the Supreme Court has never confronted the issue of whether employees can attack employer practices under 42 U.S.C. § 2000e-2 (a)(1) by pointing to terms or conditions of employment that adversely affect a protected group, lower courts have held before and after the passage of the 1991 Civil Rights Act that litigants can employ disparate impact theory to attack terms and conditions of employment having an adverse effect on a protected group under Section 2000e-2 (a) (1) of the Act (*Johnson v. AK Steel Corp.* 2008; *E.E.O.C. v. Beauty Enterprises, Inc.* 2005; *E.E.O.C. v. Premier Operator Services, Inc.* 2000; *Garcia v. Woman's Hospital of Texas* 1996; *Garcia v. Spun Steak Co.* 1993; *Scherr v. Woodland School Community Consolidated District No. 50* 1988; *E.E.O.C. v. J. C. Penney Co.* 1988; *Colby v. J.C. Penney Co.* 1987; *Lynch v. Freeman* 1987; *Wambheim v. J.C. Penny Co.* 1983).[2]

In cases challenging English-only rules (*E.E.O.C. v. Beauty Enterprises, Inc.* 2005; *E.E.O.C. v. Premier Operator Services, Inc.* 2000; *Garcia v. Spun Steak* 1993) and the failure to provide clean rest room facilities (*Johnson v. AK Steel Corp.* 2008; *DeClue v. Central Illinois Light Co.* 2000; *Lynch v. Freeman* 1987), for example, courts have resisted the defense that a disparate impact cause of action can be brought only to attack barriers to hiring and promotions under Section 2000e-2 (a)(2) of Title VII, which prohibits discriminatory classification or segregation of employees.[3] Moreover, the legislative history of the 1991 Civil Rights Act appears to presume that disparate impact litigation can challenge terms and conditions of employment under 2000e-2 (a)(1) (137 Congressional Record S15,489; Jolls 2001; Chen 1994). The EEOC appears to agree with this conclusion (EEOC Guidelines on Discrimination Because of National Origin, 29 C.F.R. 16067.7 and 45 FR 85635).

Because the plaintiffs' challenge under 2000e-2(a)(1) is that the terms or conditions of employment have an adverse effect on women, the plaintiffs would use their own testimony combined with social science expert testimony of the harm caused by the training program to demonstrate that the employer's practice has a disparate impact on women at work (*E.E.O.C. v. Beauty Enterprises Inc.* 2005; *E.E.O.C. v. Premier Operators Services Inc.* 2000; *Lynch v. Freeman* 1987). Statistics that prove a differential in success rates in the training program between women and men would be helpful, but not necessary. When the challenge is to terms or conditions of employment, the best evidence may be the testimony of the plaintiffs, combined with expert testimony.

In *Lynch v. Freeman*, for example, the Sixth Circuit accepted the female employees' testimony in a case alleging that dirty removable toilets had a disparate impact on women because women testified that they had difficulty using the toilets in a sanitary fashion and presented expert medical testimony about the disparate effect the unsanitary conditions had on female workers (*Lynch v. Freeman* 1987). Likewise, in *Johnson v. AK Steel*, the court held that the plaintiff's testimony that the defendant provided no break time over a twelve-hour shift to visit restrooms, that the male employees urinated over the side of the truck, and that she was told to urinate in the same manner created a genuine issue of material fact as to whether the failure to provide break time and restrooms created a disparate impact on women (*Johnson v. AK Steel Corp.* 2008).

In *E.E.O.C. v. Premier Operator Services*, the court held that English-only rules created a disparate impact on bilingual Latino telephone operators who were hired to speak Spanish to clients on the telephone but who were forbidden from speaking Spanish between the telephone calls and during breaks. The plaintiff class established that the rule caused a disparate impact on workers whose national origin was a Spanish-speaking country through the expert testimony of a linguist who testified that native speakers unconsciously engage in "code-switching" into their native language with other native speakers and that class members switched from one language to another unknowingly. Because this "code-switching" was unconscious, Hispanic employees were subjected to risk of reprimands or firings on the basis of their speaking Spanish inadvertently, and the English-only policy posed no such comparable risk to non-Hispanic employees (*E.E.O.C. v. Premier Operator Services Inc.* 2000; *see also E.E.O.C. v. Beauty Enterprises Inc.* 2005 (permitting plaintiffs to prove disparate impact caused by "English only" rule by using testimony of expert on code-switching)).

In a case brought by women challenging the training in the police academy, similar expert testimony from masculinities experts that attacks discriminatory terms and conditions of employment under 2000e-2(a)(1) would make masculine practices in police training visible and detail the effects of the hidden curricula in the police academy on women. This testimony should establish a disparate impact based on sex or gender, either alone or in combination with race, class, sexual orientation, or gender identity.

Once the disparate impact is established, the burden of proof shifts to the defendant to demonstrate that the training program is job related and consistent with business necessity. While the training program is concededly job related and necessary to the business of policing, the plaintiffs attack the hidden curriculum that sends the message to their male colleagues and to the female trainees that women are inferior; they do not attack the fact of training itself. It would be highly unlikely that the defendant could argue that the hidden curriculum is job related or consistent with business necessity. Nevertheless, if the court were to look at the entire training program and conclude that it is job related and consistent with business necessity, the burden would shift to the plaintiffs to prove that a less discriminatory training program was available to the defendant and the defendant refused to adopt it. This proof should not be difficult. There is no issue that the training program, absent the hidden curriculum, would be less discriminatory and would be equally effective.

Defendant's responsibility for the hidden curriculum in the training is obvious. The hidden curriculum is part of a program required for entry into the police force. If the employer claims that it is impossible to screen out the hidden gender bias in the curriculum, the employees would have a good argument that the employer condoned the behaviors used by male students and instructors to resist the female students' presence, to establish superiority of men in the job, and to discourage women from continuing in the profession. The hidden curriculum also reifies a particular species of aggressive, heterosexual, and, at times, violent masculinity over other types of masculinity. Students and instructors use terms such as "pussy" to refer to nonmasculine men, a term that refers in derogatory fashion to a woman's genitals, and show students a film with a man dreaming about a sexually available and attractive woman (Prokos and Padavic 2002). This behavior, which is unrelated to the content of the training, not only threatens the dignity of the women but also may have an adverse effect on men who do not subscribe to violent, aggressive sexuality because of their gender.

Police recruits may also have success attacking the training program through a disparate treatment/sex- or gender-based harassment analysis, by arguing that the training program created a hostile work environment for the women because of their sex. I discuss hostile work environment law in part II above, but in short, to make a prima facie case, the plaintiffs would have to demonstrate that the behavior was unwelcome, severe or pervasive, and that it occurred because of their sex (*Faragher v. City of Boca Raton* 1988). While the training program should fit the hostile work environment model, and employees challenging the training program should allege hostile work environment and disparate impact, courts have aggressively granted summary judgment in hostile work environment cases, holding as a matter of law that the behavior is insufficiently severe or pervasive to alter the terms or conditions of employment (McGinley 2008; Beiner 2005, 1999).

Some courts may conclude that the training program in this case creates a disparate impact on the women recruits but does not reach the level of a hostile work environment that is sufficiently severe or pervasive to alter the terms and conditions of employment. Moreover, the different remedies provided in disparate treatment and disparate impact cases may justify different standards. Plaintiffs may collect punitive and compensatory damages in disparate treatment cases in addition to the equitable remedies traditionally granted, including back pay, injunctive relief, declaratory relief, and attorney's fees and costs (Civil Rights Act 1991). Punitive and compensatory damages are not available, however, upon a showing of disparate impact (ibid.). Thus, it would make sense for courts to hold employers liable for disparate impact in some cases where they are hesitant to find the employer liable for a hostile work environment.

Hiring and Promotion Qualifications Reflecting Hegemonic Masculinity: Competitiveness and Aggressiveness

Masculinities research may also aid employees arguing that the employer's neutral hiring and promotion qualifications have a disparate impact based on the intersection of race and gender. These qualifications, as interpreted by an employer through a stereotyped lens, will disparately affect the hiring and promotion opportunities of women or men who do not conform to the hegemonic view of masculinity because of their gender and race.

Consider the hiring of personnel to sell used cars. The employer's image of a used car salesman is a white man who acts in a competitive and aggressive fashion. Thus, the employer searching for new sales personnel may consider aggression and competitiveness as qualifications for the job. These qualifications are gender and race neutral, but they will probably have a disparate effect on white, Asian, and Latino women, black men and women, and gender-nonconforming white men and those men of color, particularly Asian men, who are perceived as effeminate (Chang 2012).

Identity studies explain that because of stereotypes, human beings expect different behaviors from different people. Society expects white women to be less competitive and aggressive than their male counterparts, but it attributes anger to black women and expects them to be more aggressive than white women (McGinley 2009a). Nonetheless, in contrast to an aggressive and competitive white man who would receive a job offer, a black woman who is equally aggressive and competitive would probably not receive the offer because of the negative stereotype of black women as angry, dangerous, and hypersexual. Society expects black men to be threatening, violent, angry, and aggressive but expects Asian men to be passive, quiet, and effeminate (Cooper 2009, 2006; Carbado and Gulati 2001; Chen 1996).

These stereotypes affect our perception of how a job applicant would behave at work and distort the employer's view of the applicant when the employer is matching the applicant to the stated qualifications of competitiveness and aggressiveness. Of course, much of this screening may occur in the unconscious cognitive processing of the person doing the hiring. Expert evidence of implicit bias and masculinities research would be useful to explain to the jury how the employer's procedures may encourage supervisors to engage in discrimination. Some plaintiffs who are rejected for the job may prove that the specific employment requirements of competitiveness and aggressiveness harmed them. But for others, the plaintiffs may have to demonstrate that is it a combination of the stated qualifications and the application of those qualifications to particular identities that caused their rejection. The plaintiffs would argue that the qualifications, combined with implicit biases, poisoned the hiring decisions, thereby creating a preference for white men and having a disparate impact on women and men of color.

The stereotype that white women are passive, caring, unaggressive, and uncompetitive is both descriptive and prescriptive. People believe that white women fit the stereotype and that white women *should* fit the stereotype. So, a white woman who applies for a job as salesperson will be presumed to be inadequately aggressive and competitive to do the job. If, however, she demonstrates aggression and competitiveness equal to the men applying for the job, because of the prescriptive stereotype, the employer will probably judge her differently for her failure to comply with the stereotypes of white women (Heilman et al. 2004; Eagly and Karau 2002; Foschi, Lai, and Sigerson 1994; Butler and Geis 1990). In this event, the interviewer will probably refuse to hire her precisely because she meets the job qualifications. This scenario is similar to that in *Price Waterhouse*, where Ann Hopkins experienced a double bind because her job required her to act aggressively but the partners did not like aggressive women.

Chicanas and other Latina women may have an even more difficult experience than white women. The good/bad woman stereotypes are particularly compelling in the Mexican American community, so a Chicana who resists the stereotype of passivity and submissiveness in the business world to prove that she can perform the job may risk disapproval not only of a potential employer but also of her community, and even a threat to her own self-identity (Niemann 2001).

Unlike those of white women, stereotypes of black women and men are descriptive, but not prescriptive. Thus, the black man and black woman may have to play a role to defeat the negative stereotypes of danger, aggression, and anger. A black man applying for the job who demonstrates equal competitiveness and aggression to that of the white male applicants because of the descriptive stereotypes of black males may be considered more aggressive and competitive than the white male applicants. He may not get the job because his perceived aggressiveness and competitiveness make him appear to his interviewer as threatening (Carbado and Gulati 2013, 2001; Cooper 2009, 2006). Black women, although stereotypically considered aggressive, a quality that the job description may call for, may also be considered angry and dangerous and therefore unacceptable to the employer. The black female applicant is in a double bind because to the extent that she plays the "good black woman"—the motherly Aunt Jemima type—she will probably not be considered appropriate for the job.

Asian men suffer from a "good Asian" and "bad Asian" stereotype of their own. Good Asian men are feminine and child-like, never aggressive. Bad Asian men are devious and violent (Chen 1996). In both cases, the stereotypes will make it very difficult for Asian men to compete for the job of car salesman. Anthony Chen explained that the Asian American men he interviewed dealt with the hegemonic ideal by using four different coping methods, some of which actually reinforced the hegemony of white men. They engaged in compensation, deflection, denial, and repudiation. Only the last coping method countered the hegemonic ideal and fought the oppression that the Asian American men experienced (Chen 1999).

The stereotypes of white women and persons of color will affect the way they are viewed, how they respond to certain behaviors, and how those responses are interpreted. Thus, job or promotional requirements that are linked unconsciously or consciously to the dominant white male, such as aggression and competitiveness, are problematic.

Masculinities and other social science studies can demonstrate that the qualifications of competitiveness and aggression required by the car dealership have a disparate impact on white women and persons of color. In fact, these standards are based on the hegemonic white man as the measuring stick, and while they may predict success in white men, they are not the only qualities that predict success.

The employer will respond by attempting to demonstrate that aggressiveness and competitiveness are job related and consistent with business necessity. Because judges often state that they do not sit as "super personnel officers," they may be likely to conclude that employers had made out the affirmative defense (*Kipp v. Missouri Highway and Transportation Commission* 2002; *Harvey v. Anheuser-Busch, Inc.*1994). This holding would shift the burden to the plaintiffs to prove that a less discriminatory alternative exists.

The opportunity to prove that a less discriminatory alternative exists may offer these plaintiffs a chance to demonstrate that even without characteristics such as competitiveness or aggression, a salesperson can perform the job well. In fact, men's attempts to prove their masculinity through aggression and competitiveness may lead to less, rather than more, productive work environments.

Studies by organizational experts Robin Ely and Debra Meyerson may aid plaintiffs in proving less discriminatory alternatives where the employer requires or tolerates masculine behaviors. In *An Organizational Approach to Undoing Gender*, Ely and Meyerson theorize that organizations have the capacity to "undo gender" (Ely and Meyerson 2010). They studied the working environments of two oil rigs (the "safety-first" oil rigs) whose management had adopted strong safety policies and compared them to the working atmospheres of oil rigs that had not adopted the safety policies (the "conventional" oil rigs). On the conventional oil rigs, the men showed off their physical prowess, idealized physical strength and likened weakness to being a woman, demonstrated bravado in the presence of physical dangers, projected images of sexual potency and technical competence, and displayed emotional detachment toward others. The men working on the safety-first rigs described by Ely and Meyerson, in contrast, developed close interpersonal relationships, openly admitted their mistakes, and showed sensitivity toward others. Ely and Meyerson found that the safety-first initiative led to an 84 percent decline in the accident rate and a simultaneous increase in productivity (ibid.).

If Ely and Meyerson's results can be replicated in other workplaces, they would suggest that eliminating masculine aggression and competition is a less discriminatory alternative because it improves relationships among workers and enhances productivity. Expert testimony by these researchers or others who have made similar findings would help plaintiffs prove that there are less discriminatory, effective alternatives to aggressive, competitive behaviors.

Ameliorating Masculinities through Disparate Impact

This chapter proposes the use of disparate impact theory under Title VII of the Civil Rights Act to challenge the presence of masculine structures and practices in workplaces that create barriers to women, men of color, and gender-nonconforming men. Because the harm done by masculine structures and practices is often invisible and unintentional, disparate impact theory, which holds employers responsible for facially neutral policies or practices that unintentionally create a disparate impact on protected groups, is a vehicle that may prove successful in attacking invisible but harmful structures and practices.[4]

Next, part IV discusses the theoretical, legal, and practical aspects of educating judges and juries to the key role that concepts of masculinity play in the workforce. It also discusses how employers should eliminate masculine structures and practices.

Practical Considerations

Experts and Evidentiary Constructs

Chapters 1 through 8 described the law and legal constructs applied to Title VII cases and discussed how masculinities theory can provide valuable information to judges and juries deciding employment discrimination cases. In this part, chapter 9 deals with the theoretical, legal, and practical considerations surrounding the use of masculinities research to provide a different lens or perspective through which judges and juries can view the occurrences in these cases. Specifically, it explains that common sense alone is not a sufficient tool with which to analyze employment discrimination cases involving race and gender issues, and argues that legal actors need to rely on expert witnesses to understand hidden gendered and racialized structures and actions. Moreover, it explains why and under what conditions these expert opinions should be presented in court. Finally, it argues that judges should receive judicial education on masculinities theory so that they are informed to decide motions to dismiss, and for summary judgment, and that judges and lawyers should work together to create jury instructions that would incorporate understandings from masculinities theory. The conclusion analyzes how employers should eliminate masculinities from their workforces.

9

Educating Judges and Juries about Masculinities

The Necessity of Experts to Counter Common Sense

All lawyers know that expert testimony is necessary to help fact finders and judges understand the science in a patent case, or whether a surgeon followed a procedure that is acceptable to the surgical community in a medical malpractice case. But many lawyers and judges assume that fact finders and judges can deploy their own common sense, without aid from expert testimony, when deciding cases brought under the antidiscrimination laws. The claim is that because all members of society make judgments in their daily work lives about the behaviors and motivations of others, fact finders and judges should also employ their common sense in determining whether the defendant discriminated against the plaintiff because of the individual's sex, gender, or race. The assumption is that deciding whether a person has discriminated against another on the basis of her protected characteristics is a simple calculus.

But research demonstrates that this decision is not at all simple (Fiske and Borgida 2011). There is established and increasingly more complicated science behind human motivation, intent, and behavior (Banaji and Greenwald 2013; Greenwald and Banaji 1995; Kimmel 2013; Greenwald et al. 2009). In essence, the view that antidiscrimination law needs no expert testimony operates on assumptions, often hidden or unconscious, about the prevalence of discriminatory decision making in workplaces (Weiss 2011; Calloway 1994). These assumptions include views that we live in a postracial society and that sex discrimination is a thing of the past. On the basis of lived experience, each juror brings assumptions into the jury box. Judges and lawyers make assumptions about the meanings and causes of certain employer behaviors that may affect lawyers' strategies, the way judges rule on motions and instruct juries, and the way fact finders decide whether discrimination has occurred.

Common sense can lead lawyers, judges, and juries astray. Masculinities experts must explain how the plaintiff's mistreatment in the workplace

is linked to gender, combined with race and other factors. This testimony is
often crucial to the courts' and juries' understanding of the workplace and
the way they should draw inferences in a discrimination suit.

Testimony of masculinities research by a qualified expert sociologist or social psychologist is admissible, relevant, and highly probative. Although the Supreme Court expressed some hesitancy about
the use of social framework evidence in *Wal-Mart v. Dukes* (2011), it
is still possible to use reliable expert testimony in these cases to get
to the truth.

Admissibility of Expert Testimony

The trial court acts as a responsible gatekeeper to assure exclusion of
unreliable expert testimony (Advisory Committee Notes 2000; *Kumho
Tire Co. Ltd. v. Carmichael* 1999; *Daubert v. Merrell Dow Pharmaceuticals, Inc.* 1993). Federal Rule of Evidence 702 governs the admissibility of
expert testimony; it assures knowledge and expertise of the expert, use
of accepted principles and methodology, that the testimony is based on
sufficient facts, and that the expert has applied accepted principles to
the facts (Federal Rules of Evidence 2011 Amendments, Rule 702). The
rule permits the use of testimony by sociologists and social psychologists who rely on peer-reviewed articles and methodologies acceptable
to their professions (*Tyus v. Urban Search Management* 1996) (overturn-
ing the lower court's failure to admit a sociologist's expert testimony
about the effect of television advertising on African American viewers
in a housing discrimination case).

Moreover, the 2000 amendment to Rule 702 did not alter "the venerable practice of using expert testimony to educate the fact finder on general principles" (ibid.). For this generalized type of expert testimony, the
party offering the expert merely needs to demonstrate that (1) the expert
is qualified; (2) the testimony addresses a subject matter on which an
expert can assist the fact finder; (3) the testimony is reliable; and (4) the
testimony fits the facts of the case (ibid.).

Given these standards, expert testimony by reputable, well-trained
sociologists or social psychologists who are engaged in empirical or
ethnographic research or who use other social scientists' peer-reviewed
empirical or ethnographic research to reach conclusions about the pres-

ence of masculine structures, performances, or practices in workplaces in a Title VII suit will normally be reliable under Rule 702 and helpful to the judge and jury.

Social Framework Evidence

In accordance with the standards of Rule 702, if properly instructed by the judge, jurors should receive expert social framework evidence offered by a party at trial and incorporate it into their decision making. "Social framework evidence" is not a scientific term; the term relates to the use of social science evidence in litigation (Brief of *Amici Curiae* of the American Sociological Association and the Law and Society Association in *Wal-Mart Stores, Inc. v. Dukes* 2011). When used in litigation, social framework testimony is offered by an expert who gives a background of social science research that meets the criteria of reliability to the fact finder and may or may not link that research to the employer's workplace. If it does not link the research to the workplace, this is the "venerable" use of the expert to educate the jury on general principles, a practice that the Rules Committee clearly approved of when it wrote the 2000 amendment to Rule 702 (Advisory Committee Notes 2000).

In *Wal-Mart v. Dukes*, the plaintiffs alleged that supervisors' use of discretionary, subjective decision making caused a pattern and practice of discriminatory decisions against women (*Wal-Mart Stores, Inc. v. Dukes* 2011). The issue before the U.S. Supreme Court was whether the lower court correctly certified a class of 1.5 million women. Specifically, the defendant argued that the class action plaintiffs could not meet the "commonality" of claims requirement of Federal Rule of Civil Procedure 23, the provision that provides for certification of class actions, given that the plaintiffs did not share a common supervisor or work in the same stores. The Court stated that to prove commonality, the plaintiffs would have to demonstrate that Wal-Mart "operated under a general policy of discrimination'" (ibid., 2553). In fact, the Court noted, there was no explicit policy of discrimination, and the statistics demonstrating that women were left behind in promotions and pay were insufficient to conclude that there were common questions of fact in the case.

In that setting, five justices of the Supreme Court criticized the plaintiffs' use of an expert, Dr. William Bielby, a sociologist, who testified that Wal-Mart has a "'strong corporate culture'" that makes it "'vulnerable'" to "gender bias'" (ibid.). Justices Roberts, Scalia, Alito, Thomas, and Kennedy concluded that because Dr. Bielby could not estimate the percentages of employment decisions that were caused by stereotypes, the Court did not have to consider Dr. Bielby's testimony. This decision led to discussion among scholars and practitioners about the admissibility of social framework evidence.

"Applied" and "Pure" Social Framework Evidence

While there is dispute about the terminology used to describe the evidence, I use the terms introduced by Deborah Weiss: "pure" social framework evidence and "applied" social framework evidence (Weiss 2011).

Experts present "pure" social framework evidence in court to give jurors and judges a background on an issue in the case without commenting on how that evidence would apply to the particular case. There seems to be little or no disagreement about the legitimacy of pure social framework evidence, but there is concern that some courts have ruled out this evidence as irrelevant or, if they conclude that the evidence is relevant, have found that the prejudicial effect outweighs its relevancy under Federal Rules of Evidence 402 and 403 (ibid.). Nonetheless, the Advisory Committee Notes to Amended Federal Rule of Evidence 702 clarify that it contemplates the continued use of "pure" social framework evidence when it states that the 2000 amendment did not alter the "venerable" practice of using an expert to educate the jury on general principles, using general information (Advisory Committee Notes 2000). If the expert testimony meets the four requirements of the rule noted above, this evidence should be admitted. An objection that the prejudicial value of the evidence outweighs its probative value should ordinarily not succeed in this situation because this objection appears to be interposed merely to create doubt about the intrinsic value of the opinion or the conclusion itself.

"Applied" social framework evidence goes one step beyond "pure" social framework evidence. The expert explains the research and, *without opining as to the bottom line in the case*—whether the defendant illegally discriminated against the plaintiff or plaintiffs—loosely links the social framework evidence to other evidence concerning the employer's behavior in the particular case (Weiss 2011). For example, the plaintiffs' expert in a class action may explain to the jury about the prevalence of hidden bias and stereotypes that affect decision making in society and in organizations and testify that defendant's particular policies may have permitted its supervisors to resort to hidden prejudices or stereotypes in promotional decisions. It is this latter type of "applied" social framework evidence that the Supreme Court appears to have rejected for purposes of determining whether to certify the class in *Wal-Mart*.

In *Wal-Mart*, the Court cited to a 2008 article, "Contextual Evidence of Gender Discrimination: The Ascendance of 'Social Frameworks,'" by John Monahan, Laurens Walker, and Gregory Mitchell, who argue that Dr. Bielby's testimony legitimately offered statements about the research into implicit biases and stereotypes, but went beyond this pure evidence and illegitimately applied it to the facts specific to Wal-Mart's mode of operation. While Monahan and his coauthors agree that pure social framework evidence can be used to give background information about research results to the fact finders, they conclude that applied social framework evidence does "not meet the standards expected of social scientific research into stereotyping and discrimination" (Monahan, Walker, and Mitchell 2008, 1745). To meet those standards, the authors conclude, the plaintiff's expert would have to conduct scientific research on a specific issue before the fact finder.

Monahan, Walker, and Mitchell agree that experts can present pure social framework evidence under Federal Rule of Evidence 702, which requires that the testimony be based on "sufficient facts or data" (Federal Rules of Evidence 2015). But they argue that applied social framework evidence is inapplicable and inadmissible under Rule 702 because it does not follow the prescribed scientific methods that assure validity (ibid.).

Social Facts versus Social Frameworks

Monahan, Walker, and Mitchell argue that there are approved scientific methods that experts can use that would ensure the reliability of specific testimony related to the defendant's workplace without compromising scientific accuracy (Mitchell, Walker, and Monahan 2011). They call this type of applied evidence "social facts." They argue that "because social facts involve case-specific claims, social facts require the application of sound methods and principles to case-specific data to reach descriptive and causal conclusions about the case at hand" (ibid., 1117–18). An example of "social facts" data that is used widely in employment discrimination cases is a statistical analysis of the workforce conducted by an expert statistician, which is often used in pattern and practice cases to demonstrate that the employer discriminates as a course of conduct based on the protected characteristic.

Besides statistical studies, they argue, plaintiffs' experts may use testers to apply for positions in the workplace, perform observational studies of case records by systematically coding the records with reference to a research hypothesis, or conduct a study of a third party that is similar to the defendant when it comes to the research subjects, setting, and timing. Some coding studies would not require the collection of new data, they contend, but would require that data already in existence and produced to the plaintiffs through discovery be "systematically reviewed using reliable qualitative *and* quantitative social science techniques" (ibid., 1127–28).

Of course, many of these suggestions may not be feasible in many employment discrimination cases. In individual cases and class actions, issues of cost, potential contamination of the evidence, and defendants' refusal to grant access to their workforces for experimentation may arise if plaintiffs were to ask permission from their opponents to permit experts to conduct observations of or experiments on employees at the defendant's workplace (Hart and Secunda 2009).

Judging Reliability of Social Science Research

Monahan, Walker, and Mitchell's contentions, however, are controversial in the scientific community. A significant number of well-known social scientists and their scholarly organizations disagree with Monahan, Walker, and Mitchell. Scholars who are engaged in substantial research have successfully used applied social framework evidence in a number of high-profile employment discrimination cases (ibid.). Moreover, scholarly scientific associations vouch for the scientific reliability of well-executed social science research that can be presented in court (Brief of *Amici Curiae* American Sociological Association and the Law and Society Association in *Wal-Mart Stores, Inc. v. Dukes* 2011).

Psychologists who are engaged in both research and expert testimony concerning the issue of stereotyping stress that their work is scientifically reliable and methodologically sound. Under *Daubert v. Merrell Dow Pharmaceuticals, Inc.* (1993) and its progeny, the work of the expert must be "empirically tested, peer-reviewed and published, represent scientific consensus, and have a known error rate" (Fiske and Borgida 2011). Susan Fiske and Eugene Borgida, very active social science researchers who testified at the trials in *Price Waterhouse v. Hopkins* (1989) and *Jenson v. Eveleth Taconite Co.* (1997), respectively, maintain that they and other social scientists attain quality control through peer review, scientific consensus shown through surveys of experts, quantitative review literature or meta-analysis, qualitative review, adversarial collaboration, and/or the commission of consensus documents by professional societies (Fiske and Borgida 2011).

Fiske and Borgida conclude that these methods go well beyond the "commonsense" approach to behavior that happens in legal cases absent scientific expert testimony (ibid.). In other words, the assumptions that judges and juries employ when using their "common sense" about human behavior are often contradicted by controlled scientific experiments. Fiske and Borgida also conclude that experts "can offer research knowledge and identify 'characteristics of policies challenged in the particular workplace that research has linked with higher likelihood of bias and stereotype or lower likelihood of correction for bias'" (ibid., 875, quoting Hart and Secunda 2009). Fiske and Borgida warn that scientists do not perceive a sharp distinction between pure and applied social framework evidence. Rather, scientists view pure (general causation) versus applied (specific causation) research as falling on a continuum (Fiske and Borgida 2011). They conclude,

> A sharp distinction between general and specific causation is alien to psychologists and most scientists. The ability to generalize to specific circumstances is probabilistic, and applying knowledge in court is not different in principle from applying scientific evidence in other contexts. However, the confidence with which experts can generalize varies, depending on the state of available, relevant science. . . . Qualified social scientists who provide general, relevant knowledge and apply ordinary scientific reasoning may offer informed opinion about the individual

case, but *probabilistically*. None of this usurps the triers of fact of their role, as they are capable of drawing their own conclusions, with scientific judgments as one input. (ibid., 876)

The American Sociological Association and the Law and Society Association agree. They explain that sociological research that is well executed "provides systemic research methodologies for analyzing data on individual and organizational behavior. [It] meets rigorous disciplinary standards that include blind peer review and professional accountability for published work" (Brief of *Amici Curiae* American Sociological Association and the Law and Society Association in *Wal-Mart Stores, Inc. v. Dukes* 2011, 2–3).

Social sciences employ the scientific method, which is highly reliable "because it permits researchers to replicate, refine, and further test empirical findings" (ibid., 5). Sociologists who use proper case study method analyze aggregate data, perform case studies, publish their results in peer-reviewed journals, and, on the basis of this accumulation of information and learning, apply this knowledge to a particular situation. A sociologist who uses the proper case study methodology will be reluctant to draw causal connections in a particular case, but on the basis of high-quality peer-reviewed research in the literature, he or she can assess whether the company's practices "were likely to have prevented, permitted, promoted or encouraged discrimination" (ibid., 8).

A sociologist who uses a proper method will cite to published peer-reviewed research that is broadly supported in the social science literature and that informs the sociologist's analysis of the employer's workplace. The expert must also review the statistical results (if any) provided by other experts, and refer to qualitative evidence that includes the testimony of company owners and managers (ibid.). Adherence to this methodology confirms the reliability of the expert's testimony as required by Federal Rule of Evidence 702. While social scientists do not opine about the bottom line in a case, it is *not* contrary to scientific method to offer links between the general scientific evidence and the facts of the particular case. In other words, leading psychologists, the American Sociological Association, and the Law and Society Association agree: use of applied social framework evidence, when properly analyzed, is consistent with good scientific practice.

After *Price Waterhouse* and *Wal-Mart*, What Next?

The Supreme Court has not wholeheartedly endorsed the use of social science testimony in employment discrimination cases, but neither has it rejected its use. In fact, the lower court in *Hopkins v. Price Waterhouse* (1985) admitted the testimony of expert Dr. Susan Fiske, who concluded that the plaintiff was vulnerable to stereotyping about women because the workplace was male dominated and the plaintiff was the only woman considered for partnership. When the case reached the Supreme Court, the four-justice plurality refused to "adopt the dissent's dismissive attitude toward Dr. Fiske's field of study and toward her own professional integrity" (*Price Waterhouse v. Hopkins* 1989, 255), and along with Justice O'Connor, who concurred in the judgment, adopted the expert's analysis that the negative comments made about Ann Hopkins resulted from gender stereotyping. This evidence supported the conclusion that the firm rejected Hopkins's bid for partnership because of her sex (ibid.).

Wal-Mart v. Dukes, decided twenty-two years after *Price Waterhouse*, however, seems to signal that at least for the purposes of determining class certification, applied social framework evidence may not be used, *absent other evidence*, to support a finding of commonality. Some have read the five-justice opinion to conclude that applied social framework evidence should not be admissible to prove the substantive claim—that the employer engaged in illegal sex discrimination under Title VII. But *Wal-Mart v. Dukes'* pronouncement about Dr. Bielby's testimony may be limited to the class certification process because of the particularly odd facts in that case. The justices appeared to be particularly troubled by the size of the class—1.5 million women—who alleged sex discrimination against Wal-Mart and the procedural and practical problems that such a class action would create.

Moreover, in *Wal-Mart*, there was no unifying policy or group of policies governing the promotion and pay processes under attack. It appears that the Court was not making a pronouncement about the future of all applied social framework evidence, when used either to support a class that is limited in size and scope or to prove the underlying claim of discrimination in an individual suit or an appropriately sized class action. In fact, in *Ellis v. Costco Wholesale Corp.*, where a smaller class in size and scope existed and there was evidence of discrete policies affecting the plaintiffs' promotions, the court distinguished the facts in *Wal-Mart* and accepted the applied social framework evidence that supported the plaintiff's claim, concluding that the testimony was admissible and useful in determining that the plaintiff met the commonality requirement (*Ellis v. Costco Wholesale Corp.* 2012). Ellis is a particularly well written and well analyzed opinion that demonstrates to future litigants how to bring class actions that will survive the certification process. It stands for the proposition that applied social framework testimony, if used to buttress other evidence of discrimination in a moderately sized class action, can be useful in determining issues concerning commonality. If this is the case, it is also likely that applied social framework evidence, if appropriately used and if faithful to scientific methodology and principles, can continue to support plaintiffs' claims in employment discrimination cases.

Given the uncertainty that *Wal-Mart* created about the use of applied social framework evidence, and the disagreement of social scientists about what reliably constitutes scientific method, lower courts will have to make their own judgments about the value of the expert evidence before them. But one thing is certain: all sides agree that social scientists may offer "pure" social framework testimony—general information that does not link the research to the employer's workplace but that explains about stereotyping, masculinity, race, and gender in workplaces. Even assuming that *Wal-Mart* is ultimately interpreted to limit the use of expert testimony to "pure" social framework testimony, the research of masculinities studies should be admissible in trial courts.

Using Social Framework Testimony

Let's return to the hypothetical lawsuit of Jonathan Martin versus the NBA and the Miami Dolphins to review this concept. If Martin sues, the defendants will argue that there is no evidence that his teammates' harassment occurred because of sex or race. Martin should respond by introducing an expert, a sociologist who specializes in masculinities, to explain to the jury that masculinity is often invisible because it is "how things are." He should also explain that men, particularly when working in all-male environments, harass other men because the victim is considered insufficiently masculine or to demean the victim's masculinity and/or to demonstrate the harasser's masculinity. When a group of men harasses a male victim, individual men engage in the harassment to prove their masculinity to the group and to assure that the group maintains its masculine boundaries. The expert could also discuss the way masculinity, race, and work intersect, and the way men demonstrate their masculinity through behaviors at work. By focusing on how black male masculinity is perceived and performed, the expert can explain that black men engaged in tough blue-collar jobs are expected not to demonstrate vulnerability and to perform hypermasculinity. This is pure social framework evidence. If the court permits, the expert could apply the social framework to the individual case by opining that especially in all-male, hypermasculine environments such as the NFL, men need to compete to prove their masculinity to one another; the expert could relate this scientifically acquired knowledge to the facts of Martin's case and the atmosphere in the Miami Dolphins' locker rooms to conclude that in such an environment, men who are considered to be less masculine because they are quiet, educated, or effeminate in other ways will often become the victims of their more macho colleagues.

This testimony will prepare the jury for the judge's instruction that explains that discrimination because of sex includes discrimination based on a failure to live up to masculine stereotypes as well as discrimination based on biological sex. Moreover, on the basis of the evidence, the judge can instruct the jury that if the motivation for the harassment is Martin's teammates' interest in defining the boundaries of masculine behavior on the team, this harassment occurred because of sex. The judge can also explain that if the jury finds that the teammates harassed Martin because as a black man he did not live up to the stereotype of bad black masculine man, the harassment occurred because of both race and gender. Finally, if the defendant argues that Martin welcomed the behavior, and refers to Martin's failure to complain to the team managers and owners about the behavior, Martin can offer the testimony of a psychologist who can explain the psychology behind why people who are victims of harassment often fail to complain about it. All of this testimony will probably counter the common sense of the jury and the judge, and will allow judge and jurors to evaluate the case with the necessary scientific background that will enable a fair resolution.

A similar strategy would take place in a case of a previously all-male blue-collar working environment where men harass their female colleagues. The defendants may argue that there is no harassment of women based on sex because both men and women are subjected to the same treatment; the "girlie" magazine photos had always been displayed in the workplace even before the women began working there, and the crude discussion of sexual positions was always a part of the way the men related to one another. Consequently, the defendant will agree that the behavior is harassing, but will deny that it occurs because of sex. Women can offer the expert testimony of a sociologist who will demonstrate that men harass women in formerly all-male environments to support the men's sense of masculinity by preserving the worksite as an all-male environment. Men use the "girlie" magazines and other props to denigrate women, and, even before the arrival of the women, to denigrate men who are insufficiently masculine. This behavior supports the group's sense of power and masculinity. When directed at women, the behavior occurs to force them out of the job. This may be presented as pure social framework evidence without the expert's commenting on the evidence before him or, if the judge permits, the expert could comment on the evidence and relate the social science to the facts before him.

In a case where the employer refuses to hire a young black man to serve as a nurse in a nursing home, the plaintiff may use an expert to testify that society sees young black men as angry, hypermasculine, and dangerous. It may be difficult to prove race discrimination because there are black female nurses working at the home. And, it may be difficult to prove sex discrimination because there are also white male nurses working at the home. Expert testimony about the stereotypes of black men, combined with evidence of the demographics of the employer's workforce, the lack of black males in the nursing home, and comments made by the employer, can be used to explain to the jury that human beings have multidimensional identities and that the discrimination occurs because of the intersection of race and gender in the nursing home. Once again, the evidence can be presented as pure or applied social framework evidence, depending on the judge's ruling.

In sum, these are just some examples of the use of expert testimony regarding masculinities research to help the plaintiff prove a Title VII sex and/or race discrimination case. The testimony should be particularly effective if the trial judge instructs the jury as to the issues regarding masculinities in the case. Judges need judicial education to be able to comprehend these issues and to open their minds to understanding that relying on commonsense assumptions about human behavior leads to injustice. In essence, judges and juries need to view the cases before them through a different lens.

Judicial Education

Up to this point, I have argued that social science expert evidence of masculinities theory should be admitted into evidence in order to educate judges and juries in employment discrimination cases. I have also advocated the use of jury instructions that include an understanding of masculinities theory. But so few cases go to trial that these reforms, even if successful, would not reach a large percentage of the Title VII cases filed. Courts decide many cases on defendants' motions to dismiss and for summary judgment. Therefore, it is necessary for courts to understand masculinities theory earlier in the litigation process so that judges can use the information in their adjudication of these procedural motions.

Deciding Procedural Motions: Expert Information Is Crucial

MOTIONS TO DISMISS

Courts need information to assure fair judicial decisions. This is particularly true in employment discrimination cases that are fact intensive, especially at procedural junctures when courts decide motions to dismiss, motions for summary judgment, and motions for judgment as a matter of law. Since *Twombly* and *Iqbal*, the standard for motions to dismiss requires that a judge determine the plausibility of inferences to be drawn from the facts pled in the complaint (*Ashcroft v. Iqbal* 2009; *Bell Atlantic Corp. v. Twombly* 2007). This analysis requires federal judges to reach decisions in the individual case on the basis of the complaint without additional information in the record (Thomas 2010).

It is particularly problematic for judges to make the plausibility determination on the basis of commonsense assumptions about how discriminators do or don't operate without any information about implicit bias and decision making, and in cases where masculinities are relevant, without understanding how masculinities work. It is especially important that judges receive training in advance about implicit bias as well as masculinities theory so that they will understand which inferences are plausible when considering motions to dismiss.

MOTIONS FOR SUMMARY JUDGMENT AND FOR JUDGMENT AS A MATTER OF LAW

In determining motions for summary judgment and motions for judgment as a matter of law, judges make determinations based on the evidence before them. Many of these determinations are particularly fact intensive, thereby creating the possibility that the courts deciding the motion will interpret the facts through a lens that is significantly different from that of juries. But these motions require judges to exercise constraint and respect for jury decision making. The courts decide whether there is sufficient evidence for the fact finder to conclude that the defendant discriminated against the plaintiff because of the plaintiff's protected characteristic. In other words, they determine whether a reasonable jury could conclude that the defendant illegally discriminated against the plaintiff. These decisions should not be decided on the basis of a judge's commonsense assumption about how "most managers" operate or on judges' instincts that discrimination is a thing of the past. The implicit bias research, combined with masculinities theory, reveals that discrimination based on stereotyped assumptions about gender and race continues to affect managerial decision making. It also suggests that judges themselves harbor implicit biases that may affect their judging. Judges need additional information to inform their first natural reactions to the fact patterns before them.

STEREOTYPES AND IMPLICIT BIAS

There is significant research concluding that implicit bias is common and that it affects human behavior (Banaji and Greenwald 2013; Fiske and Borgida 2011). Additionally, substantial research demonstrates that, due to stereotypes about women, their peers and superiors judge female leaders more harshly. If women act contrary to stereotype, they are unlikeable, but if they conform to stereotype, they are considered weak and incapable of leadership (Heilman et al. 2004; Rudman 2001). Stereotypes, whether conscious or unconscious, and implicit bias can affect decision making in a way that is detrimental to a plaintiff alleging employment discrimination. (Gertner and Hart 2012). In "Does Unconscious Racial Bias Affect Trial Judges?" the authors report on a study they conducted on trial judges to determine whether they harbor racial biases (Rachlinski et al. 2009). The study results demonstrated that trial judges carry implicit racial bias that can affect their judgments about how to sentence a criminal defendant. But the study also demonstrates that when judges were made aware of their biases, at least in the experimental setting, they were able to control the effect of their biases on their sentencing decisions (ibid.).

Additionally, a recent study demonstrates that panels of the U.S. courts of appeal overturn decisions by federal trial judges who are of color at a rate that is much higher than the reversal rate of white trial judges, even when taking into account the trial judges' prior professional and judicial experience, ratings by the American Bar Association, and composition of the court of appeals panel (Sen 2015). This study suggests that the panels deciding whether to overturn the lower court judges' decisions may be engaging in implicit bias, fully unaware that they are doing so.

There are a number of ways to counter the very natural human reaction to form inaccurate commonsense assumptions about behaviors, and to apply them to judicial decision making. Judges should receive sustained and repeated judicial education and training about stereotyping, implicit bias, human behavior, and masculinities theory. The National Center for State Courts, for example, provides training programs on implicit bias and has a number of reports describing implicit bias and the research supporting it, including a report on strategies that can be used to reduce the effect of implicit bias (NCSC 2012). The Kirwin Institute for the Study of Race and Ethnicity at Ohio State University also has information on implicit bias, including a report on the science of implicit bias that would be useful to judges (Staats 2014).

Attorneys can also educate judges through the use of attorneys' or amicus briefs that contain citations to law review articles and books relating to social science information about human interactions and unconscious bias and masculinities research. They can also introduce expert testimony on social framework evidence. Moreover, judges and lawyers can work together to construct jury instructions that acknowledge the important influence of biases and stereotypes in decision making.

In sum, lawyers, judges, and juries are all human. Nearly all human beings harbor stereotypes and biases as a result of natural cognitive processing. When lawyers, judges, and juries make decisions about an employee's or applicant's discrimination claim, they often rely on common sense and perception, which are tainted with stereotypes and biases. Masculinities research, which is still a developing area of study, can help educate lawyers, judges, and juries to make just and accurate decisions in discrimination cases.

Conclusion

The Future of Masculinities

This book explains masculinities research, its application to discrimination in workplaces, and the way understanding this body of work can aid lawyers, judges, and juries in making just and accurate decisions in employment discrimination claims brought under Title VII of the Civil Rights Act of 1964. It explains theory using real-life examples, applies theory to create new interpretations of Title VII antidiscrimination law, and makes practical suggestions for how legal actors can use masculinities research to enhance their understanding of the phenomena surrounding discrimination in the workplace and to communicate it in litigation.

Articulating Theory

The *theory* in this book relies largely on ethnographic, empirical, and theoretical work performed by social scientists over a period of approximately the last forty-five years. I combine masculinities research with feminist legal theory, critical race theory, and intersectionality and multidimensionality theories to enhance understandings of multidimensional masculinities theory, a new concept that Frank Rudy Cooper and I articulated in *Masculinities and the Law: A Multidimensional Approach* (Cooper and McGinley 2012; McGinley and Cooper 2012). Multidimensional masculinities theory is a critical theory of law that "assumes that law distributes power by relying upon assumptions about human behavior that reproduce preexisting social relations. Law and culture are co-constitutive: cultural norms influence law and legal norms simultaneously influence culture" (McGinley and Cooper 2012, 1) (citations omitted). Multidimensional masculinities theory differs from masculinities studies in that it takes a multidimensional approach in a legal environment: it considers not only gender but also other identities, as they are performed *in context*. Thus, in the case of Title VII, the workplace context is central to an understanding of how and why masculine structures affect performances at work.

Applying Theory to Title VII

The book then *applies* multidimensional masculinities theory to the employment discrimination law of Title VII of the Civil Rights Act. It explains Title VII law and proof mechanisms that judges use to determine whether discrimination has occurred, and recommends, with examples from real cases, how multidimensional masculinities theory can benefit that interpretation. In a number of situations, it makes law reform proposals, based on a multidimensional masculinities analysis, to change the standards used by the courts to determine whether plaintiffs have suffered illegal discrimination.

Two concepts are key to understanding the application of multidimensional masculinities theory to law reform proposals in this book. First, employment discrimination law should provide a broad remedy to those experiencing discrimination based on race, sex, gender, and other covered identity characteristics. Courts should not limit Title VII remedies to victims who suffer adverse employment consequences as a result of individual employers' conscious discriminatory views. Rather, the law should remedy discriminatory structures that cause unequal treatment at work as well as individual animus and hidden biases reflected in individual actions. Moreover, the law should create incentives to employers to deter themselves and their employees from endorsing, using, and responding to structures and behaviors that cause discrimination against members of protected groups. Second, human beings often rely on common sense to make decisions about whether behaviors are race, sex, national origin, or gender based. Masculinities theory demonstrates that employers' and judges' reliance on common sense to make and evaluate workplace decisions can be problematic because it allows persons' implicit biases to distort their perception, and may lead to inaccurate decision making. This decision making tends to underestimate the prevalence of discriminatory actions, in large part because of cultural understandings that are embedded in society and translated into law.

Admitting Expert Evidence

The book also explains the law surrounding the ability to introduce expert evidence in court to help judges and juries determine whether discrimination has taken place. It argues that judges should admit into evidence reliable, probative expert testimony on masculinities to counter hidden biases that occur unconsciously when fact finders and judges use their common sense. Common sense, while often useful in directing a person's judgment, is problematic because it relies on embedded and unconscious biases communicated to individual actors through culture. The law, when it endorses the exclusive use of common sense, can often embed discriminatory structures into its analysis.

The book also argues that judicial education should include information on multidimensional masculinities theory in order to assure understanding and just procedural responses to pretrial motions and adjudication during and after trial.

Future Considerations

In the fifty-odd years since its enactment, Title VII has had enormous positive effects on workplaces. Consider the number of white women and persons of color who work today in jobs that were formerly predominantly held by white men. But if Title VII is to continue to further the economic interests of white women and persons of color, the law must be responsive to new, hidden forms of bias and discrimination. It should interpret Title VII to hold employers responsible for these new forms of discrimination in an effort to deter discriminatory structures and behavior in workplaces. Employers, in turn, should respond to economic deterrence created by Title VII, and create processes and structures to avoid discriminatory decisions at work. There has been much talk of stereotypes and hidden bias among legal scholars, but few scholars and legal actors have also recognized the importance of masculine structures and performances in the workplace to employee success.

Even in the absence of court action adopting masculinities theory, employers should become familiar with masculinities research and then work to eliminate masculine structures and performances from workplaces. Employers should consider the work of the theorists discussed in this book. In particular, they should acquaint themselves with the work of David Collinson, Jeff Hearn, Jennifer Pierce, and Patricia Yancey Martin. Collinson and Hearn's work will educate employers on the prevailing masculine practices that are invisible in many white-collar workplaces: authoritarianism, paternalism, entrepreneurialism, informalism, and careerism (Collinson and Hearn 1994). Pierce's studies demonstrate invisible gendering in the legal profession (Pierce 1999, 1995), and Martin's work explains the importance of the "doing" of masculinities in workplaces and the effect of masculine practices on women at work, even though there may be no purpose to harm women (Martin 2003, 2001).

To understand blue-collar masculinities where men harass both women and men at work, employers should read David Collinson's work on shop culture (Collinson 1988) and my work, which analyzes much of the literature on bullying and masculinities, especially that concerning harassment by men of other men (McGinley 2008).

Armed with this information, employers should consider whether invisible, gender-based practices occur in their workplaces. To the extent that an employer exposes women or gender-nonconforming men to masculine structures and standards, future employees may bring discrimination lawsuits against them. It is possible that courts would require employers to justify these masculine standards by demonstrating that living up to the standards is a bona fide occupational qualification for the job. Courts rarely, however, recognize this defense, and it would be very difficult for an employer to prove that playing baseball with the company team, for example, is related to job performance. While courts may not be ready to conclude that masculine practices violate Title VII, a savvy employer will attempt to eliminate them from the workplace because doing so will be likely to create a more productive and happier workplace, and save employers money.

One example of invisible masculine practices prevalent in workplaces is "clubby" behavior among men that grants an advantage to white male employees who fit the masculinity norms. A woman or gender-nonconforming man who is excluded from promotions due to a failure to adapt to the informal behavior of male workers may, in the future, have a cause of action under Title VII. Another example is the hazing and harassment of new male and female employees in blue-collar workplaces. Structures and behaviors that expect men of color or white women to perform their gender in ways that either reject stereotypes about gender or race or adhere to them offer another example.

Most important, employers should create productive workplaces that feel safe and supportive. An understanding of masculinities research should enable employers to see invisible harms and to assure that the workplace is comfortable for all workers. Employers can achieve this goal by looking at their workplaces *through a different lens*, and considering how standards and practices affect out-groups at work.

NOTES

NOTES TO ACKNOWLEDGMENTS

1 During this time period, I published the following law review articles that dealt with masculinities and Title VII issues: *How Masculinities Distribute Power: The Influence of Ann Scales*, 91 DENV. U. L. REV. 187 (2014) (with Frank Rudy Cooper); *Masculinity, Labor, and Sexual Power*, 93 BOSTON U. L. REV. 795 (2013); *Masculine Law Firms*, 8 FLA. INT'L U. L. REV. 423 (2013); *Introduction: Men, Masculinities, and Law: A Symposium on Multidimensional Masculinities Theory*, 13 NEV. L. J. 315 (2013); *Identities Cubed: Perspectives on Multidimensional Masculinities Theory*, 13 NEV. L. J. 326 (2013) (with Frank Rudy Cooper); *Reasonable Men*, 45 U. CONN. L. REV. 1 (2012); *Cognitive Illiberalism, Summary Judgment, and Title VII*, 57 N.Y.L.S. L. REV. 865 (2012/13); Ricci v. DeStefano: *Diluting Disparate Impact and Redefining Disparate Treatment*, 12 NEV. L. J. 626 (2012); *Work, Caregiving, and Masculinities*, 34 SEATTLE U. L. REV. 703 (2011); Ricci v. DeStefano: *A Masculinities Theory Analysis*, 33 HARV. J. LAW & GENDER 581 (2010); *Discrimination Redefined*, 75 MO. L. REV. 441 (2010); *Erasing Boundaries: Masculinities, Sexual Minorities, and Employment Discrimination*, 43 U. MICH. J. LAW REFORM 1 (2010); *Reproducing Gender on Law School Faculties*, 2009 BYU L. REV. 99; *Hillary Clinton, Sarah Palin, and Michelle Obama: Performing Gender, Race, and Class on the Campaign Trail*, 86 DENV. U. L. REV. 709 (2009); *Creating Masculine Identities: Bullying and Harassment "Because of Sex,"* 79 U. COLO. L. REV. 1151 (2008); *Harassing "Girls" at the Hard Rock: Masculinities in Sexualized Environments*, 2007 U. ILL L. REV. 1229; *Discrimination in Our Midst: Law Schools' Potential Liability for Employment Practices*, 14 UCLA WOMEN'S L.J. 1 (2005); *Masculinities at Work*, 83 ORE. L. REV. 359 (2004), and *Viva la Evolución! Recognizing Unconscious Motive in Title VII*, 9 CORNELL J. L. & PUB. POL'Y 415 (2000). I am very thankful to the publications and to the students on the law reviews who worked on editing these works.

NOTES TO CHAPTER 1

1 Portions of this chapter are derived from the following articles and are reprinted or revised with permission from the publishers: Ann C. McGinley, *Work, Caregiving, and Masculinities*, 34 SEATTLE U. L. REV. 703 (2011); Ann C. McGinley, *Erasing Boundaries: Masculinities, Sexual Minorities, and Employment Discrimination*, 43 U. MICH. J. LAW REFORM 1 (2010); Ann C. McGinley, *Reproducing*

Gender on Law School Faculties, 2009 BYU L. REV. 99; Ann C. McGinley, *Creating Masculine Identities: Bullying and Harassment "Because of Sex*," 79 U. COLO. L. REV. 1151 (2008); Ann C. McGinley, *Masculinities at Work*, 83 ORE. L. REV. 359 (2004).

2 The following description comes from the allegations in the complaint. Amended Complaint and Jury Demand, *Ayanna v. Dechert LLP*, 2012 WL 5064041 (D. Mass. Oct. 17, 2012) (No. 10-12155-NMG) and from depositions taken during the discovery process. I assume for the sake of discussion that the plaintiff would have been able to prove these allegations had the case gone to trial. Because the case upon which this story is based settled before trial, I cannot confirm that Ayanna's side of the case is accurate, but the record leads me to the conclusion that there was sufficient evidence for Ayanna to go to trial on his Family Medical Leave Act of 1993 (FMLA) (29 U.S.C. § 2615(a)(2) (2006) and Massachusetts Anti-Discrimination law counts. The trial court granted summary judgment on the sex discrimination claim but denied the defendant's summary judgment motion on the FMLA claim (McGinley 2013a).

3 The following description comes from the allegations in the complaint. Because they are allegations, they have not been proven, but I use the allegations as illustrative of the types of cases that describe hostile working environments based on women's gender in male-dominated workforces.

NOTE TO CHAPTER 2

1 In *Baldwin v. Foxx*, the EEOC, in an appeal from a Department of Transportation decision, stated, "[W]e conclude that sexual orientation is inherently a 'sex-based consideration,' and an allegation of discrimination based on sexual orientation is necessarily an allegation of sex discrimination under Title VII" (*Baldwin v. Foxx* 2015).

NOTES TO CHAPTER 3

1 Portions of this chapter are reprinted with permission of the publisher from Ann C. McGinley, *Creating Masculine Identities: Bullying and Harassment "Because of Sex*," 79 U. COLO. L. REV. 1151 (2008).

2 The 1991 Civil Rights Act overturned the portion of the case concerning proof of a mixed-motives case, but the statutory amendment does not affect the Court's conclusion that sex stereotyping may constitute sex discrimination under Title VII.

3 There are a few cases where groups of female coworkers harass male coworkers. In most of the cases reported of this type, the women appear to harass the men due to the men's participation in harassment of female coworkers. Whether this behavior occurs because of sex is doubtful. There are also some cases in which a group of women harasses individual women. If the purpose is to harass a woman for her failure to live up to gender or sexual norms or stereotypes, this behavior probably occurs because of sex under *Price Waterhouse v. Hopkins* (1989) (holding

that discriminatory treatment occurred because of sex where the employer treated the female plaintiff differently because she did not live up to feminine gender stereotypes).

4 For more discussion of this category where men are both the harassers and the victims, *see* McGinley, *supra* note 1, at 1219–30.

5 Because of the procedural posture, the question was whether the lower court had properly denied the defendant's motion for judgment as a matter of law. The en banc court concluded that there was sufficient evidence of differential treatment.

NOTES TO CHAPTER 4

1 Portions of this chapter are reprinted with permission of the publishers from Ann C. McGinley, *Reasonable Men*, 45 U. CONN. L. REV. 1 (2012).

2 The final question is whether a "reasonable response" standard would make a difference. For a discussion of whether this proposal would have a positive effect, and the literature supporting the discussion, *see* McGinley, *supra* note 1, at 35–38.

NOTES TO CHAPTER 6

1 Portions of this chapter are derived from Ann C. McGinley, *Discrimination Redefined*, 75 MO. L. REV. 441 (2010) and from Ann C. McGinley, *Viva la Evolución: Recognizing Unconscious Motive in Title VII*, 9 CORNELL J. L. & PUB. POL'Y 415 (2000), and are reprinted or revised with permission of the publishers.

2 For examples of how the *McDonnell Douglas/Reeves* construct can sanction a finding of liability based on implicit bias, *see* McGinley, *Viva la Evolución*, *supra* note 1, at 447–65.

3 For discussion of how pattern and practice cases can be won on implicit bias, *see* McGinley, *Viva la Evolución*, *supra* note 1, at 465–67.

4 For a description of these doctrines, *see* Nancy Gertner and Melissa Hart, *Implicit Bias in Employment Litigation*, in IMPLICIT RACIAL BIAS ACROSS THE LAW (eds. Justin D. Levinson and Robert J. Smith, 2012), 80–94.

NOTES TO CHAPTER 7

1 Portions of this chapter are reprinted with permission of the publishers from Ann C. McGinley, *Masculine Law Firms*, 8 FLA. INT'L. U. L. REV. 423 (2013), Ann C. McGinley, *Work, Caregiving, and Masculinities*, 34 SEATTLE U. L. REV. 703 (2011), and Ann C. McGinley, *Masculinities at Work*, 83 ORE. L. REV. 359 (2004).

2 Title VII provides a "BFOQ" defense for sex or gender discrimination where sex is a "bona fide occupational qualification." This defense has been construed extremely narrowly by the U.S. Supreme Court (*International Union et al. v. Johnson Controls* 1991).

NOTES TO CHAPTER 8

1 Portions of this chapter are reprinted by permission of the publishers from Ann C. McGinley, *Masculinities and Disparate Impacts* in EXPLORING MASCULINI-

TIES: FEMINIST LEGAL THEORY REFLECTIONS (eds. Martha Albertson Fineman and Michael Thomson, 2013), 201–22.

2 Section 2000e-2 (a) (1) makes it illegal for an employer

to fail or refuse to hire or to discharge any individual, or otherwise to discriminate against any individual with respect to his compensation, terms, conditions, or privileges of employment, because of such individual's race, color, religion, sex, or national origin.

3 Section 2000e-2 (a) (2) makes it illegal for an employer

to limit, segregate, or classify his employees or applicants for employment in any way which would deprive or tend to deprive any individual of employment opportunities or otherwise adversely affect his status as an employee, because of such individual's race, color, religion, sex, or national origin.

4 These scenarios may also create disparate treatment causes of action for sex discrimination if there is proof that the employer consciously relied on stereotypes about women or persons of color in failing to hire or promote them or in firing them. Even if the employer's decision is unconsciously based on stereotypes, but there is proof that the stereotype caused the plaintiff's rejection, the plaintiff should prevail in a disparate treatment case. *See* chapter 7.

REFERENCES

137 Cong. Rec. 29051-52 (1991) (statement of Sen. Kennedy).

Abrams, Kathryn. 2000. Cross-Dressing in the Master's Clothes. *Yale Law Journal* 109:745–82 (reviewing Joan Williams, *Unbending Gender: Why Family and Work Conflict and What to Do about It*).

———. 1995. The Reasonable Woman: Sense and Sensibility in Sexual Harassment Law. *Dissent* 42:48–54.

Advisory Committee Notes, *Notes of Advisory Committee on Rules* (2000 Amendment), http://federalevidence.com/node/1335.

Age Discrimination in Employment Act (ADEA), 29 U.S.C.A. § 621.

Albemarle Paper Co. v. Moody, 422 U.S. 405 (1975).

Alfano v. Costello, 294 F.3d 365 (2d Cir. 2002).

Amalfe, Christine A., Gibbons PC. 2013. The Limitations on Implicit Bias Testimony Post-*Dukes*, http://www.americanbar.org/content/dam/aba/events/labor_law/2013/03/employment_rightsresponsibilitiescommitteemidwintermeeting/1_amalfe.authcheckdam.pdf.

American Association of University Professors (AAUP). 2006a. 1940 Statement of Principles on Academic Freedom and Tenure with 1970 Interpretive Comments, in *AAUP Policy Documents and Reports*, 10th ed. American Association of University Professors.

———. 2006b. Statement of Principles on Family Responsibilities and Academic Work, in *AAUP Policy Documents and Reports*, 10th ed. American Association of University Professors.

Americans with Disabilities Act (ADA), 42 U.S.C.A. § 12101.

Anderson v. Zubieta, 180 F.3d 329 (D.C. Cir. 1999).

Armenti, Carmen. 2004. Women Faculty Seeking Tenure and Parenthood: Lessons from Previous Generations. *Cambridge Journal of Education* 34(1):65–83.

Ash v. Tyson Foods, Inc., 129 Fed. Appx. 529 (11th Cir. 2005) (unpublished).

Ash v. Tyson Foods, Inc., 546 U.S. 454 (2006).

Ashcroft v. Iqbal, 556 U.S. 662 (2009).

Ayanna v. Dechert, LLP, 914 F. Supp. 2d 51 (D. Mass. 2012).

———. Amended Complaint and Jury Demand, *Ayanna v. Dechert, LLP*, 914 F. Supp. 2d 51 (D. Mass. 2012) (No. 10-12155-NMG), ECF No. 13.

———. Complaint and [sic] Jury Demand at intro, *Ayanna v. Dechert, LLP*, 914 F. Supp. 2d 51 (D. Mass. 2012) (No. 10-12155-NMG), ECF No. 1.

———. Defendant Dechert LLP's Memorandum of Law in Support of Its Motion for Summary Judgment, *Ayanna v. Dechert, LLP*, 914 F. Supp. 2d 51 (D. Mass. 2012) (No. 10-12155-NMG), ECF No. 68.

———. Deposition of Ariel M. Ayanna, Oct. 6, 2011, Exhibit A to Appendix of Deposition Excerpts in Support of Defendant Dechert LLP's Motion for Summary Judgment, *Ayanna v. Dechert, LLP*, 914 F. Supp. 2d 51 (D. Mass. 2012) (No. 10-12155-NMG), ECF Nos. 71-1 to 71-3.

Back v. Hastings on Hudson Free School District, 365 F.3d 107 (2d Cir. 2004).

Baldwin v. Foxx, EEOC Appeal No. 120133080 (July 15, 2015), www.eeoc.gov/decisions/0120133080.pdf.

Banaji, Mazarin R., and Anthony G. Greenwald. 2013. *Blindspot: Hidden Biases of Good People*. New York: Delacorte Press.

Barnes v. Costle, 561 F.2D 983 (D.C. Cir. 1977).

Bartlett, Katharine T. 2009. Making Good on Good Intentions: The Critical Role of Motivation in Reducing Implicit Workplace Discrimination. *Virginia Law Review* 95:1893–1972.

Battiata, Mary. 1986a. Mechelle Vinson's Tangled Trials: After the Supreme Court, Pursuing Harassment Case. *Washington Post*, August 11, at C1.

———. 1986b. Mechelle Vinson's Long Road to Court: A Disputed Tale of Sexual Harassment in the Office. *Washington Post,* August 12, at C1.

Bazemore v. Friday, 478 U.S. 385 (1986).

Beiner, Theresa M. 2014. Theorizing Billable Hours. *Montana Law Review* 75:1–35.

———. 2005. *Gender Myths v. Working Realities: Using Social Science to Reformulate Sexual Harassment Law*. New York: New York University Press.

———. 1999. The Misuse of Summary Judgment in Hostile Environment Cases. *Wake Forest Law Review* 34:71–134.

Bell Atlantic Corp. v. Twombly, 550 U.S. 544 (2007).

Benson, Katherine A. 1984. Comments on Crocker's "An Analysis of University Definitions of Sexual Harassment," *Signs: Journal of Women and Culture* 9:516–17.

Bernstein, Anita. 1997. Treating Sexual Harassment with Respect. *Harvard Law Review* 111:445–527.

Bibby v. Philadelphia Coca-Cola Bottling Co., 260 F.3d 257 (3d Cir. 2001).

Blair, Irene V. 2002. The Malleability of Automatic Stereotypes and Prejudice. *Personality and Social Psychology Review* 6(3):242–61.

Blair, Irene V., Jennifer E. Ma, and Alison P. Lenton. 2001. Imagining Stereotypes Away: The Moderation of Implicit Stereotypes through Mental Imagery. *Journal of Personality and Social Psychology* 81(5):828–41.

Bodenhausen, Galen V. 1993. Emotions, Arousal, and Stereotypic Judgments: A Heuristic Model of Affect and Stereotyping, in *Affect, Cognition, and Stereotyping*, eds. Diane M. Mackey and David L. Hamilton. San Diego: Academic Press, 13–14.

Bornstein, Stephanie. 2012. The Law of Gender Stereotyping and the Work-Family Conflicts of Men. *Hastings Law Journal* 63:1297–1344.

Bradley v. City of Lynn, 443 F.Supp. 2d 145 (D. Mass. 2006).

Brinson, Will. 2013. Doug Baldwin: "Disappointing" to Call Jonathan Martin, Stanford "Soft." *CBS Sports*, November 6, http://www.cbssports.com/nfl/eye-on-football/24195620/doug-baldwin-disappointing-to-call-jonathan-martin-stanford-soft.

Burlington Industries, Inc. v. Ellerth, 524 U.S. 742 (1998).

Burlington Northern and Santa Fe Railroad Co. v. White, 548 U.S. 53 (2006).

Butler, Dore, and Florence L. Geis. 1990. Nonverbal Affect Responses to Male and Female Leaders: Implications for Leadership Evaluations. *Journal of Personality and Social Psychology* 58:48–59.

Cahn, Naomi. 1992. Symposium: The Looseness of Legal Language; The Reasonable Woman Standard in Theory and in Practice. *Cornell Law Review* 77:1398–1445.

Calanchini, Jimmy, Karen Gonsalkorale, Jeffrey W. Sherman, and Karl Christoph Klauer. 2013. Counter-Prejudicial Training Reduces Activation of Biased Associations and Enhances Response Monitoring. *European Journal of Social Psychology* 43:321–25.

Calloway, Deborah. 1994. *St. Mary's Honor Center v. Hicks*: Questioning the Basic Assumption. *Connecticut Law Review* 26:997–1038.

Carbado, Devon W., and Mitu Gulati. 2013. *Acting White? Rethinking Race in Post-Racial America*. New York: Oxford University Press.

———. 2001. The Fifth Black Woman. *Journal of Contemporary Legal Issues* 11:701–29.

———. 2000. Working Identity. *Cornell Law Review* 85:1260–1308.

Carbone, June, and Naomi Cahn. 2014. *Marriage Markets: How Inequality Is Remaking the American Family*. New York: Oxford University Press.

Carino v. University of Oklahoma Board of Regents, 750 F.2d 815 (10th Cir. 1984).

Carnes, Molly, Patricia G. Devine, Carol Isaac, Linda B. Manwell, Cecelia E. Ford, Angela Byars-Winston, Eve Fine, and Jennifer Sheridan. 2012. Promoting Institutional Change through Bias Literacy. *Journal of Diversity in Higher Education* 5:63–77.

Case, Mary Ann. 1995. Disaggregating Gender from Sex and Sexual Orientation: The Effeminate Man in the Law and Feminist Jurisprudence. *Yale Law Journal* 105:1–105.

Chamallas, Martha. 2010. Gaining Some Perspective in Tort Law: A New Take on Third-Party Criminal Attack Cases. *Lewis and Clark Law Review* 14:1351–1400.

Chambers, Henry L., Jr. 2002. (Un)Welcome Conduct and the Hostile Work Environment. *Alabama Law Review* 53:733–87.

Chang, Robert. 2012. Rescue Me, in *Masculinities and the Law: A Multidimensional Approach*, eds. Frank Rudy Cooper and Ann C. McGinley. New York: New York University Press, 119–33.

Chen, Anthony. 1999. Lives at the Center of the Periphery, Lives at the Periphery of the Center: Chinese American Masculinities and Bargaining with Hegemony. *Gender and Society* 13:584–607.

Chen, Chiung H. 1996. Feminization of Asian (American) Men in the U.S. Mass Media: An Analysis of the Ballad of Little Jo. *Journal of Communication Inquiry* 20:57–71.

Chen, Edward M. 1994. *Garcia v. Spun Steak Co.*: Speak-English-Only Rules and the Demise of Workplace Pluralism. *Asian American Law Journal* 1:155–88.

Cochran, Augustus B. 2004. *Sexual Harassment and the Law: The Mechelle Vinson Case.* Lawrence: University Press of Kansas.

Civil Rights Act of 1991, Pub. L. No. 102-166, 105 Stat. 1071.

Colby v. J.C. Penney Co., 811 F.2d 119 (7th Cir. 1987).

Collier, Richard. 2013. Rethinking Men and Masculinities in the Contemporary Legal Profession: The Example of Fatherhood, Transnational Business Masculinities, and Work-Life Balance in Large Law Firms. *Nevada Law Journal* 13:410–37.

Collinson, David L. 1988. Engineering Humor: Masculinity, Joking, and Conflict in Shop-Floor Relations. *Organization Studies* 9:181–99.

Collinson, David L., and Jeff Hearn. 1994. Naming Men as Men: Implications for Work, Organization, and Management. *Gender, Work, and Organization* 1:2–22.

Collinson, Margaret, and David Collinson. 1996. "It's Only Dick:" The Sexual Harassment of Women Managers in Insurance Sales. *Work, Employment, and Society* 10:29–56.

Connecticut v. Teal, 457 U.S. 440 (1982).

Connell, R. W. 2005. *Masculinities*, 2nd ed. Berkeley: University of California Press.

Cooper, Frank Rudy. 2010. Masculinities, Post-Racialism, and the Gates Controversy: The False Equivalence between Officer and Civilian. *Nevada Law Journal* 11:1–43.

———. 2009. Our First Unisex President? Black Masculinity and Obama's Feminine Side. *Denver University Law Review* 86:633–61.

———. 2006. Against Bipolar Masculinity: Intersectionality, Assimilation, Identity Performance, and Hierarchy. *University of California Davis Law Review* 39:853–906.

Cooper, Frank Rudy, and Ann C. McGinley, eds. 2012. *Masculinities and Law: A Multidimensional Approach.* New York: New York University Press.

Corbett, William R. 2003. McDonnell Douglas, 1973–2003: May You Rest in Peace? *University of Pennsylvania Journal of Labor and Employment Law* 6:199–219.

Corcoran, Katja, Tanja Hundhammer, and Thomas Mussweiler. 2009. A Tool for Thought! When Comparative Thinking Reduces Stereotyping Effects. *Journal of Experimental Social Psychology* 45(4):1008–11.

Crenshaw, Kimberle W. 1993. Mapping the Margins: Intersectionality, Identity Politics, and Violence against Women of Color. *Stanford Law Review* 43:1241–99.

Cummins, Justin D. 2007. Effective Legal Strategy and Litigation Tactics in the Wake of *Desert Palace v. Costa. Minnesota Trial Lawyers Association Employment Law Report* Spring:32–35.

Cunningham, William A., Marcia K. Johnson, Carol L. Raye, J. Chris Gatenby, John C. Gore, and Mahzarin R. Banaji. 2004. Separable Neural Components in the Processing of Black and White Faces. *Psychological Science* 15:806–13.

Cunningham-Parmeter, Keith. 2013. Men at Work: Uncovering the Masculine Face of Caregiving Discrimination. *Columbia Journal of Gender and Law* 24:253–301.

Czopp, Alexander M., and Margo J. Monteith. 2003. Confronting Prejudice (Literally): Reactions to Confrontations of Racial and Gender Bias. *Personality and Social Psychology Bulletin* 29:532–44.

Dahl, Melissa. 2013. Big Man Bullied: Jonathan Martin Reminds Us That Victims Aren't Always the Little Guys. *NBC News*, No-

vember 5, http://www.nbcnews.com/health/mental-health/
   big-man-bullied-jonathan-martin-reminds-us-victims-arent-always-f8C11519754.
Dasgupta, Nilanjana, and Shaki Asgari. 2004. Seeing Is Believing: Exposure to Coun-
   terstereotypic Women Leaders and Its Effect on the Malleability of Automatic
   Gender Stereotyping. *Journal of Experimental Social Psychology* 40:642–58.
Daubert v. Merrell Dow Pharmaceuticals, Inc., 509 U.S. 579 (1993).
DeClue v. Central Illinois Light Co., 223 F.3d 434 (7th Cir. 2000).
Derum, Chad, and Karen Engle. 2003. The Rise of the Personal Animosity Presump-
   tion and the Return to "No Cause" Employment. *Texas Law Review* 81:1177–1247.
Desert Palace, Inc. v. Costa, 539 U.S. 90 (2003).
Devine, Dennis J., Laura D. Clayton, Benjamin B. Dunford, Rasmy Seying, and Jenni-
   fer Pryce. 2001. Jury Decision Making: 45 Years of Empirical Research on Deliberat-
   ing Groups. *Psychology, Public Policy, and Law* 7(3):622–27.
The Dirksen Congressional Center. 2006. Major Features of the Civil Rights Act of
   1964. Public Law 88-352, http://people.bu.edu/smarks/LegislationWeb/Civil-Rights-
   Act/1964%20Act.htm.
Doe v. City of Belleville, Ill., 119 F.3d 563 (7th Cir. 1997).
Doneff, Andrea. 2014. Social Framework Studies Such As Women Don't Ask and It Does
   Hurt to Ask Show Us the Next Step toward Achieving Gender Equality—Eliminating
   the Long-Term Effects of Implicit Bias—but Are Not Likely to Get Cases Past Sum-
   mary Judgment. *William and Mary Journal of Women and the Law* 20:573–623.
Dothard v. Rawlinson, 433 U.S. 321 (1977).
Dowd, Nancy E. 2012. Fatherhood and Equality: Reconfiguring Masculinities. *Suffolk
   University Law Review* 45:1047–81.
———. 2010. *The Man Question: Male Subordination and Privilege,* New York: New
   York University Press.
Dowd, Nancy E., Nancy Levit, and Ann C. McGinley. 2012. Feminist Legal Theory
   Meets Masculinities Theory, in *Masculinities and the Law: A Multidimensional
   Approach,* eds. Frank Rudy Cooper and Ann C. McGinley. New York: New York
   University Press, 25–50.
Durkin v. Verizon N.Y., Inc., 678 F. Supp. 2d 124 (S.D.N.Y. 2009).
Eagly, Alice H., and Steven J. Karau. 2002. Role Congruity Theory of Prejudice toward
   Female Leaders. *Psychological Review* 109:573–89.
Eagly, Alice H., Mona G. Makhijani, and Bruce G. Klonsky. 1992. Gender and the
   Evaluation of Leaders: A Meta-Analysis. *Psychological Bulletin* 111:3–22.
Eberhardt, Jennifer L. 2005. Imaging Race. *American Psychologist* 60:181–90.
E.E.O.C. Guidelines on Discrimination Because of Sex, 29 C.F.R. § 1604.11(a)(3) (2015).
E.E.O.C. Guidelines on Discrimination Because of National Origin, 29 C.F.R. § 16067.7
   (2015).
E.E.O.C. Guidelines on Discrimination Because of National Origin, 45 Fed. Reg.
   85,632, 85,635 (Dec. 29, 1980) (to be codified at 29 C.F.R. pt. 1606).
E.E.O.C. 2007. *Enforcement Guidance: Unlawful Disparate Treatment of Workers with
   Caregiving Responsibilities,* http://www.eeoc.gov/policy/docs/caregiving.html.

———. 1990. *Policy Guidance on Current Issues of Sexual Harassment*, http://www.eeoc. gov/policy/docs/currentissues.html.

———. 1979. *Adoption of Questions and Answers to Clarify and Provide a Common Interpretation of the Uniform Guidelines on Employee Selection Procedures*, http://www.eeoc.gov/policy/docs/qanda_clarify_procedures.html.

E.E.O.C. v. Beauty Enterprises, Inc., 3:01CV378 (AHN), 2005 WL 2764822 (D. Conn. 2005).

E.E.O.C. v. Boh Bros. Construction Co., LLC, 731 F.3d 444 (5th Cir. 2013) (en banc).

E.E.O.C. v. Harbert-Yeargin, Inc., 266 F.3d 498 (6th Cir. 2001).

E.E.O.C. v. J.C. Penney Co., 843 F.2d 249 (6th Cir. 1988).

E.E.O.C. v. National Education Association, 422 F.3d 840 (9th Cir. 2005).

E.E.O.C. v. Premier Operator Services, Inc., 113 F. Supp. 2d 1066 (N.D. Tex. 2000).

E.E.O.C. v. Prospect Airport Services, Inc., 621 F.3d 991 (9th Cir. 2010).

E.E.O.C. v. Prospect Airport Services, Inc., 2:05-01125KJDGWF, 2007 WL 2875155 (D. Nev. 2007).

Ehrenreich, Nancy S. 1990. Pluralist Myths and Powerless Men: The Ideology of Reasonableness in Sexual Harassment Law. *Yale Law Journal* 99:1177–1234.

Ellis v. Costco Wholesale Corp., 285 F.R.D. 492 (N.D. Cal. 2012).

Ellison v. Brady, 924 F.2d 872 (9th Cir. 1991).

Ely, Robin. 1994. The Effects of Organizational Demographics and Social Identity on Relationships among Professional Woman. *Administrative Science Quarterly* 39(2):203–38.

Ely, Robin J., and Debra E. Meyerson. 2010. An Organization Approach to Undoing Gender: The Unlikely Case of Offshore Oil Platforms. *Research in Organizational Behavior* 30:3–34.

Engelhart, Mike. 2011. Trial Tips for Plaintiff Employment Lawyers, http://www.justex.net/JustexDocuments/10/Preparation%20and%20Trial%20of%20the%20Employment%20Case%206-2011.pdf.

Erin Brockovich. 2000. DVD. Directed by Steven Soderbergh. Universal Pictures.

Eskridge, William N., Jr. 1994. *Dynamic Statutory Interpretation*. Cambridge, MA: Harvard University Press.

Family Medical Leave Act (FMLA) of 1993, 29 U.S.C. §§2601 et seq.

Faragher v. City of Boca Raton, 524 U.S. 775 (1998).

Federal Rules of Evidence. 2011 Amendments. Rule 702.

Federal Rules of Evidence. 2015. Rule 702.

Fineman, Martha A., and Michael Thomson, eds. 2013. *Exploring Masculinities: Feminist Legal Theory Reflections*. Farnham, UK: Ashgate.

Fiske, Susan T. 2005. What We Know about the Problem of the Century: Lessons from Social Science to the Law and Back. In *Handbook of Employment Discrimination Research*, eds. L. B. Nielsen and R. L. Nelson. Netherlands: Springer, 59–71.

Fiske, Susan T., and Eugene Borgida. 2011. Standards for Using Social Psychological Evidence in Employment Discrimination Cases. *Temple Law Review* 83:867–76.

Fletcher, Joyce K. 2001. *Disappearing Acts: Gender, Power, and Relational Practice at Work*. Cambridge, MA: MIT Press.

Foschi, Martha, Larissa Lai, and Kirsten Sigerson. 1994. Gender and Double Standards in Assessment of Job Applicants. *Social Psychology Quarterly* 57:326–37.

Garcetti v. Ceballos, 126 S.Ct. 1951 (2006).

Garcia, Kelli K. 2012. The Gender Bind: Men as Inauthentic Caregivers. *Duke Journal of Gender Law and Policy* 20:1–43.

Garcia v. Spun Steak Co., 998 F.2d 1480 (9th Cir. 1993).

Garcia v. Woman's Hospital of Texas, 97 F.3d 810 (5th Cir. 1996).

General Electric Co. v. Gilbert, 429 U.S. 125 (1976).

General Telephone Co. of Southwest. v. Falcon, 457 U.S. 147 (1982).

Gertner, Nancy, and Melissa Hart. 2012. Implicit Bias in Employment Litigation, in *Implicit Racial Bias across the Law*, eds. Justin D. Levinson and Robert J. Smith. Cambridge: Cambridge University Press, 80–94.

Giele, Janet Z. 2008. Homemaker or Career Woman: Life Course Factors and Racial Influences among Middle-Class Americans. *Journal of Comparative Family Studies* 39:393–411.

Glenn v. Brumby, 632 F. Supp. 2d 1308 (N.D. Ga. 2009).

Gray v. Genlyte Group, Inc., 289 F.3d 128 (1st Cir. 2002).

Green, Tristin K. 2003. Discrimination in Workplace Dynamics: Toward a Structural Account of Disparate Treatment Theory. *Harvard Civil Rights–Civil Liberties Law Review* 38:91–157.

Greenwald, Anthony G., and Mahzarin R. Banaji. 1995. Implicit Social Cognition: Attitudes, Self-Esteem, and Stereotypes. *Psychological Review* 102:4–27.

Greenwald, Anthony G., and Linda Hamilton Krieger. 2006. Implicit Bias: Scientific Foundations. *California Law Review* 94:945–68.

Greenwald, Anthony G., Andrew T. Poehlman, Eric Luis Ulhmann, and Mahzarin R. Banaji. 2009. Understanding and Using the Implicit Association Test: III Meta-Analysis of Predictive Validity. *Journal of Personality and Social Psychology* 97:17–41.

Griggs v. Duke Power Co., 401 U.S. 424 (U.S., 1971).

Gutek, Barbara A., and Maureen Ann O'Connor. 1995. The Empirical Basis for the Reasonable Woman Standard in Sexual Harassment Law. *Journal of Social Issues: Gender Stereotyping, Sexual Harassment, and the Law* 51(1):151–66.

Gutek, Barbara A., Maureen Ann O'Connor, Renée Melacon, Margaret S. Stockdale, Tracey M. Geer, and Robert S. Done. 1999. The Utility of the Reasonable Woman Legal Standard in Hostile Environment Sexual Harassment Cases: A Multimethod, Multistudy Examination. *Psychology, Public Policy, and Law* 5(3):596–629.

Habib v. NationsBank, 279 F.3d 563 (8th Cir. 2001).

Hamilton, David L., and Diane M. Mackie. 1993. Cognitive and Affective Processes in Intergroup Perception: The Developing Interface, in *Affect, Cognition, and Stereotyping*, eds. Diane M. Mackey and David L. Hamilton. San Diego: Academic Press.

Hamilton, David L., and Tina K. Trolier. 1986. Stereotypes and Stereotyping: An Overview and Cognitive Approach, in *Prejudice, Discrimination, and Racism*, eds. John F. Dovidio and Samuel L. Gaertner, New York: Academic Press, 127–63.

Hamm v. Weyauwega Milk Products, Inc. 323 F.3d 1058 (7th Cir 2003).

Harper, Michael C. 2010. The Causation Standard in Federal Employment Law: *Gross v. FBL Financial Services, Inc.*, and the Unfulfilled Promise of the Civil Rights Act of 1991. *Buffalo Law Review* 58:69–145.

Harris, Lasana T., and Susan T. Fiske. 2009. Social Neuroscience Evidence for Dehumanised Perception. *European Review of Social Psychology* 20:192–94.

Harris v. Forklift Systems, Inc., 510 U.S. 17 (1993).

Hart, Alan J., Paul J. Whalen, Lisa M. Shin, Sean C. McInerney, Haêkan Fischer, and Scott L. Rauch. 2000. Differential Response in the Human Amygdala to Racial Outgroup vs. Ingroup Face Stimuli. *NeuroReport* 11:2351–55.

Hart, Melissa. 2005. Subjective Decisionmaking and Unconscious Discrimination. *Alabama Law Review* 56:741–91.

Hart, Melissa, and Paul M. Secunda. 2009. A Matter of Context: Social Framework Evidence in Employment Discrimination Class Actions. *Fordham Law Review* 78:37–70.

Harvey v. Anheuser-Busch, Inc., 38 F.3d 968 (8th Cir. 1994).

Hastings, Deborah. 2015. Seattle-Area High School Football Players Charged with Attempted Rape of Special Needs Student. *Daily News,* February 7, http://www.nydailynews.com/news/national/ wash-football-players-charged-attempted-rape-article-1.2106649.

Hazelwood School Disrict v. United States, 433 U.S. 299 (1977).

Hazen Paper Co. v. Biggins, 507 U.S. 604 (1993).

Heilman, Madeline. 2012. Gender Stereotypes and Workplace Bias. *Research in Organizational Behavior* 32:113–35.

Heilman, Madeline E., Caryn J. Block, Richard F. Martell, and Michael C. Simon. 1989. Has Anything Changed? Current Characterizations of Men, Women, and Managers. *Journal of Applied Psychology* 74:935–42.

Heilman, Madeline E., Aaron S. Wallen, Daniella Fuchs, and Melinda M. Tamkins. 2004. Penalties for Success: Reactions to Women Who Succeed at Male Gender-Typed Tasks. *Journal of Applied Psychology* 89:416–27.

Henson v. City of Dundee, 682 F.2d 897 (11th Cir. 1982).

Herbert, Melissa. 1998. *Camouflage Isn't Only for Combat: Gender, Sexuality, and Women in the Military.* New York: New York University Press.

Hernández, Tanya K. 2014. One Path for "Post-Racial" Employment Discrimination Cases: The Implicit Association Test Research as Social Framework Evidence. *Journal of Law and Inequality* 32:307–44.

———. 2011. "What Not to Wear": Race and Unwelcomeness in Sexual Harassment Law; The Story of *Meritor Savings Bank v. Vinson,* in *Women and the Law Stories,* eds. Elizabeth Schneider and Stephanie Wildman. St. Paul, MN: Foundation Press, 277–306.

Hernandez v. Brand FX Body Co., Inc., 13-cv-3058-MWB, Complaint and Jury Demand.

Heymann, Laura A. 2010. The Grammar of Trademarks. *Lewis and Clark Law Review* 14:1313–50.

Hochschild, Arlie. 1989. *The Second Shift: Working Families and the Revolution at Home.* London: Penguin.

Holbrook v. Reno, 196 F.3d 255 (D.C. Cir. 1999).

Holman v. Indiana, 211 F.3d 399 (7th Cir. 2000).

Hopkins v. Price Waterhouse, 618 F. Supp. 1109 (D.D.C. 1985).

Howe v. City of Akron, 723 F.3d 651 (6th Cir. 2013).

Hoyle v. Freightliner, LLC, 650 F.3d 321 (4th Cir. 2011).

Hurley v. Atlantic City Police Dept., 174 F.3d 95 (3d Cir. 1999).

Information on Impact, 29 C.F.R. § 1607.4.

In re Smurfit-Stone Container Corp., 122 Lab. Arb. Rep. (BNA) 33, 41 (2005).

International Brotherhood of Teamsters v. United States, 431 U.S. (1977).

International Union, United Automobile, Aerospace and Agricultural Implement Workers of America UAW v. Johnson Controls, Inc., 499 U.S. 187 (1991).

Jenson v. Eveleth Taconite Co., 130 F.3d 1287 (8th Cir. 1997).

Johnson, Margaret E. 2007. "Avoiding Harm Otherwise": Responses to the Harms of Sexual Harassment. *Temple Law Review* 80:743–807.

Johnson v. AK Steel Corp., 1:07-CV-291, 2008 WL2184230 (W.D. Ohio 2008).

Johnson v. Ready Mixed Concrete Co., 424 F.3d 806 (8th Cir. 2005).

Jolls, Christine. 2001. Antidiscrimination and Accommodation. *Harvard Law Review* 115:642–99.

Jones v. Pacific Rail Services, 2001 WL 127645 (N.D. Ill. Feb. 14, 2001).

Juliano, Ann. 2007. Contra-Power Harassment: The Case of Subordinate-Initiated Harassment. *Boston University Law Review* 87:491–560.

Juliano, Ann, and Stewart J. Schwab. 2001. The Sweep of Sexual Harassment Cases. *Cornell Law Review* 86:548–602.

Kahan, Dan M., David A. Hoffman, and Donald Braman. 2009. Whose Eyes Are You Going to Believe? *Scott v. Harris* and the Perils of Cognitive Illiberalism. *Harvard Law Review* 122:837–905.

Kahan, Dan M., David A. Hoffman, Donald Braman, Danieli Evans, and Jeffrey J. Rachlinski. 2012. "They Saw a Protest": Cognitive Illiberalism and the Speech Conduct Distinction. *Stanford Law Review* 64:851–905.

Kang, Jerry. 2005. Trojan Horses of Race. *Harvard Law Review* 118:1489–1593.

Kang, Jerry, Mark Bennett, Devon Carbado, Pam Casey, Nilanjana Dasgupta, David Faigman, Rachel Godsil, Anthony G. Greenwald, Justin Levinson, and Jennifer Mnookin. 2012. Implicit Bias in the Courtroom. *University of California–Los Angeles Law Review* 59:1124–86.

Karjanen, David. 2008. Gender, Race, and Nationality in the Making of Mexican Migrant Labor in the United States. *Latin American Perspective* 35:51–63.

Karst, Kenneth L. 1991. The Pursuit of Manhood and the Desegregation of the Armed Forces. *University of California–Los Angeles Law Review* 38:499–581.

Katz, Roger C., Roseann Hannon, and Leslie Whitten. 1996. Effects of Gender and Situation on the Perception of Sexual Harassment. *Sex Roles* 34(1/2):35–42.

Katz v. Dole, 709 F.2d 251 (4th Cir. 1983).

Kerfoot, Deborah, and David Knights. 1998. Managing Masculinity in Contemporary Organizational Life: A Managerial Project. *Organization* 5:7–26.

Kimmel, Michael. 2013. *Angry White Men: American Masculinity at the End of an Era.* New York: Nation Books.

———. 2004. Masculinity as Homophobia: Fear, Shame, and Silence in the Construction of Gender Identity, in *Feminism and Masculinities*, ed. Peter F. Murphy. Oxford: Oxford University Press.

King, Allan G., and Carole F. Wilder. 2012. *Dukes v. Wal-Mart:* Some Closed Doors and Open Issues. *Littler Report,* http://www.littler.com/files/press/pdf/TheLittlerReport-DukesVsWalMartSomeClosedDoorsAndOpenIssues.pdf.

King v. Board of Regents of University of Wisconsin System, 898 F.2d 533 (7th Cir. 1990).

Kipp v. Missouri Highway and Transportation Commission, 280 F.3d 893 (8th Cir. 2002).

Kopp v. Samaritan Health Servs. Inc., 13 F.3d 264 (8th Cir. 1993).

Krieger, Linda H. 1995. The Content of Our Categories: A Cognitive Bias Approach to Discrimination and Equal Employment Opportunity. *Stanford Law Review* 47:1161–1248.

Kumho Tire Company, Ltd. v. Carmichael, 526 U.S. 137 (1999).

Lebrecht, Sophie, Lara J. Pierce, Michael J. Tarr, and James W. Tanaka. 2009. Perceptual Other-Race Training Reduces Implicit Racial Bias. *PloS ONE* 4(1):e4215. Doi:10.1371/journal/pone.0004215.

Lefkowitz, Bernard. 1998. *Our Guys: The Glen Ridge Rape and the Secret Life of the Perfect Suburb.* New York: Vintage.

Legault, Lisa, Jennifer N. Gutsell, and Michael Inzlicht. 2011. Ironic Effects of Antiprejudice Messages: How Motivational Interventions Can Reduce (but Also Increase) Prejudice. *Psychological Science* 22(12):1472–77.

Levit, Nancy, and Robert M. Verchick. 2006. *Feminist Legal Theory: A Primer.* New York: New York University Press.

Lidge, Ernest F., III. 2002. The Courts' Misuse of the Similarly Situated Concept in Employment Discrimination Law. *Missouri Law Review* 67:831–82.

Lieder, Michael. 2014. Employment Discrimination and Wage and Hour Class and Collective Actions after *Dukes* and *Behrend*: A Plaintiff Lawyer's Perspective. *American Law Institute,* http://files.alicle.org/thumbs/datastorage/skoobesruoc/pdf/CV037_chapter_03_thumb.pdf.

Lopez v. River Oaks Imaging & Diagnostic Group, Inc., 542 F. Supp. 2d 653 (S.D. Tex. 2008).

Lorber, Judith. 1994. *Paradoxes of Gender.* New Haven, CT: Yale University Press.

Lynch v. Freeman, 817 F.2d 380 (6th Cir. 1987).

Macerollo, Andrea. 2008. The Power of Masculinity in the Legal Profession: Women Lawyers and Identity Formation. *Windsor Review of Legal and Social Issues* 25:121–44.

MacKinnon, Catharine A. 1979. *Sexual Harassment of Working Women: A Case of Sex Discrimination.* New Haven, CT: Yale University Press.

Martin, Natasha. 2008. Immunity for Hire: How the Same-Actor Doctrine Sustains Discrimination in the Contemporary Workplace. *Connecticut Law Review* 40:1117–74.

Martin, Patricia Yancey. 2003. "Said and Done" versus "Saying and Doing": Gendering Practices, Practicing Gender at Work. *Gender and Society* 17:342–66.

———. 2001. "Mobilizing Masculinities": Women's Experiences with Men at Work. *Organization* 8:587–618.

Martin, Roland S. 2008. Understanding Why You Don't Call a Black Man a Boy. *CNN*, April 15, http://ac360.blogs.cnn.com/2008/04/15/understanding-why-you-dont-call-a-black-man-a-boy/?hpt=ac_mid.

Mason, Mary Ann, and Marc Goulden. 2004. Do Babies Matter (Part II)? Closing the Baby Gap. *Academe* 90:10–15.

Massachusetts General Laws Annotated 151B § 4(1) (West 2012).

McDonnell Douglas Corp. v. Green, 411 U.S. 792 (1973).

McGinley, Ann C. 2013a. Masculine Law Firms. *Florida International University Law Review* 8:423–36.

———. 2013b. Men, Masculinities, and Law: A Symposium on Multidimensional Masculinities Theory. *Nevada Law Journal* 13:315–25.

———. 2012. *Ricci v. DeStefano*: Diluting Disparate Impact and Redefining Disparate Treatment. *Nevada Law Journal* 12:101–15.

———. 2010a. *Ricci v. DeStefano*: A Masculinities Theory Analysis. *Harvard Journal of Law and Gender* 33:581–623.

———. 2010b. Erasing Boundaries: Masculinities, Sexual Minorities, and Employment Discrimination. *University of Michigan Journal of Law Reform* 53:713–71.

———. 2009a. Reproducing Gender on Law School Faculties. *Brigham Young University Law Review* 2009:99–155.

———. 2009b. Hillary Clinton, Sarah Palin, and Michelle Obama: Performing Gender, Race, and Class on the Campaign Trail. *Denver University Law Review* 86:709–24.

———. 2008. Creating Masculine Identities: Bullying and Harassment "Because of Sex." *University of Colorado Law Review* 79:1151–1241.

———. 2007. Harassing "Girls" at the Hard Rock: Masculinities in Sexualized Environments. *University of Illinois Law Review* 2007:1229–77.

———. 2004. Masculinities at Work. *Oregon Law Review* 83:359–434.

———. 2000. *Viva la Evolucion*: Recognizing Unconscious Motive in Title VII. *Cornell Journal of Law and Public Policy* 9:415–80.

———. 1993. Reinventing Reality: The Impermissible Intrusion of After-Acquired Evidence in Title VII Litigation. *Connecticut Law Review* 26:145–205.

McGinley, Ann C., and Frank Rudy Cooper. 2012. Introduction: Masculinities, Multidimensionality, and Law; Why They Need One Another, in *Masculinities and the Law: A Multidimensional Approach*, eds. Frank Rudy Cooper and Ann C. McGinley. New York: New York University Press, 1–19.

Meltzer, Marisa. 2013. You're Cute and Fired. *New York Times*, November 29, http://www.nytimes.com/2013/12/01/fashion/Some-women-are-fired-for-being-too-attractive.html?_r=2&.

Mendoza, Saaid A., Peter M. Gollwitzer, and David M. Amodio. 2010. Reducing Expression of Implicit Stereotypes: Reflexive Control through Implementation Intentions. *Personality and Social Psychology Bulletin* 36(4):512–23.

Meritor Saving Bank v. Vinson. 477 U.S. 57 (1986).

Mitchell, Gregory, Laurens Walker, and John Monahan. 2011. Beyond Context: Social Facts as Case-Specific Evidence. *Emory Law Journal* 60:1109–51.

Mollica, Paul W. 2005. Reviewing Title VII Jury Trials under McDonnell Douglas and Desert Palace. *Bloomberg BNA Employment Discrimination Report* 24(14), https://www.bloomberglaw.com/document/XBM3IBG5GVG0.

Monahan, John, Laurens Walker, and Mitchell Gregory. 2008. Contextual Evidence of Gender Discrimination: The Ascendance of "Social Frameworks." *Virginia Law Review* 94:1715–49.

Moran, Mayo. 2010. Symposium: The Reasonable Person; A Conceptual Biography in Comparative Perspective. *Lewis and Clark Law Review* 14(4):1233–83.

———. 2003. *Rethinking the Reasonable Person: An Egalitarian Reconstruction of the Objective Standard.* Oxford: Oxford University Press.

Mulroy, Elizabeth. 1995. *The New Uprooted: Single Mothers in Urban Life.* Westport, CT: Greenwood.

Murtha, Lydon. 2013. Incognito and Martin: An Insider's Story. *Sports Illustrated*, November 7, http://mmqb.si.com/2013/11/07/richie-incognito-jonathan-martin-dolphins-lydon-murtha/.

Mutua, Athena D., ed. 2006. *Progressive Black Masculinities.* New York: Routledge.

National Association of Legal Professionals (NALP). 2015. Part-Time Lawyers, http://www.nalp.org/parttime (last visited June 28, 2015).

National Center for State Courts (NCSC). 2012. Strategies to Reduce the Influence of Implicit Bias, www.ncsc.org/ibreport.

Nelson v. James H. Knight DDS, P.C., 834 N.W.2d 64 (Iowa 2013).

Neuren v. Adduci, Mastriani, Meeks and Schill, 43 F.3d 1507 (D.C. Cir. 1995).

Nichols v. Azteca Restaurant Enterprises, Inc., 256 F.3d 864 (9th Cir. 2001).

Niemann, Yolanda F. 2001. Stereotypes about Chicanas and Chicanos: Implications for Counseling. *Counseling Psychologist* 29:55–90.

Nosek, Brian A., Mahzarin R. Banaji, and Anthony G. Greenwald. 2002. Harvesting Implicit Group Attitudes and Beliefs from the Demonstration Web Site. *Group Dynamics: Theory, Research, and Practice* 6:101–15.

Ocheltree v. Scollon Productions, Inc., 308 F.3d 351 (4th Cir. 2002).

O'Connor, Maureen, Barbara A. Gutek, Margaret Stockdale, Tracey M. Greer, and, Renée Melançon. 2004. Explaining Sexual Harassment Judgments: Looking beyond Gender of the Rater. *Law and Human Behavior* 28:69–95.

Oncale v. Sundowner Offshore Services, Inc., 523 U.S. 75 (1998).

Oppenheimer, David B. 1993. Negligent Discrimination. *University of Pennsylvania Law Review* 141:899–972.

Pedersen, Natalie B. 2012. The Hazards of Dukes: The Substantive Consequences of a Procedural Decision. *University of Toledo Law Review* 44:123–43.

Pennsylvania Department of Corrections, et al. v. Yeskey, 524 U.S. 206 (1998).

Perez, Alex. 2014. Steubenville, Ohio, Teen Returns to the Football Field after Rape Conviction. *ABC News*, August 13, http://abcnews.go.com/US/steubenville-ohio-teen-returns-football-field-rape-conviction/story?id=24958411.

Perry, Elissa L., Carol T. Kulik, and Anne C. Bourhis. 2004. The Reasonable Woman Standard: Effects on Sexual Harassment Court Decisions. *Law and Human Behavior* 28:9–27.

Petersen, Kierran. 2014. "It's Rape": Sayreville High School Players Face Charges of Abusive Hazing. *BBC News*, October 22, http://www.bbc.com/news/blogs-echochambers-2971692e3.

Petrosino v. Bell Atlantic, 99 CV 4072 (JG), 2003 WL 1622885 (E.D.N.Y. 2003).

Phelps, Elizabeth A., Kevin J. O'Connor, William A. Cunningham, E. Sumie Funayama, J. Christopher Gatenby, John C. Gore, and Mahzarin R. Banaji. 2000. Performance on Indirect Measures of Race Evaluation Predicts Amygdala Activation. *Journal of Cognitive Neuroscience* 12:729–38.

Phelps, Elizabeth A., and Laura A. Thomas. 2003. Race, Behavior, and the Brain: The Role of Neuroimaging in Understanding Complex Social Behaviors. *Political Psychology* 24:747–51.

Phillips, Brian. 2013. Man Up: Declaring a War on Warrior Culture in the Wake of the Miami Dolphins Bullying Scandal. *Grantland,* November 7, http://grantland.com/features/richie-incognito-jonathan-martin-miami-dolphins-bullying-scandal/.

Picciotto, Richard. 2003. *Last Man Down: A Firefighter's Story of Survival and Escape from the World Trade Center.* New York: Berkley.

Pierce, Jennifer L. 1999. Emotional Labor among Paralegals. *Annals of the American Academy of Political and Social Science* 561:127–42.

———. 1995. *Gender Trials: Emotional Lives in Contemporary Law Firms.* Berkeley: University of California Press.

Ponce v. Billington, 679 F.3d 840 (D.C. Cir. 2012).

The Pregnancy Discrimination Act of 1978 (PDA), 42 U.S.C. § 2000e(k).

Pribbenow, Christine M., Jennifer Sheridan, Jessica Winchell, Deveny Benting, Jo Handelsman, and Molly Carnes. 2010. The Tenure Process and Extending the Tenure Clock: The Experience of Faculty at One University. *Higher Education Policy* 23:17–38.

Price Waterhouse v. Hopkins, 490 U.S. 228 (1989).

Prokos, Anastasia, and Irene Padavic. 2002. There Oughta Be a Law against Bitches: Masculinity Lessons in Police Academy Training. *Gender, Work, and Organization* 9:439–59.

Prowel v. Wise Business Forms, Inc., 579 F.3d 285 (3d Cir. 2009).

Pudrovska, Tetyana, and Amelia Karraker. 2014. Gender, Job Authority, and Depression. *Journal of Health and Social Behavior* 55(4):421–41.

Rachlinski, Jeffrey J., Sheri Johnson, Andrew J. Wistrich, and Chris Guthrie. 2009. Does Unconscious Racial Bias Affect Trial Judges? *Notre Dame Law Review* 84:1195–1246.

Rawat, Shivani, and Katy Daigle. 2013. India Gang Rape Case: 4 Men Sentenced to Death. Associated Press, September 13, http://www.huffingtonpost.com/2013/09/13/india-gang-rape-case-deat_n_3919601.html.

Reed v. Shepard, 939 F.2d 484 (7th Cir. 1991).

Reeves v. Sanderson Plumbing Products, Inc., 530 U.S. 133 (2000).

Rene v. MGM Grand Hotel, Inc., 305 F.3d 1061 (9th Cir. 2002).

Ricci v. DeStefano, 129 S.Ct. 2658 (2009).

Ridgeway, Cecilia L. 2001. Gender, Status, and Leadership. *Journal of Social Issues* 57:637–55.

Right Said Fred. 1992. "I'm Too Sexy," by Fred Fairbrass, Richard Fairbass, Rob Manzoli, and Jimi Hendrix. Tug Records.

Robinson, Russell K. 2008. Perceptual Segregation. *Columbia Law Review* 108:1093–1180.

Robinson v. Jacksonville Shipyards, 760 F. Supp. 1486 (M.D.Fla. 1991).

Robinson v. Metro-N. Commuter Rail Road Co., 267 F.3d 147 (2d Cir. 2001).

Roche, Vaughn. 1993. Football Hazing Penalty Splits Tiny Utah Town: Student Is Threatened after His Complaint Ends His Team's Season. *New York Times*, November 22, http://articles.latimes.com/1993-11-22/news/mn-59668_1_football-hazing.

Rogers, Mary F., and C. D. Garrett. 2002. *Who's Afraid of Women's Studies? Feminisms in Everyday Life.* Walnut Creek, CA: AltaMira.

Rogers v. E.E.O.C., 454 F.2d 234 (5th Cir. 1971).

Rose, Mary R., Shari S. Diamond, and Kimberly M. Baker. 2010. Goffman on the Jury: Real Jurors' Attention to the "Offstage" of Trials. *Law and Human Behavior* 34:310–23.

Rosenman, Andrew S., and Alexandra L. Newman. 2014. The Legitimacy of "Social Framework" and "Stereotyping" Testimony from Expert Witnesses in Employment Discrimination Litigation: Background and Recent Cases, Prepared for ABA Employment and Labor Law Section, *National Conference on Equal Employment Opportunity Law*, March 28, available online.

Rudman, Laurie A. 2001. Prescriptive Gender Stereotypes and Backlash toward Agentic Women. *Journal of Social Issues* 57:743–62.

Rudman, Laurie A., Richard D. Ashmore, and Melvin L. Gary. 2001. Unlearning Automatic Biases: The Malleability of Implicit Prejudice and Stereotypes. *Journal of Personality and Social Psychology* 81(5):856–68.

Sanday, Peggy Reeves. 2007. *Fraternity Gang Rape: Sex, Brotherhood, and Privilege on Campus.* New York: NYU Press.

Scherr v. Woodland School Community Consolidated District No. 50, 867 F.2d 974 (7th Cir. 1988).

Schneider, Elizabeth M. 2007. The Dangers of Summary Judgment: Gender and Federal Civil Litigation. *Rutgers Law Review* 59:705–77.

Schroer v. Billington, 577 F. Supp. 2d 293 (D.D.C. 2008).

Schultz, Vicki. 2003. The Sanitized Workplace. *Yale Law Journal* 112:2061–2193.

———. 1998. Reconceptualizing Sexual Harassment. *Yale Law Journal* 107:1683–1805.

Scott v. Harris, 550 U.S. 372 (2007).

Seamons v. Snow, 84 F.3d 1226 (10th Cir. 1996).

Sedima, S.P.R.L. v. Imrex Co., Inc., 473 U.S. 479 (1985).

Selmi, Michael. 2014. The Evolution of Employment Discrimination Law: Changed Doctrine for Changed Social Conditions. *George Washington University Law School Legal Studies Research Paper* no. 2014-8, http://ssrn.com/abstract=2430378.

———. 2007. The Work-Family Conflict: An Essay on Employers, Men, and Responsibility. *University of St. Thomas Law Journal.* 4:573–98.

Sen, Maya. 2015. Is Justice Really Blind? Race and Appellate Review in U.S. Courts. *Journal of Legal Studies* 44(S1):187–229.

Sex, Power, and the Workplace. 2002. Lumina Productions Inc.

Shafer v. Kal Kan Foods, Inc. 417 F.3d 663 (7th Cir. 2005).

Sherwyn, David, Michael Heise, and Zev J. Eigen. 2014. Experimental Evidence that Retaliation Claims are Unlike Other Employment Discrimination Claims. *Seton Hall Law Review* 44:455–503.

Shoenfelt, Elizabeth L., Allison E. Maue, and Joanne Nelson. 2002. Reasonable Person versus Reasonable Woman: Does It Matter? *Journal of Gender, Social Policy, and the Law* 10:633–72.

Shrier, Diane K., and Lydia A. Shrier. 2009. Psychosocial Aspects of Women's Lives: Work and Family/Personal Life and Life Cycle Issues. *Obstetrics and Gynecology Clinics of North America* 36:753–69.

Silva, Cristina. 2010. Sharron Angle Tells Harry Reid to Man Up, Again. *KOLO8*, October 22, http://kolotv.com/home/headline/105530068.htlm.

Skrentny, John D. 2013. *After Civil Rights: Racial Realism in the New American Workplace.* Princeton, NJ: Princeton University Press.

Smith, Michael. 2013. Report: Jonathan Martin "Gone AWOL" from Dolphins. *NBC Sports*, October 30, http://profootballtalk.nbcsports.com/2013/10/30/report-jonathan-martin-gone-awol-from-dolphins/.

Smith v. City of Salem, 378 F.3d 566 (6th Cir. 2004).

Spalter-Roth, R., and William Erskine. 2005. Beyond the Fear Factor: Work/Family Policy in Academia: Resources or Rewards? *Change* 37:19–25.

Staats, Cheryl, ed. 2014. State of Science: Implicit Bias Review 2014. *Kirwan Institute for the Study of Race & Ethnicity*, http://kirwaninstitute.osu.edu/wp-content/uploads/2014/03/2014-implicit-bias.pdf.

Standardized Civil Jury Instructions for the 9th Circuit, No.10.1A, 10.1C (2007 ed.).

Standardized Civil Jury Instructions for the 3rd Circuit, No. 5.1.1 (2010 ed.).

Staub v. Proctor Hospital, 562 U.S. 411 (2011).

Steiner v. Showboat Operating Co., 25 F.3d 1459 (9th Cir. 1994).

Stella v. Mineta, 284 F.3d 135 (D.C. Cir. 2002).

Stempel, Jeffrey W. 2012. Taking Cognitive Illiberalism Seriously: Judicial Humility, Aggregate Efficiency, and Acceptable Justice. *Loyola University Chicago Law Journal* 43:627–87.

Stewart, Brandon D., and Keith B. Payne. 2008. Bringing Automatic Stereotyping under Control: Implementation Intentions as Efficient Means of Thought Control. *Personality and Social Psychology Bulletin* 34:1332–45.

St. Mary's Honor Center v. Hicks, 509 U.S. 502 (1993).

Stockdale, Margaret S., Cynthia Gandolfo Berry, Robert W. Schneider, and Feng Cao. 2004. Perceptions of the Sexual Harassment of Men. *Psychology of Men and Masculinity* 5:158–67.

Stoessner, Steven J., and Diane M. Mackie. 1993. Affect and Perceived Group Variability: Implications for Stereotyping and Prejudice, in *Affect, Cognition, and Stereotyping*, eds. Diane M. Mackey and David L. Hamilton. San Diego: Academic Press. 63.

Sturm, Susan. 2001. Second-Generation Employment Discrimination: A Structural Approach. *Columbia Law Review* 101:458–568.

Tabor v. Hilti, Inc., 703 F.3d 1206 (10th Cir. 2013).

Texas Dept. of Community Affairs v. Burdine, 450 U.S. 248 (1981).

Thomas, Suja A. 2010. The New Summary Judgment Motion: The Motion to Dismiss under Iqbal and Twombly. *Lewis and Clark Law Review* 14:15–42.

Thornton, Margaret. 2005. Implementing Flexible Tenure Clock Policies. *New Directions for Higher Education* 130:81–90.

Thornton, Margaret, and Joanne Bagust. 2007. The Gender Trap: Flexible Work in Corporate Legal Practice. *Osgoode Hall Law Journal* 45:773–811.

Title VII of the Civil Rights Act of 1964, 42 U.S.C. § 2000e.

Torres v. Pisano, 116 F.3d 625 (2d Cir. 1997).

Tovino, Stacey A. 2007. Functional Neuroimaging Information: A Case for Neuro Exceptionalism? *Florida State University Law Review* 34:415–22.

Tyus v. Urban Search Management, 102 F.3d 256 (7th Cir. 1996).

Uniform Services Employment and Reemployment Rights Act of 1994 (USERRA), U.S.C. § 4311.

United States v. City of New York, 683 F. Supp. 2d 225 (E.D.N.Y. 2010).

University of Michigan Center for the Education of Women. 2007. Family Friendly Policies in Higher Education: A Five-Year Report, *Center for the Education of Women*, http://www.cew.umich.edu/sites/default/files/ReduxBriefFinal5-1.pdf.

Valdes, Francisco. 1995. Queers, Sissies, Dykes, and Tomboys: Deconstructing the Conflation of "Sex," "Gender," and "Sexual Orientation" in Euro-American Law and Society. *California Law Review* 83:1–377.

Valian, Virginia. 1998. *Why So Slow? The Advancement of Woman*. Cambridge, MA: MIT Press.

Vaughn v. Westinghouse Electric Corp., 620 F.2d 655 (8th Cir. 1980), *aff'd*, 702 F.2d 137 (8th Cir. 1983).

Vinson v. Taylor, 753 F.2d 141 (D.C. Cir. 1985).

Vinson v. Taylor, 78-1793, 1980 WL 100, (D.D.C. Feb. 26, 1980).

Wallace, Jean E., and Marisa C. Young. 2008. Parenthood and Productivity: A Study of Demands, Resources, and Family-Friendly Firms. *Journal of Vocational Behavior* 72:110–22.

Wal-Mart Stores, Inc. v. Dukes, 131 S.Ct. 2541 (2011).

———. 2011. Brief of Amici Curiae of the American Sociological Association and the Law and Society Association Support of Respondents in *Wal-Mart Stores, Inc. v. Dukes*, 131 S.Ct. 2541.

Wambheim v. J.C. Penny Co., 705 F.2d 1492 (9th Cir. 1983).

Wang, Lu-in. 2010. Negotiating the Situation: The Reasonable Person in Context. *Lewis and Clark Law Review* 14:1285–1311.

Wards Cove Packing Co., Inc. v. Atonio, 490 U.S. 642 (1989).

Watson v. Fort Worth Bank & Trust, 487 U.S. 977 (1988).

Weiss, Deborah M. 2011. The Impossibility of Agnostic Discrimination Law. *Utah Law Review* 2011:1677–1748.

Weiss, Robert W. 1990. *Staying the Course: The Emotional and Social Lives of Men Who Do Well at Work*. New York: Ballantine Books.

Wells, Theodore, Jr., Brad S. Karp, Bruce Birenboim, and David W. Brown. 2014. *Report to the National Football Team concerning Issues of Workplace Conduct at the Miami Dolphins*, http://63bba9dfdf9675bf3f10-68be460ce43dd2a60dd64ca5eca4ae1d.r37.cf1.rackcdn.com/PaulWeissReport.pdf.

Wencelblat, Patricia. 2011. Social Framework Analysis after *Dukes v. Wal-Mart*, in Weil Employer Update 7–9 (July–Aug. 2011), http://www.weil.com/~/media/files/pdfs/Employer_Update_JUL_AUG_2011_.pdf.

Whalen, Charles, and Barbara Whalen. 1989. *The Longest Debate: A Legislative History of the 1964 Civil Rights Act*. Santa Ana, CA: Seven Locks Press.

Whitehead, Stephen. 1998. Disrupted Selves: Resistance and Identity at Work in the Managerial Arena. *Gender and Education* 10:199–215.

Whitley v. Peer Review Systems, Inc., 221 F.3d 1053 (8th Cir. 2000).

Wiener, Richard L., and Linda E. Hurt. 2000. How Do People Evaluate Social Sexual Conduct at Work? A Psycholegal Model. *Journal of Applied Psychology* 85:75–85.

Wildman, Stephanie. 2000. Ending Male Privilege: Beyond the Reasonable Woman. *Michigan Law Review* 98:1797–1812 (reviewing Caroline Forell and Donna Matthews, *A Law of Her Own: The Reasonable Woman as a Measure of Man*).

Williams, Joan C. 2010. *Reshaping the Work-Family Debate: Why Men and Class Matter*. Cambridge, MA: Harvard University Press.

———. 2001. *Unbending Gender: Why Family and Work Conflict and What to Do about It*. New York: Oxford University Press.

Williams, Joan C., Stephanie Bornstein, Diana Reddy, and Betsy A. Williams. 2007. Law Firms as Defendants: Family Responsibilities Discrimination in Legal Workplaces. *Pepperdine Law Review* 34:393–416.

Wilson, Robin. 2008. More Colleges Are Adding Family-Friendly Benefits. *Chronicle of Higher Education* 54:B22, http://www.chroniclecareers.com/article/More-Colleges-Are-Adding/14530/.

———. 2005. The Laws of Physics. *Chronicle of Higher Education* 52:A10, http://chronicle.com/article/The-Laws-of-Physics/35304.

Wolfinger, Nicholas H., Marc Goulden, and Mary Ann Mason. 2009. Alone in the Ivory Tower. *Journal of Family Issues* 31(12):1653–70.

Wolfinger, Nicholas H., Mary Ann Mason, and Marc Goulden. 2008. Problems in the Pipeline: Gender, Marriage, and Fertility in the Ivory Tower. *Journal of Higher Education* 79 (4):388-405.

Wollert, Terry N. 2012. Command Presence: What Is It? Why Is It Important? How Do We Measure It? *International Law Enforcement Educators and Trainers Association Journal* 2(2).

Wygant v. Jackson Board of Education, 476 U.S. 267 (1986).

Yates, Michael D. 2009. *Why Unions Matter,* 2nd ed. New York: Monthly Review Press.

Zimmer, Michael J. 2004. The New Discrimination Law: Price Waterhouse Is Dead, Whither McDonnell Douglas? *Emory Law Journal* 53:1887–1949.

INDEX

Wells, Ted, 2

Wells Report, 2–4, 8, 10, 26, 35, 103

white-collar workplaces: blue-collar work-places compared to, 20, 24, 31, 52, 64; careerism in, 7, 30; gendered male and female jobs in, 21; group harassment in, ix; masculinities in, 29–31, 164

white men: fire departments and, 18; as norm, 20; performance of masculinity by, 15–16, 23; preference for, 192; success in, 194

Williams, Joan, 27–28

women: behaviors of men compared to, x, 4, 96; biological clock of, 183; black, 8, 19, 192–93; as caregiver, 15, 152–57, 182; double bind for, 150, 167, 175, 193; fertility rates for, 181; inequality of, 6–7; lesbians, 41, 47, 182; masculine style or hyperfeminine style of, 64, 68; masculine woman as "aggressive bitch," 150–52; Mean Girls, 4; part-time work by, 20, 162; photos of, 26, 210; Queen Bee Syndromes, 4, 56; rape and mur-der of Indian woman, xiv; as sexual objects, 26, 76, 79; as siren, 63, 157–58; stereotypes of, 8, 19, 40, 41, 56, 63, 65, 133, 136, 141, 144, 149, 167, 192–94, 207, 222n3. *See also* reasonable woman

Women's Initiative (Deloitte and Touche), 145

work: definition of, 131, 165–66; women and part-time, 20, 162

workplaces: analyzing masculinity in, 34; behaviors creating Title VII liability, 12, 35; childcare and, 20, 27–28; disparate impact and challenging masculinities in, 177–95; gender and, xi, 19–22, 53–54, 66–67, 147, 149–50, 170–71; interpersonal relationships in, 62, 64, 65, 69, 115, 195; masculine practices at, x, 12, 29–34, 131; masculine structures in, 6, 34, 195; masculinity of structures, 6–7; stereotypes, 40, 54, 88, 148. *See also* blue-collar workplaces; hostile work environments; white-collar workplaces

ABOUT THE AUTHOR

Ann C. McGinley is William S. Boyd Professor of Law at the Boyd School of Law at the University of Nevada, Las Vegas. A coeditor of *Masculinities and the Law: A Multidimensional Approach*, McGinley is an expert in employment discrimination law, gender, masculinities theory, and disability law. Of the nearly fifty law review articles and book chapters she has authored, thirteen apply masculinities research to interpret Title VII of the 1964 Civil Rights Act. She lives in Henderson, Nevada, with her husband, Jeff Stempel.